THE WOODS

JAMES **TYNION IV** • MICHAEL **DIALYNAS**

VOL. 7
THE BLACK CITY

BOOM!
S T U D I O S

BOOM! STUDIOS

THE WOODS Volume Seven, July 2017. Published by BOOM! Studios, a division of Boom Entertainment, Inc. The Woods is ™ & © 2017 James Tynion IV. Originally published in single magazine form as THE WOODS No. 25-28. ™ & © 2016 James Tynion IV. All rights reserved. BOOM! Studios™ and the BOOM! Studios logo are trademarks of Boom Entertainment, Inc., registered in various countries and categories. All characters, events, and institutions depicted herein are fictional. Any similarity between any of the names, characters, persons, events, and/or institutions in this publication to actual names, characters, and persons, whether living or dead, events, and/or institutions is unintended and purely coincidental. BOOM! Studios does not read or accept unsolicited submissions of ideas, stories, or artwork.

A catalog record of this book is available from OCLC and from the BOOM! Studios website, www.boom-studios.com, on the Librarians page.

BOOM! Studios, 5670 Wilshire Boulevard, Suite 450, Los Angeles, CA 90036-5679. Printed in China. First Printing.

ISBN: 978-1-60886-989-3, eISBN: 978-1-61398-660-8

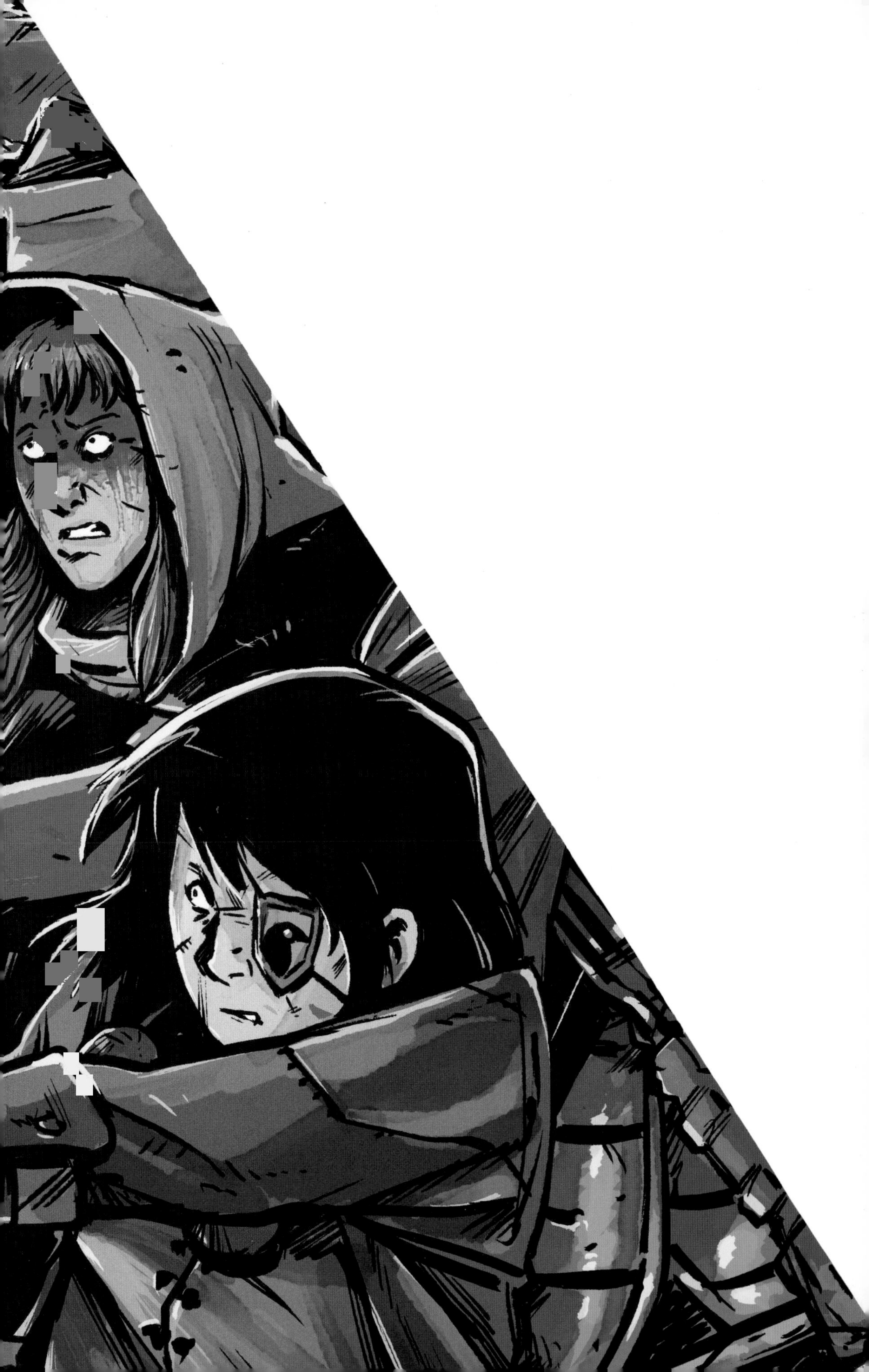

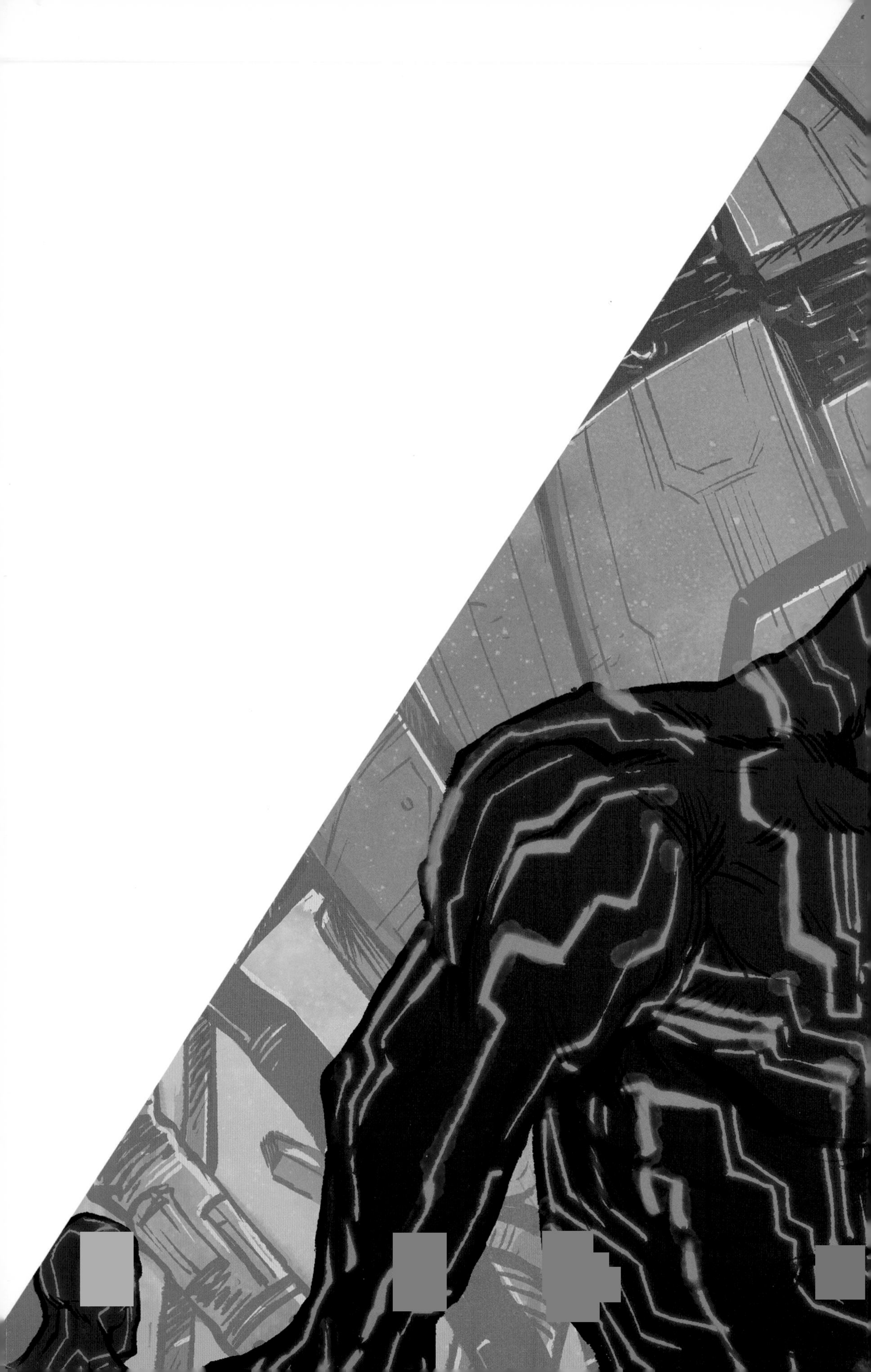

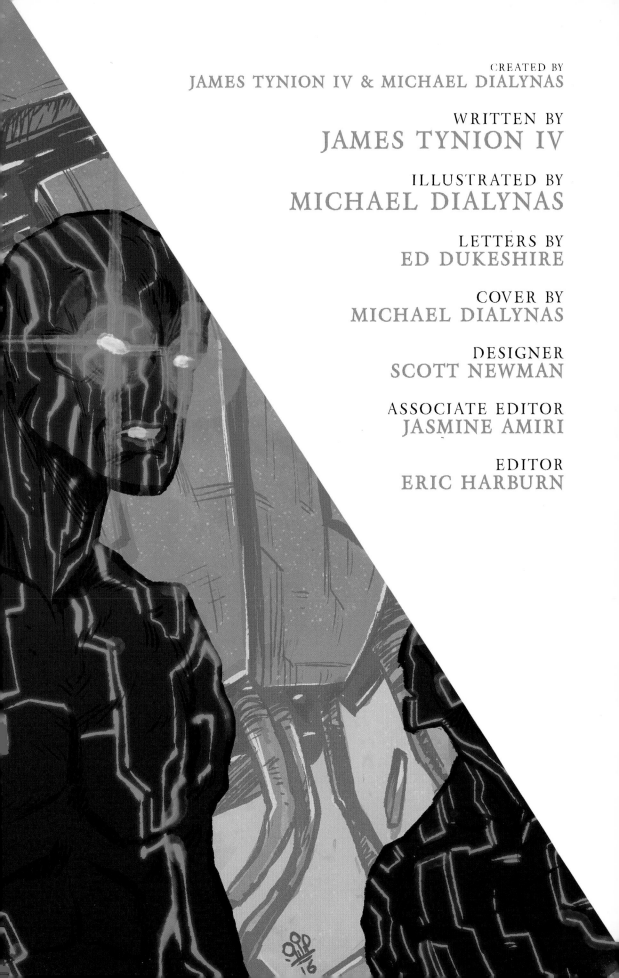

CREATED BY
JAMES TYNION IV & MICHAEL DIALYNAS

WRITTEN BY
JAMES TYNION IV

ILLUSTRATED BY
MICHAEL DIALYNAS

LETTERS BY
ED DUKESHIRE

COVER BY
MICHAEL DIALYNAS

DESIGNER
SCOTT NEWMAN

ASSOCIATE EDITOR
JASMINE AMIRI

EDITOR
ERIC HARBURN

CHAPTER
TWENTY-FIVE

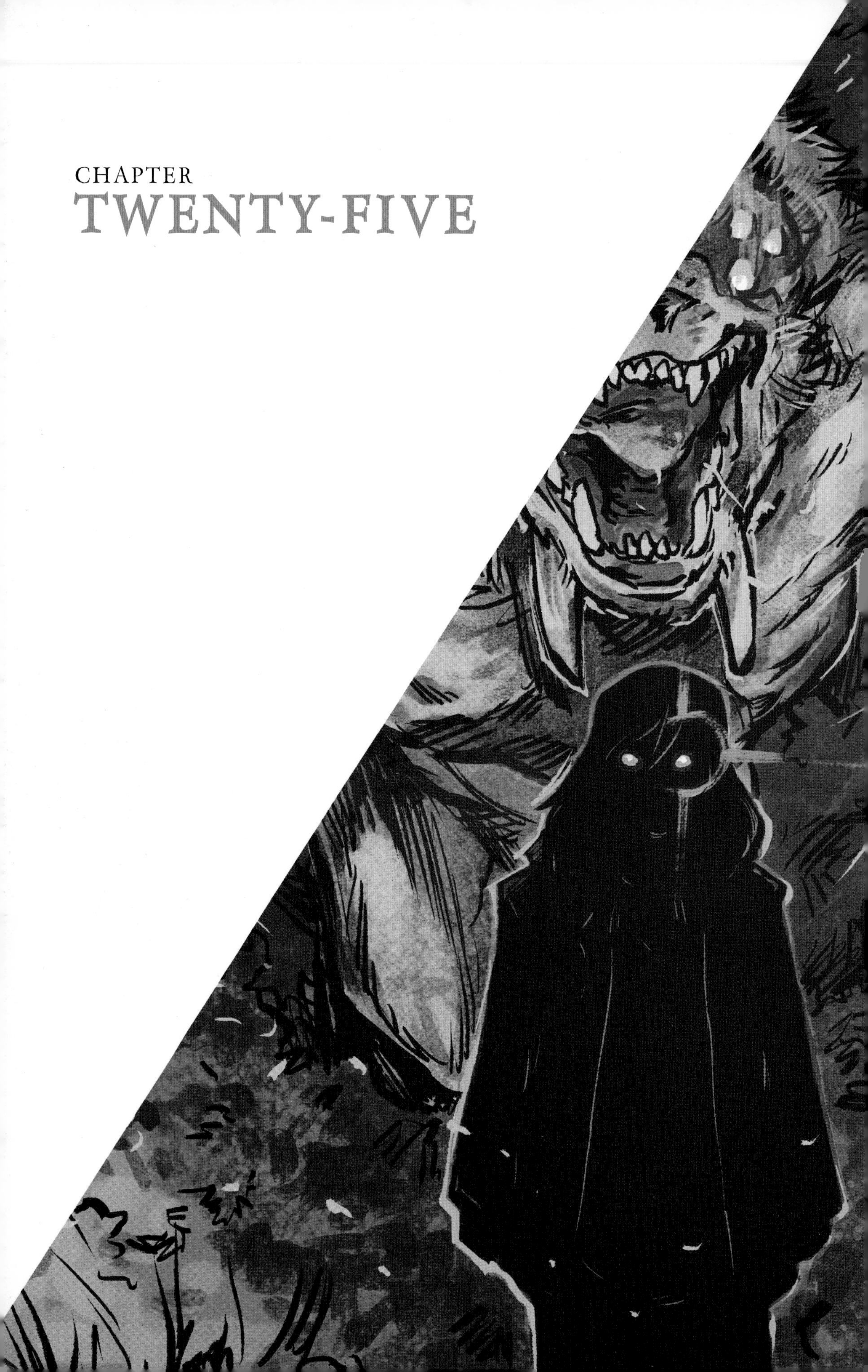

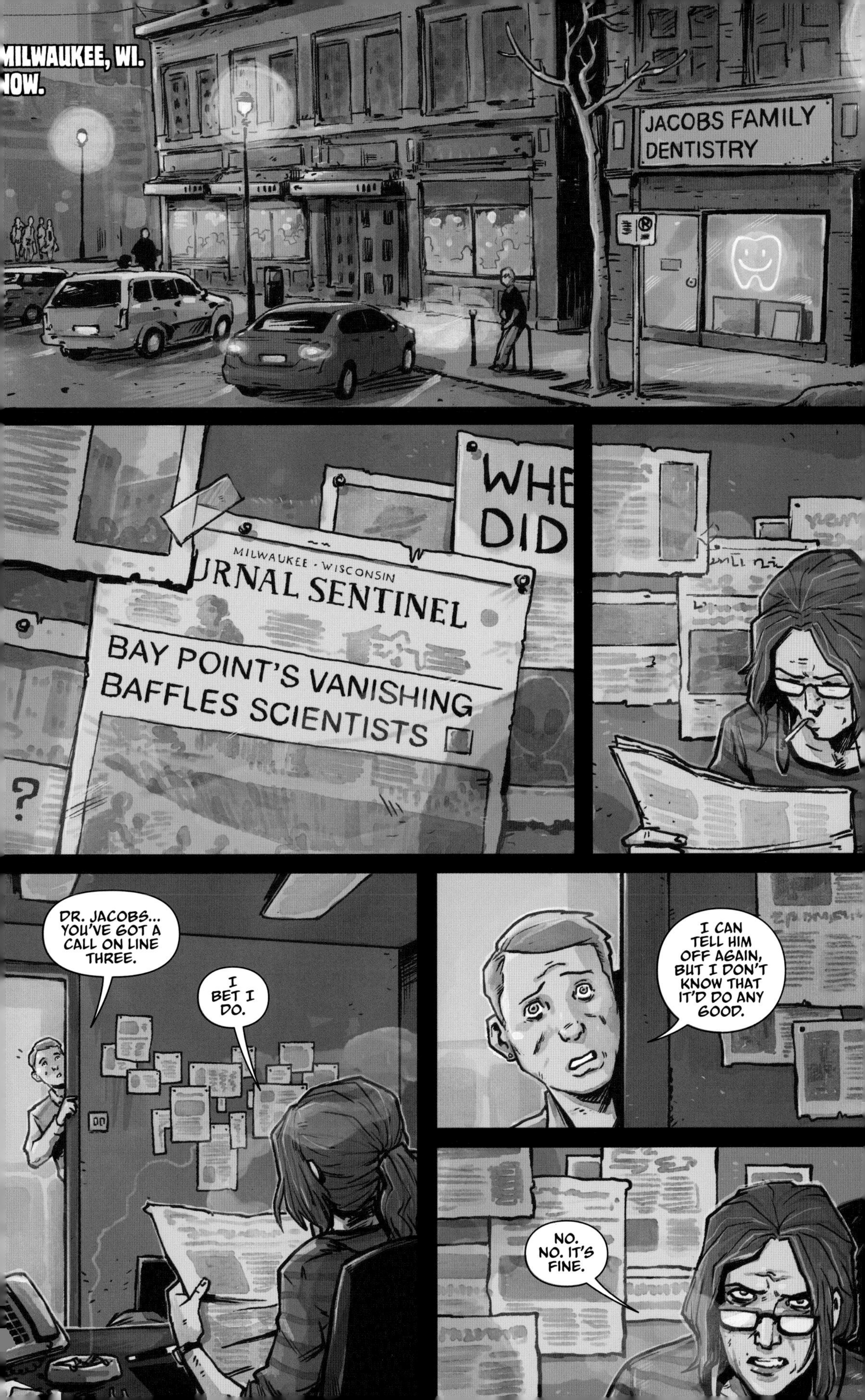
MILWAUKEE, WI.
NOW.
JACOBS FAMILY DENTISTRY
MILWAUKEE · WISCONSIN
URNAL SENTINEL
BAY POINT'S VANISHING BAFFLES SCIENTISTS
WHE
DID
DR. JACOBS... YOU'VE GOT A CALL ON LINE THREE.
I BET I DO.
I CAN TELL HIM OFF AGAIN, BUT I DON'T KNOW THAT IT'D DO ANY GOOD.
NO. NO. IT'S FINE.

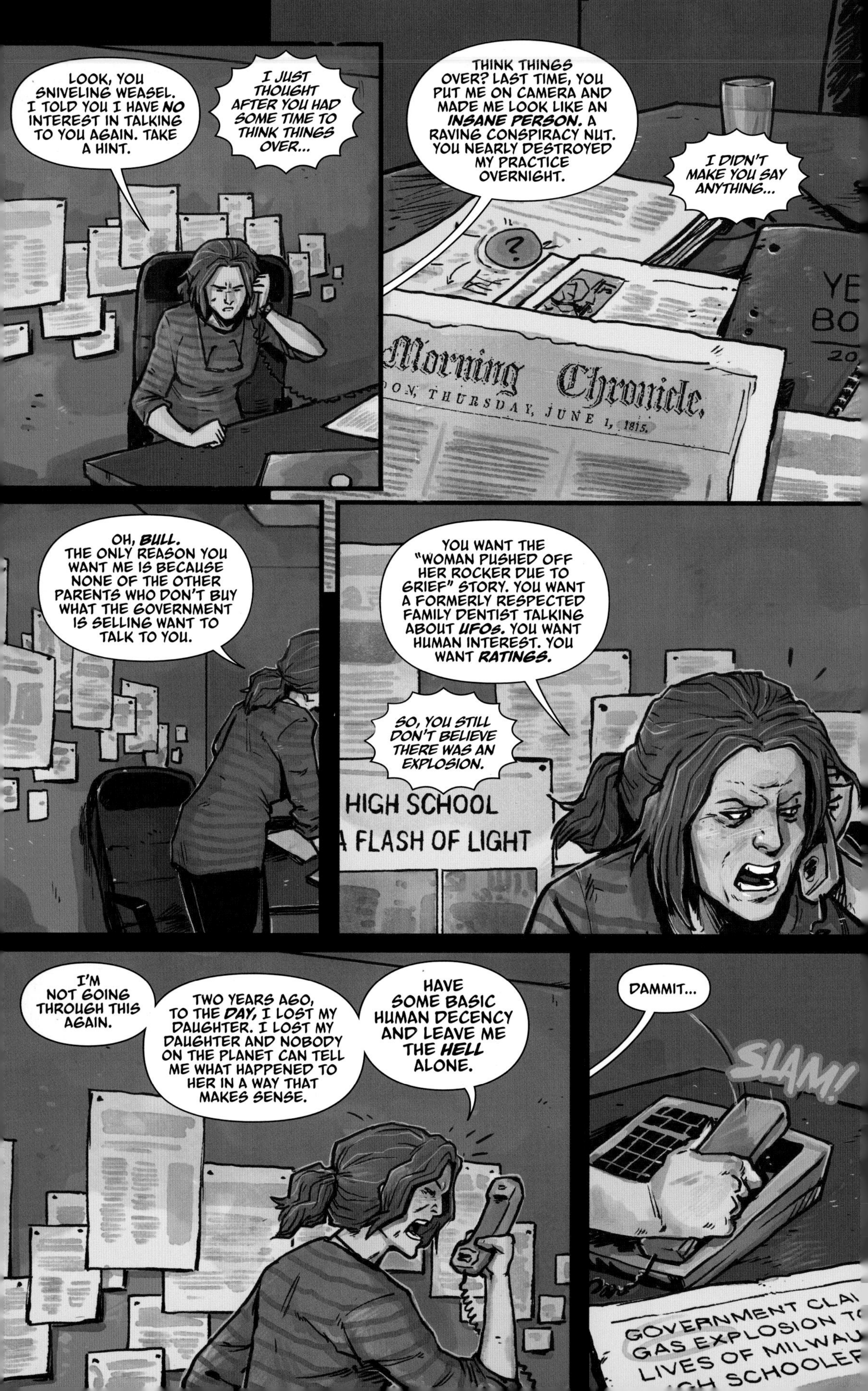
LOOK, YOU SNIVELING WEASEL. I TOLD YOU I HAVE NO INTEREST IN TALKING TO YOU AGAIN. TAKE A HINT.
I JUST THOUGHT AFTER YOU HAD SOME TIME TO THINK THINGS OVER...
THINK THINGS OVER? LAST TIME, YOU PUT ME ON CAMERA AND MADE ME LOOK LIKE AN INSANE PERSON. A RAVING CONSPIRACY NUT. YOU NEARLY DESTROYED MY PRACTICE OVERNIGHT.
I DIDN'T MAKE YOU SAY ANYTHING...
Morning Chronicle
THURSDAY, JUNE 1, 1815.
OH, BULL. THE ONLY REASON YOU WANT ME IS BECAUSE NONE OF THE OTHER PARENTS WHO DON'T BUY WHAT THE GOVERNMENT IS SELLING WANT TO TALK TO YOU.
YOU WANT THE "WOMAN PUSHED OFF HER ROCKER DUE TO GRIEF" STORY. YOU WANT A FORMERLY RESPECTED FAMILY DENTIST TALKING ABOUT UFOs. YOU WANT HUMAN INTEREST. YOU WANT RATINGS.
SO, YOU STILL DON'T BELIEVE THERE WAS AN EXPLOSION.
HIGH SCHOOL
A FLASH OF LIGHT
I'M NOT GOING THROUGH THIS AGAIN.
TWO YEARS AGO, TO THE DAY, I LOST MY DAUGHTER. I LOST MY DAUGHTER AND NOBODY ON THE PLANET CAN TELL ME WHAT HAPPENED TO HER IN A WAY THAT MAKES SENSE.
HAVE SOME BASIC HUMAN DECENCY AND LEAVE ME THE HELL ALONE.
DAMMIT...
SLAM!

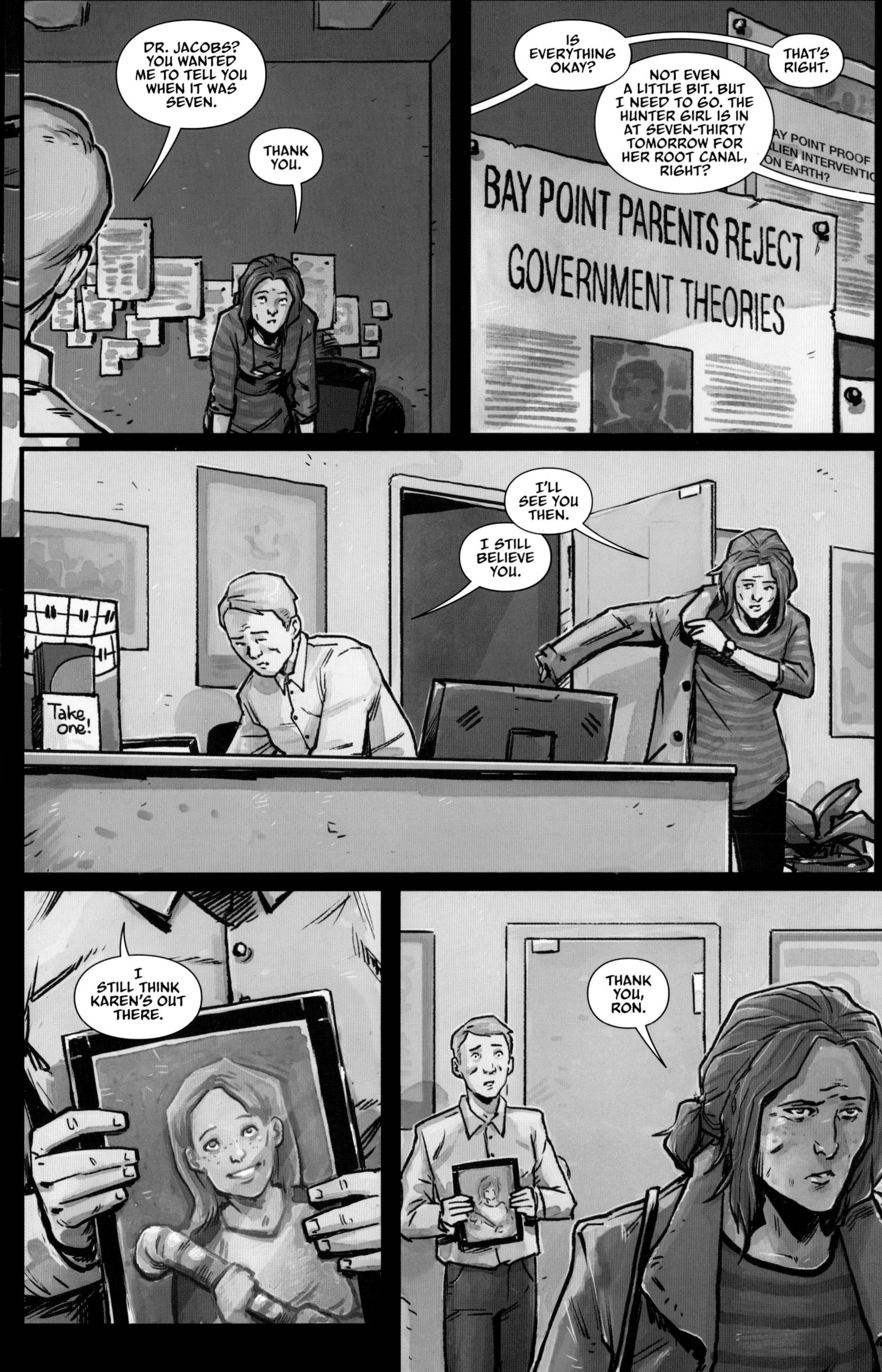
DR. JACOBS? YOU WANTED ME TO TELL YOU WHEN IT WAS SEVEN.
THANK YOU.
IS EVERYTHING OKAY?
NOT EVEN A LITTLE BIT. BUT I NEED TO GO. THE HUNTER GIRL IS IN AT SEVEN-THIRTY TOMORROW FOR HER ROOT CANAL, RIGHT?
THAT'S RIGHT.
AY POINT PROOF
LIEN INTERVENTIO
ON EARTH?
BAY POINT PARENTS REJECT GOVERNMENT THEORIES
I'LL SEE YOU THEN.
I STILL BELIEVE YOU.
Take one!
I STILL THINK KAREN'S OUT THERE.
THANK YOU, RON.

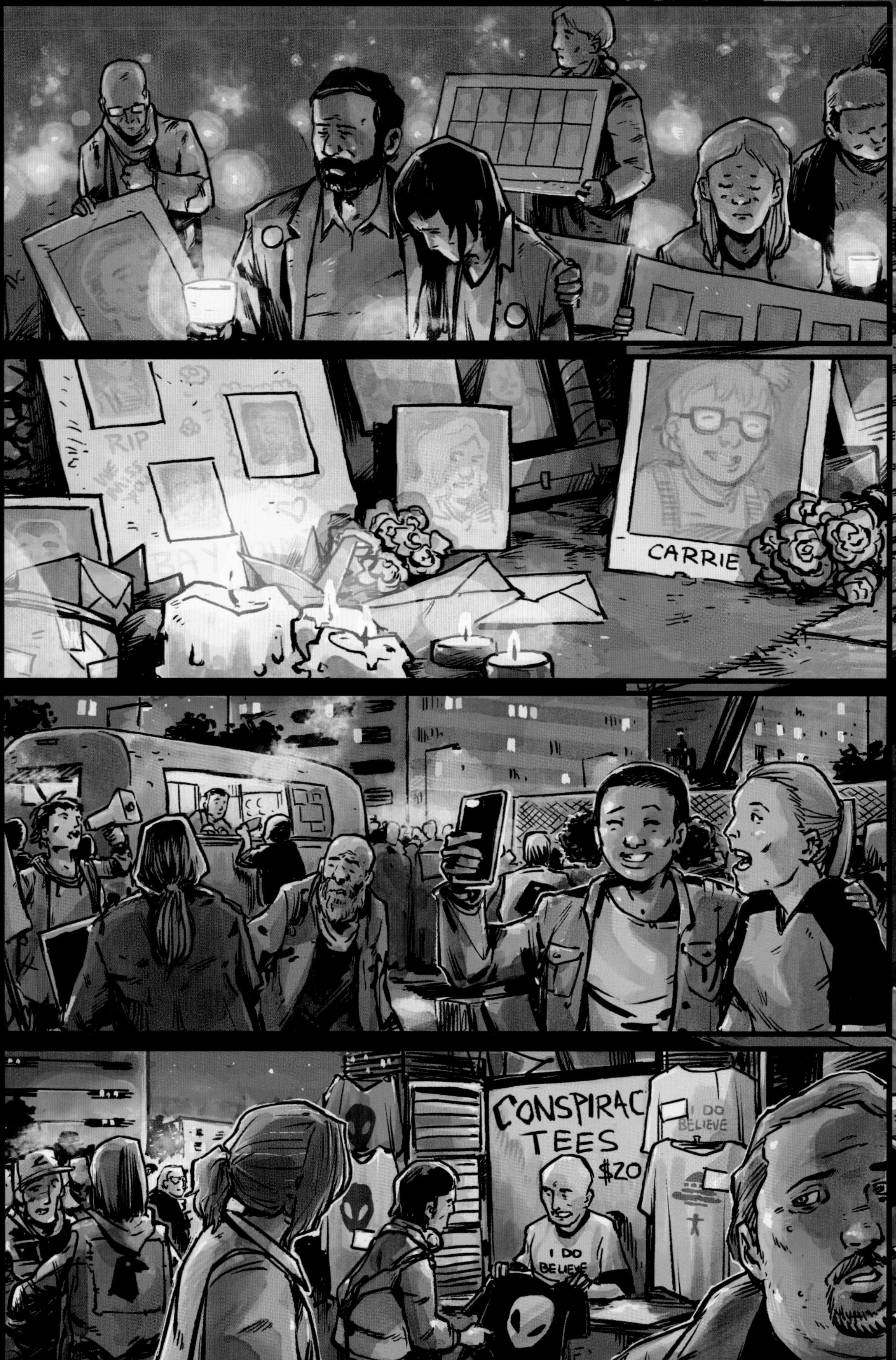
RIP
CARRIE
CONSPIRAC
TEES
$20
I DO BELIEVE
I DO BELIEVE

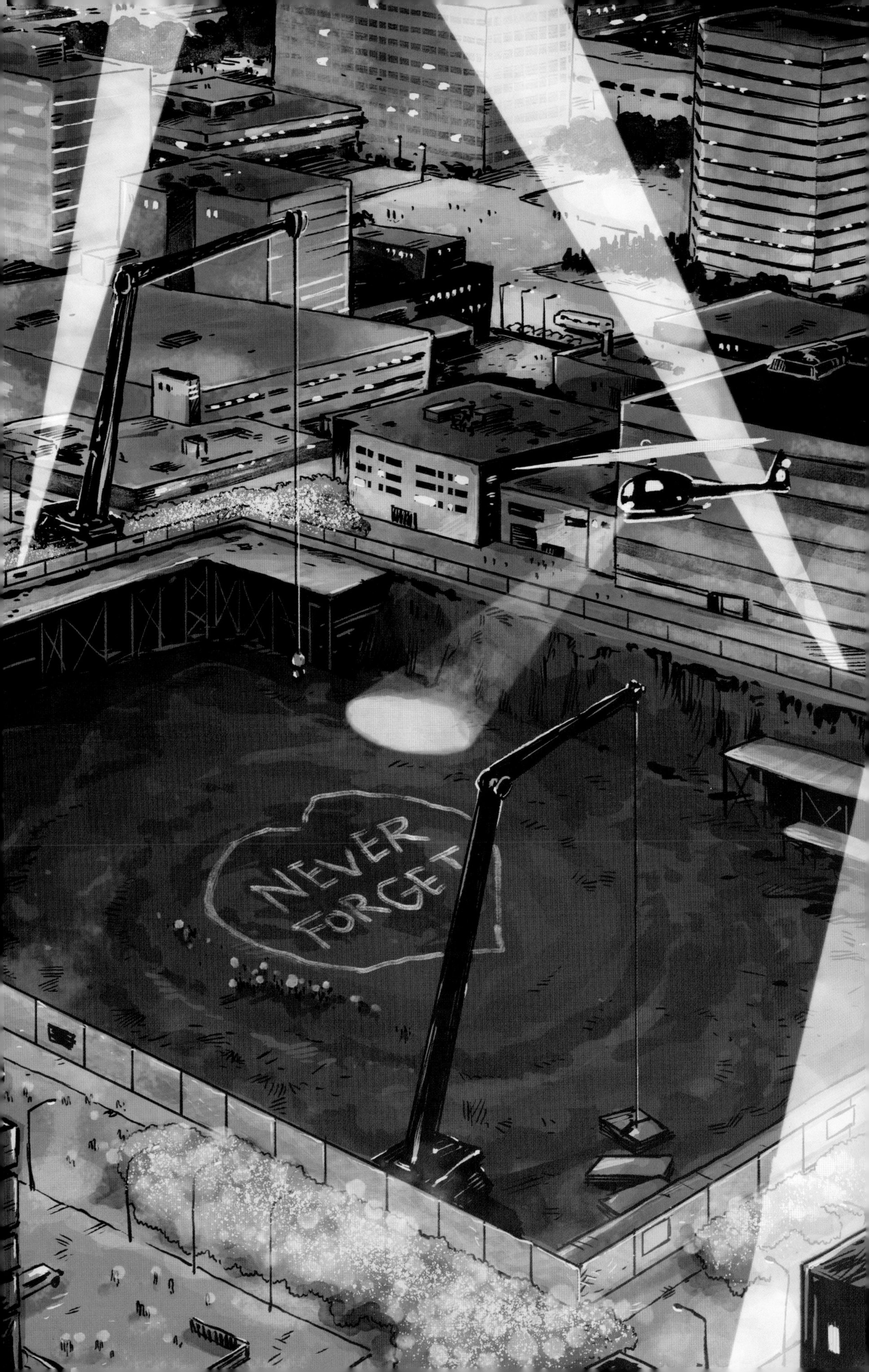
NEVER FORGET

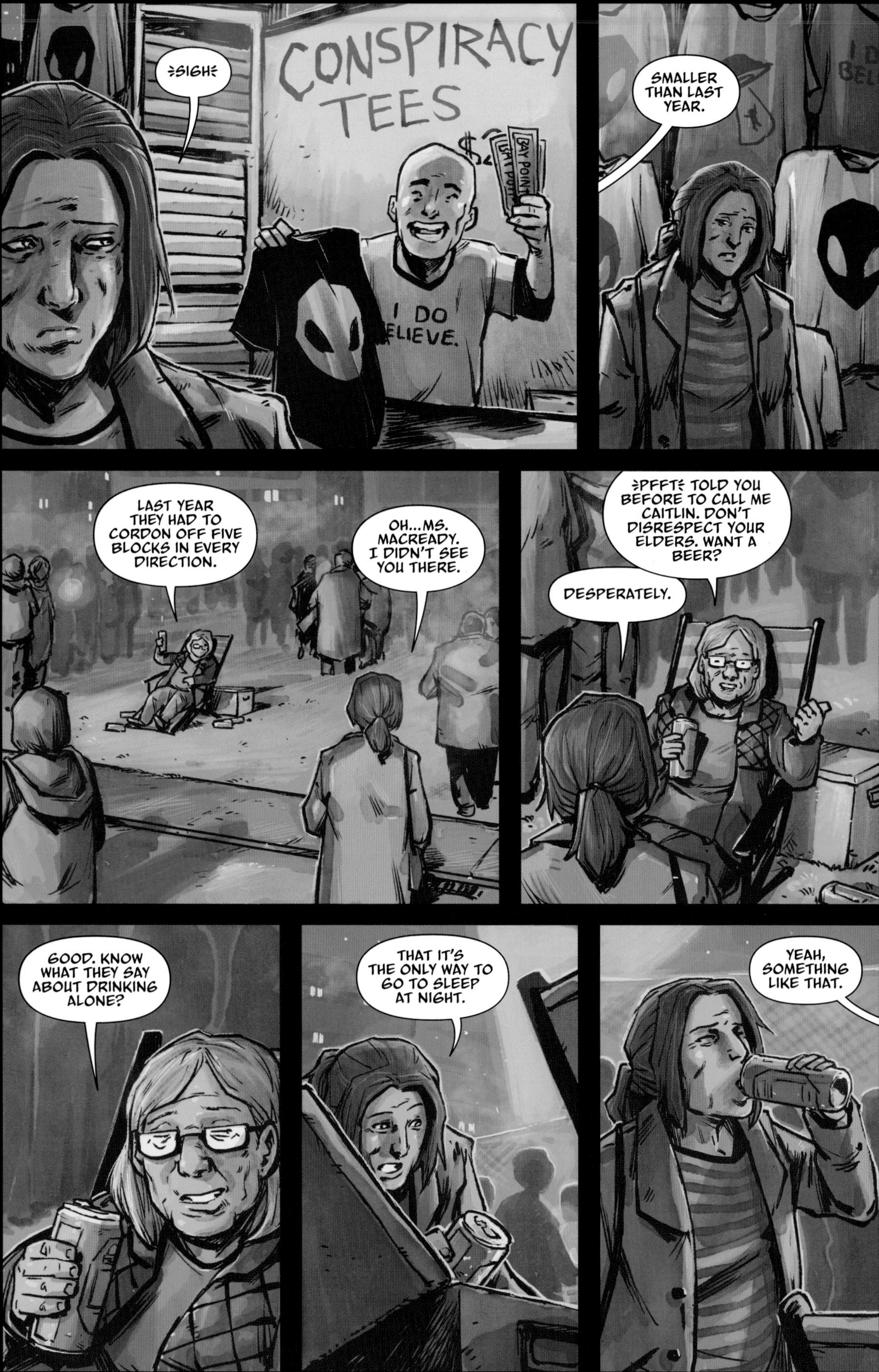

CONSPIRACY TEES
≶SIGH≷
I DO BELIEVE.
SMALLER THAN LAST YEAR.
LAST YEAR THEY HAD TO CORDON OFF FIVE BLOCKS IN EVERY DIRECTION.
OH...MS. MACREADY. I DIDN'T SEE YOU THERE.
≶PFFT≷ TOLD YOU BEFORE TO CALL ME CAITLIN. DON'T DISRESPECT YOUR ELDERS. WANT A BEER?
DESPERATELY.
GOOD. KNOW WHAT THEY SAY ABOUT DRINKING ALONE?
THAT IT'S THE ONLY WAY TO GO TO SLEEP AT NIGHT.
YEAH, SOMETHING LIKE THAT.

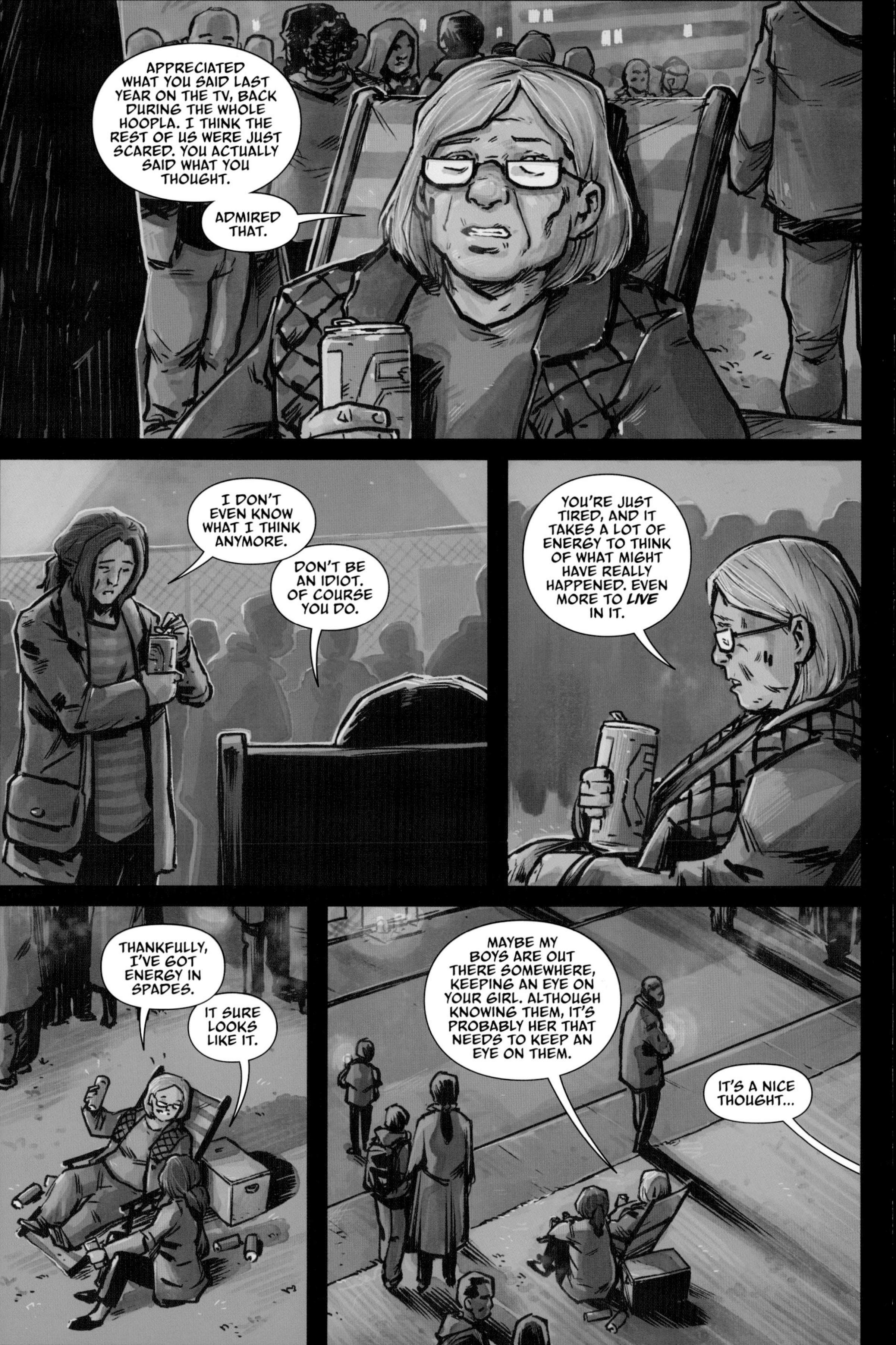
APPRECIATED WHAT YOU SAID LAST YEAR ON THE TV, BACK DURING THE WHOLE HOOPLA. I THINK THE REST OF US WERE JUST SCARED. YOU ACTUALLY SAID WHAT YOU THOUGHT.
ADMIRED THAT.
I DON'T EVEN KNOW WHAT I THINK ANYMORE.
DON'T BE AN IDIOT. OF COURSE YOU DO.
YOU'RE JUST TIRED, AND IT TAKES A LOT OF ENERGY TO THINK OF WHAT MIGHT HAVE REALLY HAPPENED. EVEN MORE TO *LIVE* IN IT.
THANKFULLY, I'VE GOT ENERGY IN SPADES.
IT SURE LOOKS LIKE IT.
MAYBE MY BOYS ARE OUT THERE SOMEWHERE, KEEPING AN EYE ON YOUR GIRL. ALTHOUGH KNOWING THEM, IT'S PROBABLY HER THAT NEEDS TO KEEP AN EYE ON THEM.
IT'S A NICE THOUGHT...

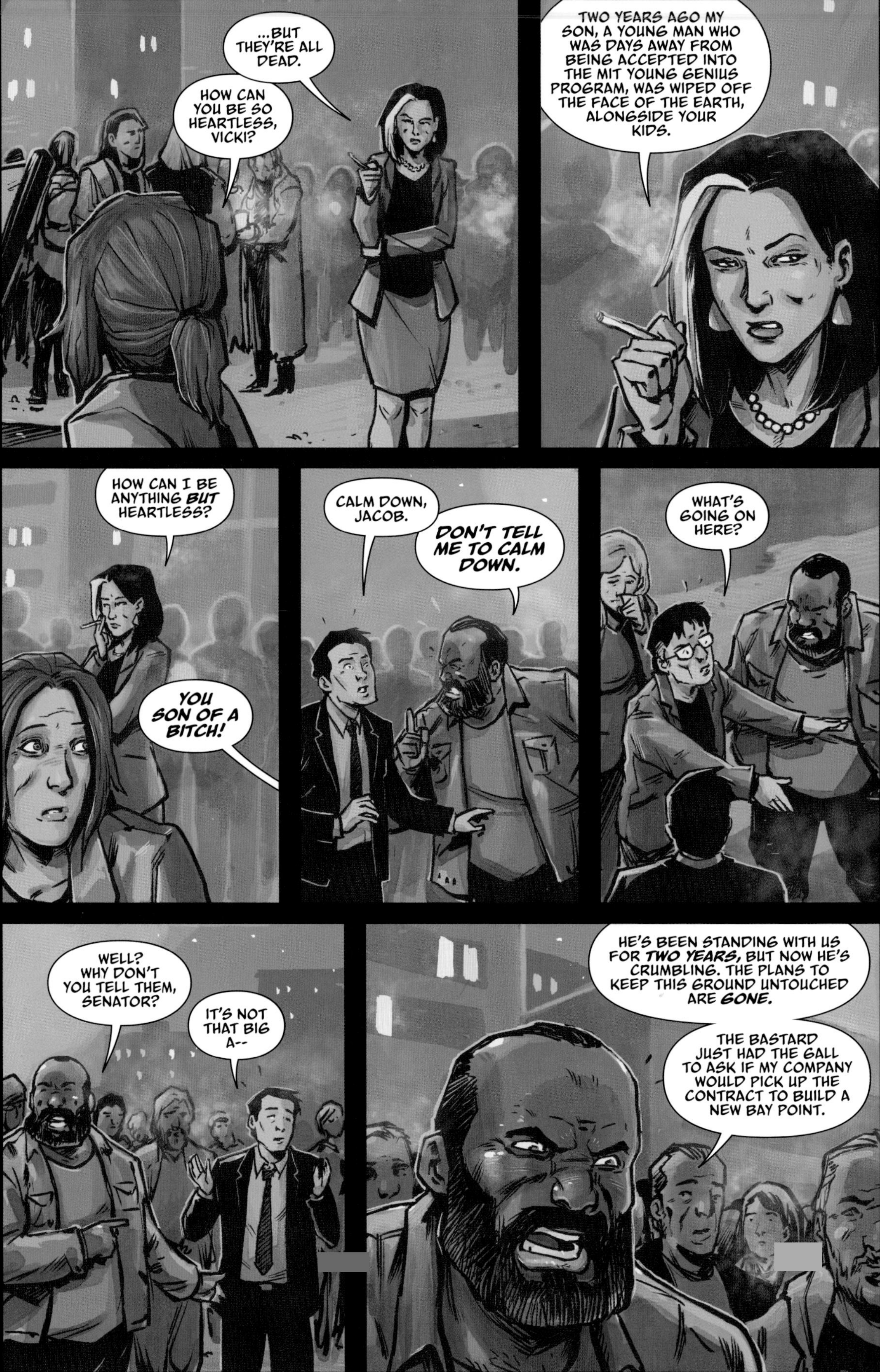

HOW CAN YOU BE SO HEARTLESS, VICKI?
...BUT THEY'RE ALL DEAD.
TWO YEARS AGO MY SON, A YOUNG MAN WHO WAS DAYS AWAY FROM BEING ACCEPTED INTO THE MIT YOUNG GENIUS PROGRAM, WAS WIPED OFF THE FACE OF THE EARTH, ALONGSIDE YOUR KIDS.
HOW CAN I BE ANYTHING *BUT* HEARTLESS?
YOU SON OF A BITCH!
CALM DOWN, JACOB.
DON'T TELL ME TO CALM DOWN.
WHAT'S GOING ON HERE?
WELL? WHY DON'T YOU TELL THEM, SENATOR?
IT'S NOT THAT BIG A--
HE'S BEEN STANDING WITH US FOR ***TWO YEARS,*** BUT NOW HE'S CRUMBLING. THE PLANS TO KEEP THIS GROUND UNTOUCHED ARE ***GONE.***
THE BASTARD JUST HAD THE GALL TO ASK IF MY COMPANY WOULD PICK UP THE CONTRACT TO BUILD A NEW BAY POINT.

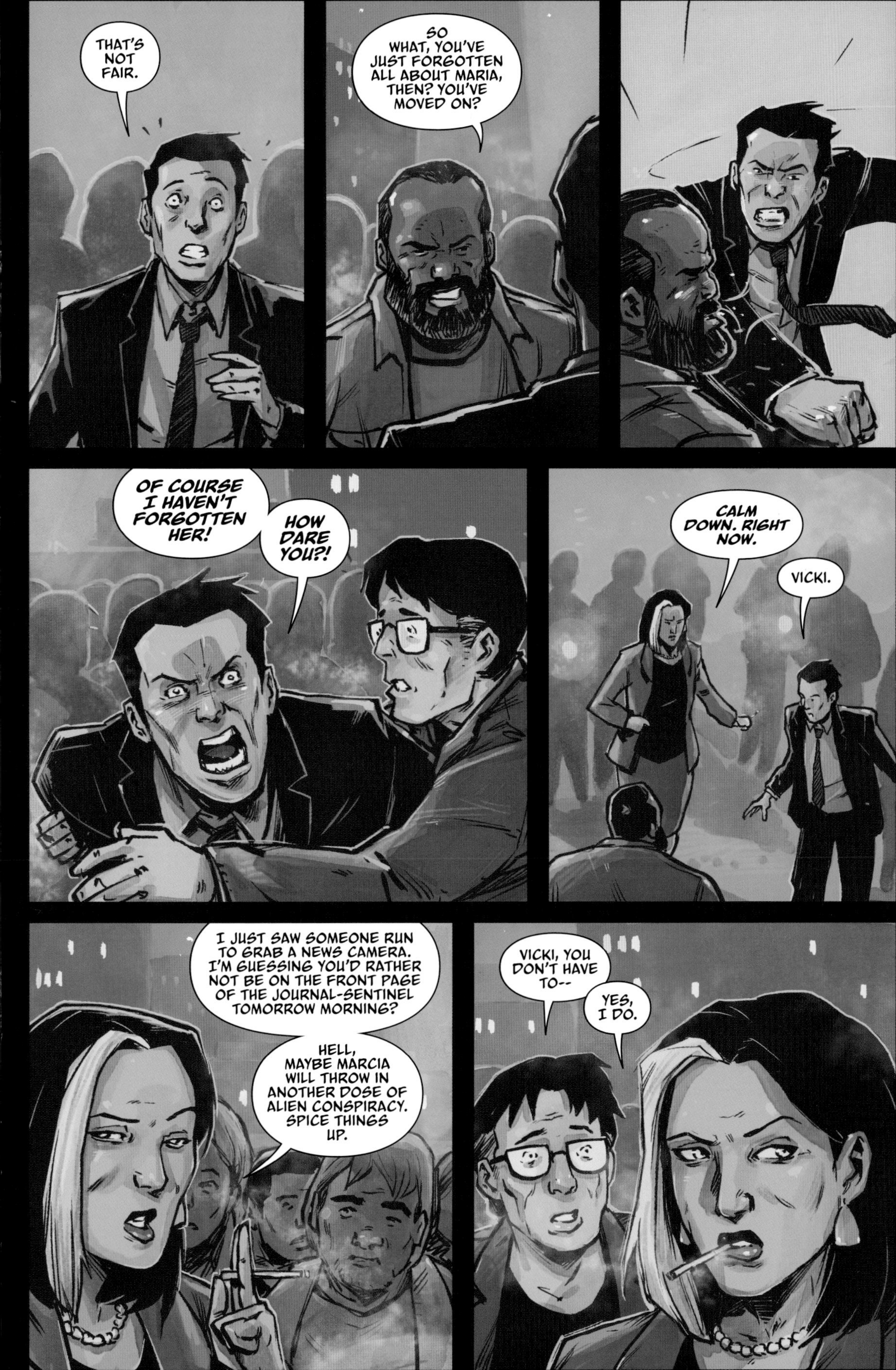
THAT'S NOT FAIR.
SO WHAT, YOU'VE JUST FORGOTTEN ALL ABOUT MARIA, THEN? YOU'VE MOVED ON?
OF COURSE I HAVEN'T FORGOTTEN HER!
HOW DARE YOU?!
CALM DOWN. RIGHT NOW.
VICKI.
I JUST SAW SOMEONE RUN TO GRAB A NEWS CAMERA. I'M GUESSING YOU'D RATHER NOT BE ON THE FRONT PAGE OF THE JOURNAL-SENTINEL TOMORROW MORNING?
HELL, MAYBE MARCIA WILL THROW IN ANOTHER DOSE OF ALIEN CONSPIRACY. SPICE THINGS UP.
VICKI, YOU DON'T HAVE TO--
YES, I DO.

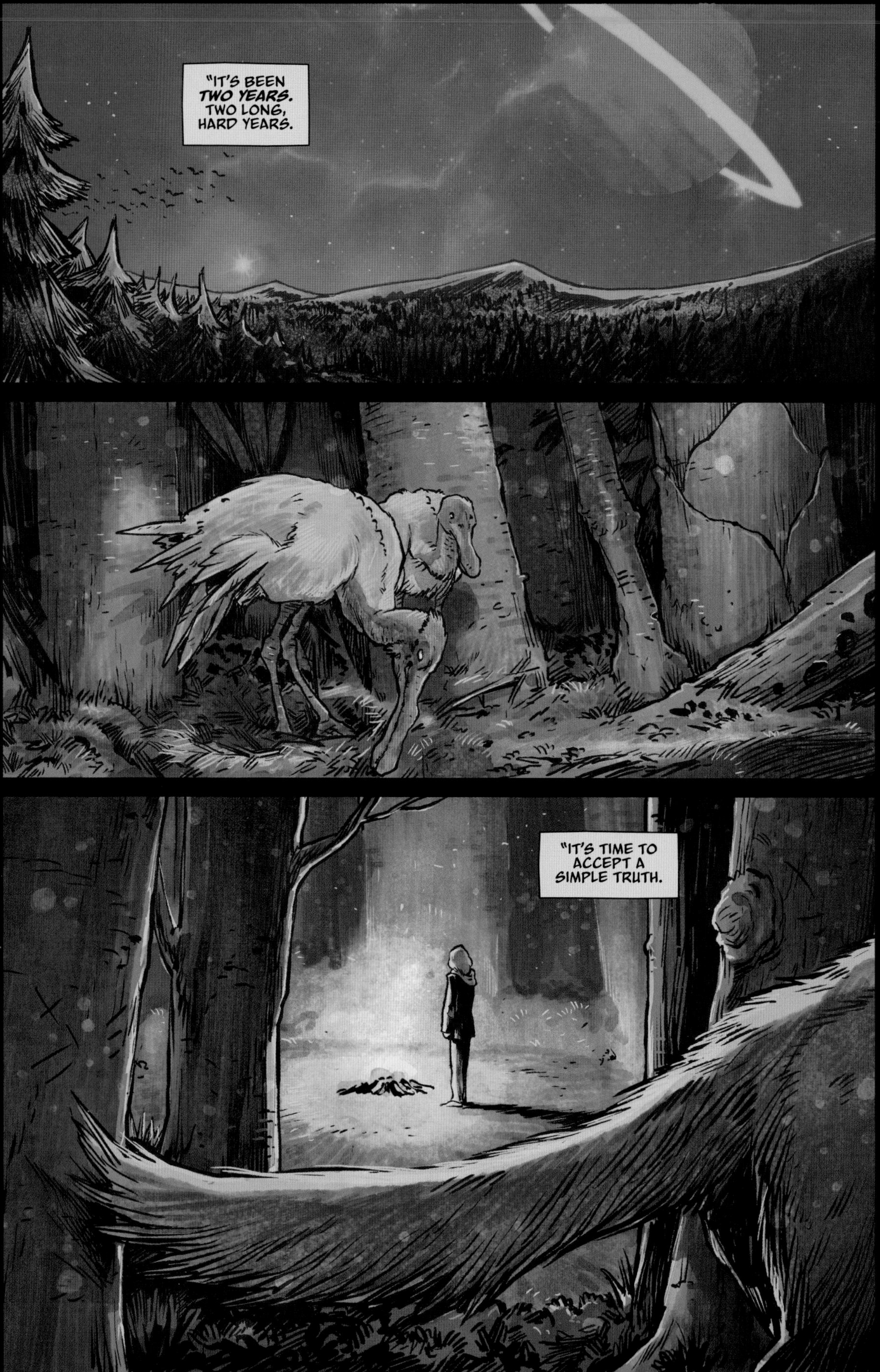
"IT'S BEEN TWO YEARS. TWO LONG, HARD YEARS.
"IT'S TIME TO ACCEPT A SIMPLE TRUTH.

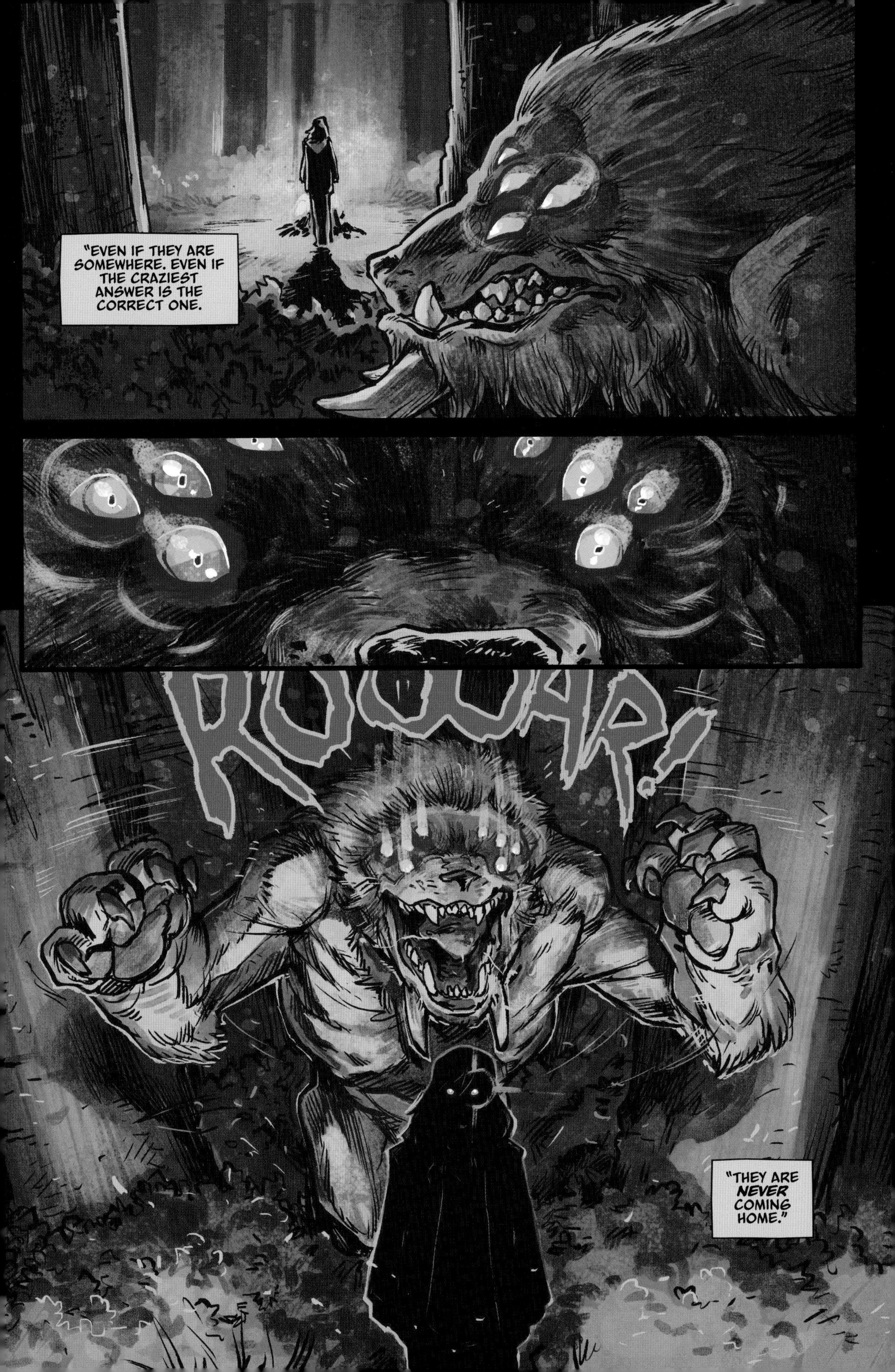
"EVEN IF THEY ARE SOMEWHERE. EVEN IF THE CRAZIEST ANSWER IS THE CORRECT ONE.
ROOOAR!
"THEY ARE *NEVER* COMING HOME."

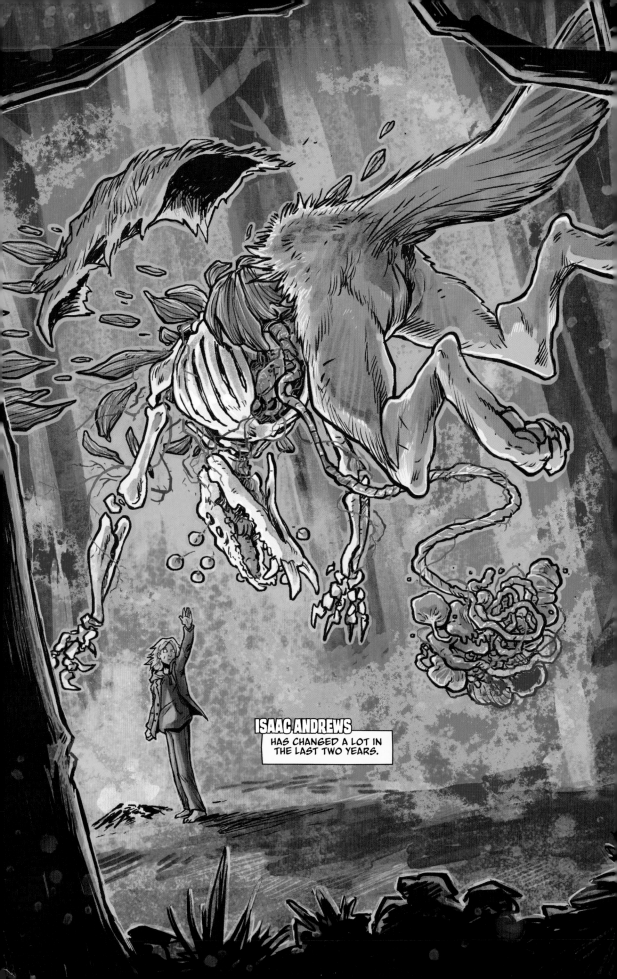

ISAAC ANDREWS

HAS CHANGED A LOT IN
THE LAST TWO YEARS.

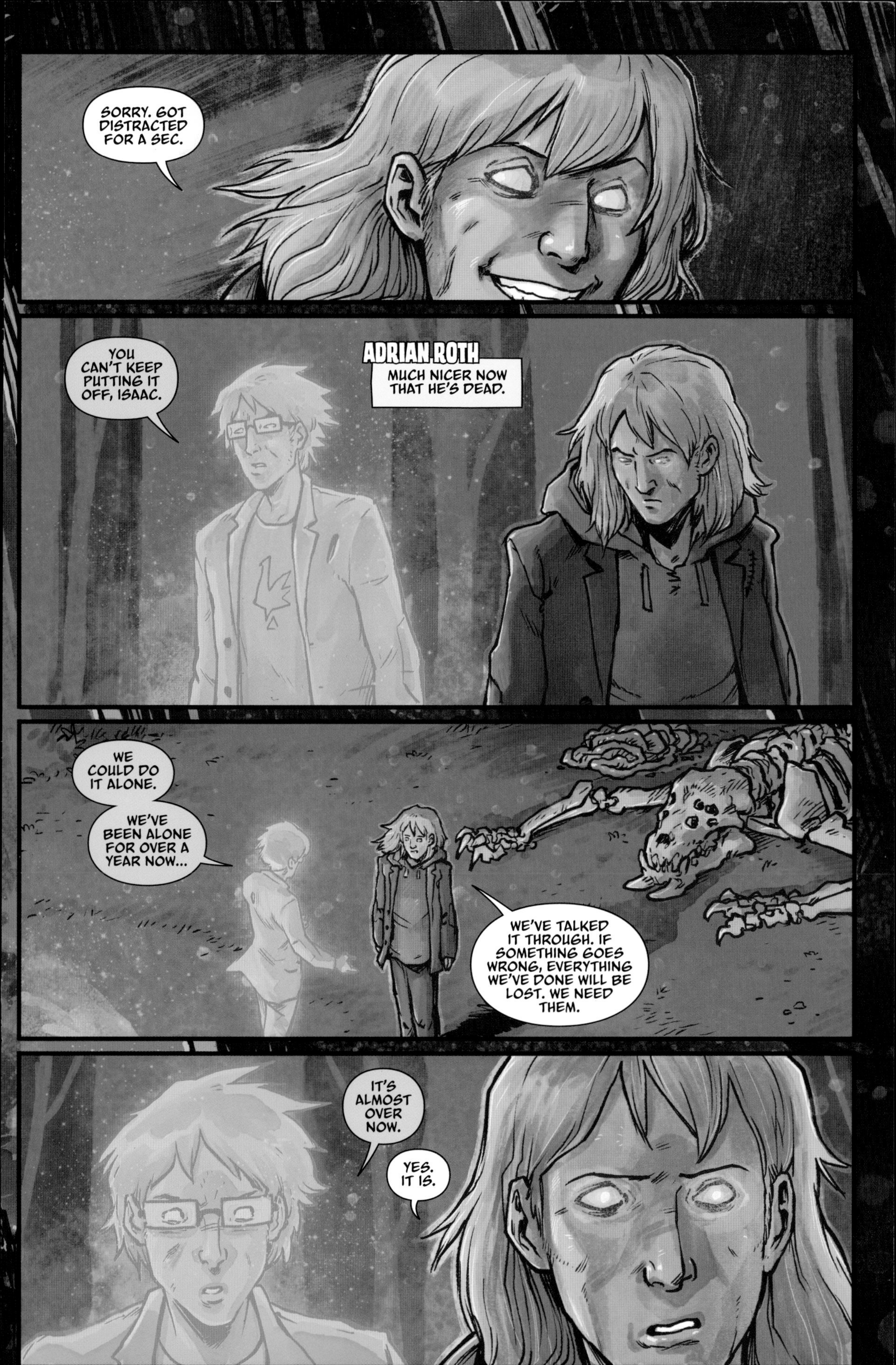
SORRY. GOT DISTRACTED FOR A SEC.
YOU CAN'T KEEP PUTTING IT OFF, ISAAC.
ADRIAN ROTH
MUCH NICER NOW THAT HE'S DEAD.
WE COULD DO IT ALONE.
WE'VE BEEN ALONE FOR OVER A YEAR NOW...
WE'VE TALKED IT THROUGH. IF SOMETHING GOES WRONG, EVERYTHING WE'VE DONE WILL BE LOST. WE NEED THEM.
IT'S ALMOST OVER NOW.
YES. IT IS.

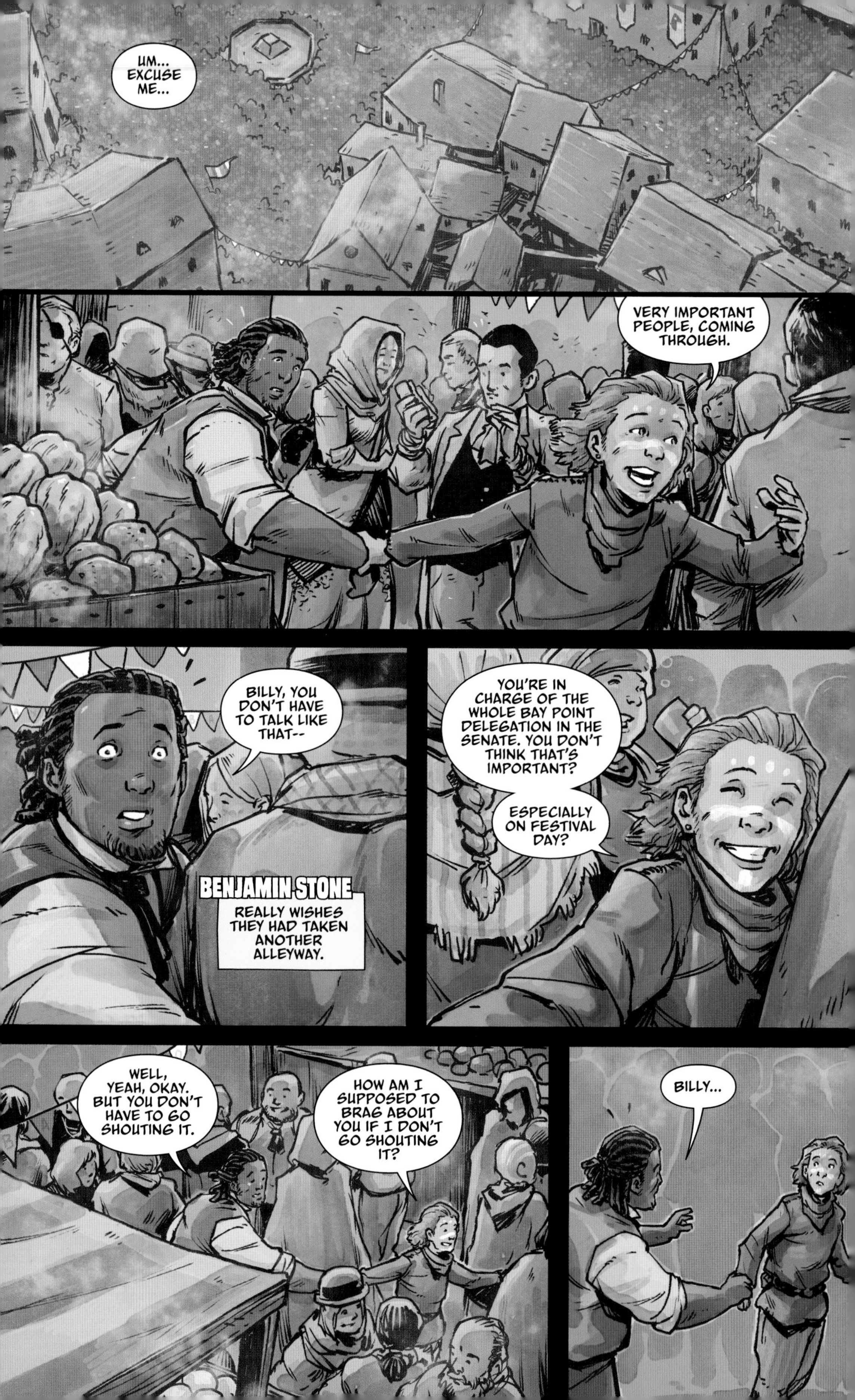
UM... EXCUSE ME...
VERY IMPORTANT PEOPLE, COMING THROUGH.
BILLY, YOU DON'T HAVE TO TALK LIKE THAT--
BENJAMIN STONE
REALLY WISHES THEY HAD TAKEN ANOTHER ALLEYWAY.
YOU'RE IN CHARGE OF THE WHOLE BAY POINT DELEGATION IN THE SENATE. YOU DON'T THINK THAT'S IMPORTANT?
ESPECIALLY ON FESTIVAL DAY?
WELL, YEAH, OKAY. BUT YOU DON'T HAVE TO GO SHOUTING IT.
HOW AM I SUPPOSED TO BRAG ABOUT YOU IF I DON'T GO SHOUTING IT?
BILLY...

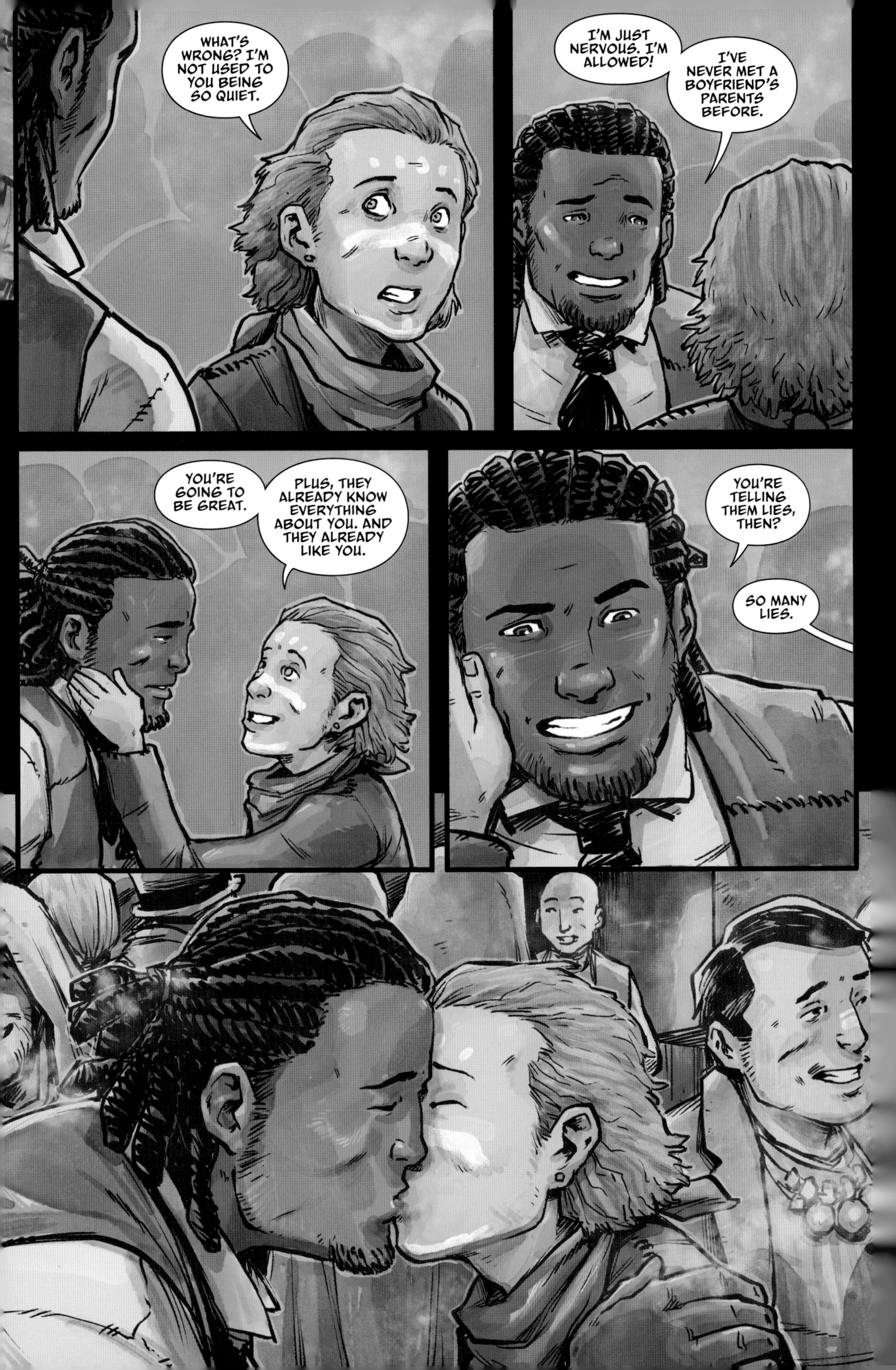
WHAT'S WRONG? I'M NOT USED TO YOU BEING SO QUIET.
I'M JUST NERVOUS. I'M ALLOWED!
I'VE NEVER MET A BOYFRIEND'S PARENTS BEFORE.
YOU'RE GOING TO BE GREAT.
PLUS, THEY ALREADY KNOW EVERYTHING ABOUT YOU. AND THEY ALREADY LIKE YOU.
YOU'RE TELLING THEM LIES, THEN?
SO MANY LIES.

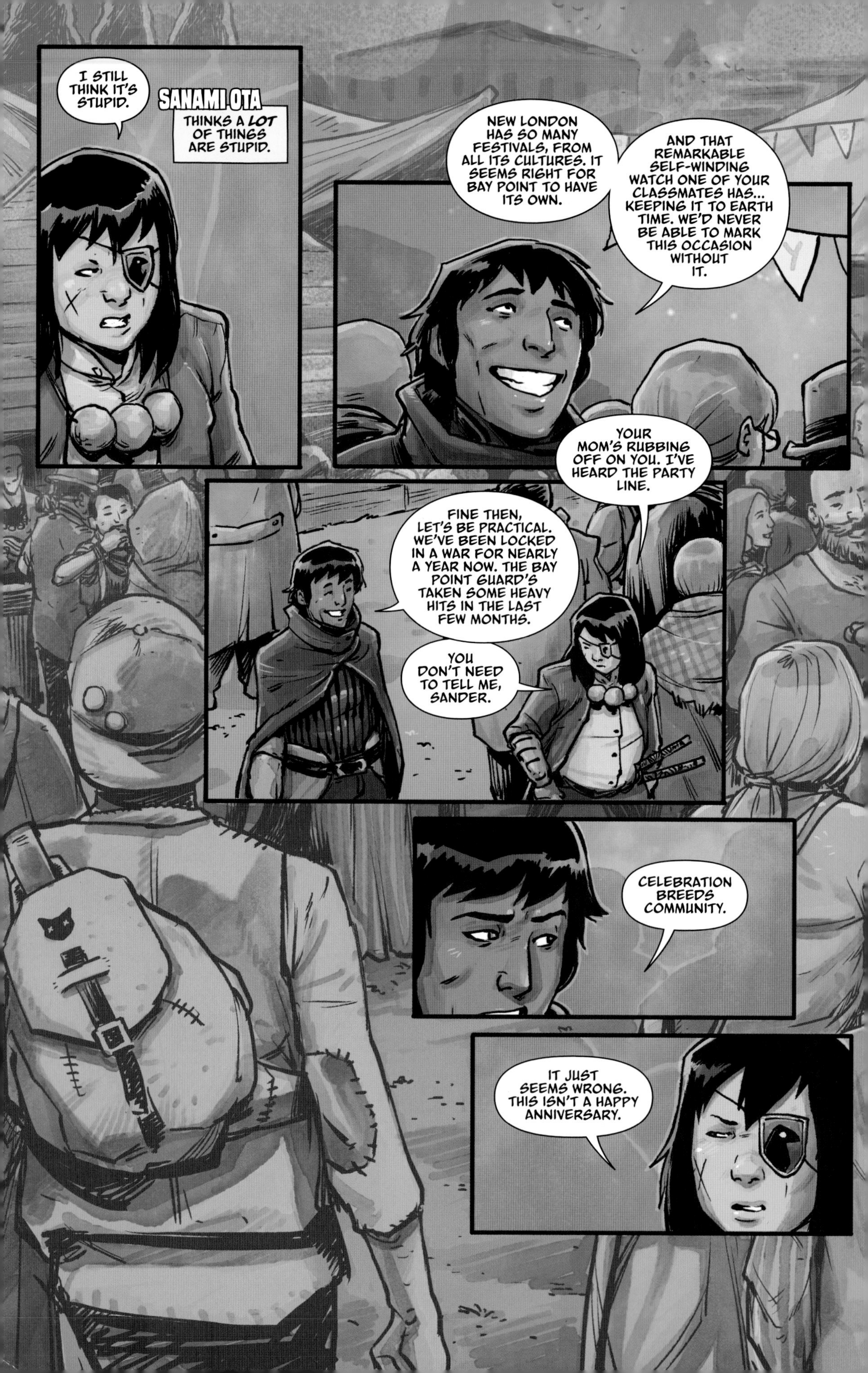
I STILL THINK IT'S STUPID.
SANAMI OTA
THINKS A LOT OF THINGS ARE STUPID.
NEW LONDON HAS SO MANY FESTIVALS, FROM ALL ITS CULTURES. IT SEEMS RIGHT FOR BAY POINT TO HAVE ITS OWN.
AND THAT REMARKABLE SELF-WINDING WATCH ONE OF YOUR CLASSMATES HAS... KEEPING IT TO EARTH TIME. WE'D NEVER BE ABLE TO MARK THIS OCCASION WITHOUT IT.
YOUR MOM'S RUBBING OFF ON YOU. I'VE HEARD THE PARTY LINE.
FINE THEN, LET'S BE PRACTICAL. WE'VE BEEN LOCKED IN A WAR FOR NEARLY A YEAR NOW. THE BAY POINT GUARD'S TAKEN SOME HEAVY HITS IN THE LAST FEW MONTHS.
YOU DON'T NEED TO TELL ME, SANDER.
CELEBRATION BREEDS COMMUNITY.
IT JUST SEEMS WRONG. THIS ISN'T A HAPPY ANNIVERSARY.

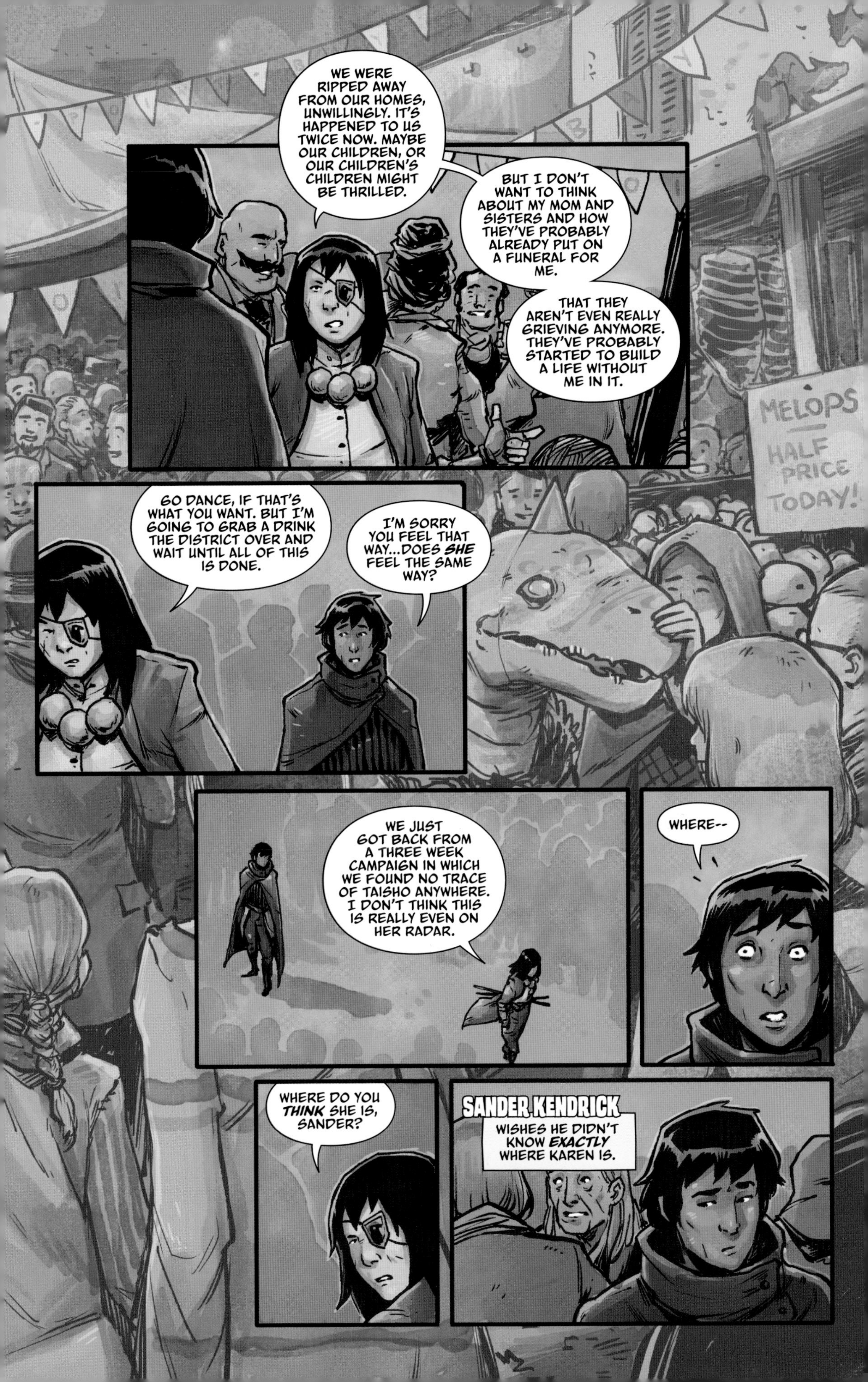
WE WERE RIPPED AWAY FROM OUR HOMES, UNWILLINGLY. IT'S HAPPENED TO US TWICE NOW. MAYBE OUR CHILDREN, OR OUR CHILDREN'S CHILDREN MIGHT BE THRILLED.
BUT I DON'T WANT TO THINK ABOUT MY MOM AND SISTERS AND HOW THEY'VE PROBABLY ALREADY PUT ON A FUNERAL FOR ME.
THAT THEY AREN'T EVEN REALLY GRIEVING ANYMORE. THEY'VE PROBABLY STARTED TO BUILD A LIFE WITHOUT ME IN IT.
MELOPS — HALF PRICE TODAY!
GO DANCE, IF THAT'S WHAT YOU WANT. BUT I'M GOING TO GRAB A DRINK THE DISTRICT OVER AND WAIT UNTIL ALL OF THIS IS DONE.
I'M SORRY YOU FEEL THAT WAY...DOES *SHE* FEEL THE SAME WAY?
WE JUST GOT BACK FROM A THREE WEEK CAMPAIGN IN WHICH WE FOUND NO TRACE OF TAISHO ANYWHERE. I DON'T THINK THIS IS REALLY EVEN ON HER RADAR.
WHERE--
WHERE DO YOU *THINK* SHE IS, SANDER?
SANDER KENDRICK
WISHES HE DIDN'T KNOW *EXACTLY* WHERE KAREN IS.

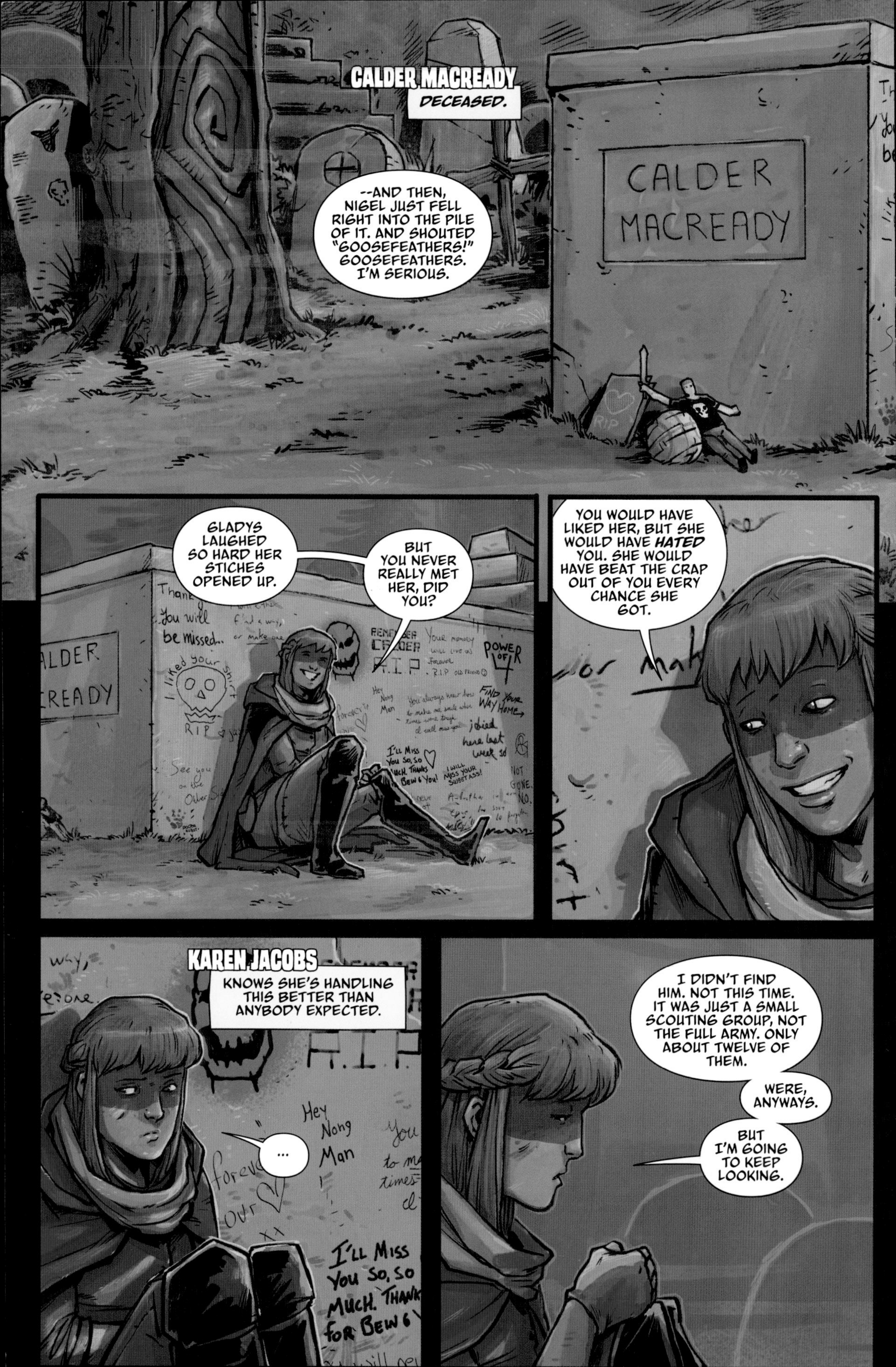

CALDER MACREADY
DECEASED.
--AND THEN, NIGEL JUST FELL RIGHT INTO THE PILE OF IT. AND SHOUTED "GOOSEFEATHERS!" GOOSEFEATHERS. I'M SERIOUS.
CALDER MACREADY
GLADYS LAUGHED SO HARD HER STICHES OPENED UP.
BUT YOU NEVER REALLY MET HER, DID YOU?
YOU WOULD HAVE LIKED HER, BUT SHE WOULD HAVE HATED YOU. SHE WOULD HAVE BEAT THE CRAP OUT OF YOU EVERY CHANCE SHE GOT.
KAREN JACOBS
KNOWS SHE'S HANDLING THIS BETTER THAN ANYBODY EXPECTED.
...
I DIDN'T FIND HIM. NOT THIS TIME. IT WAS JUST A SMALL SCOUTING GROUP, NOT THE FULL ARMY. ONLY ABOUT TWELVE OF THEM.
WERE, ANYWAYS.
BUT I'M GOING TO KEEP LOOKING.

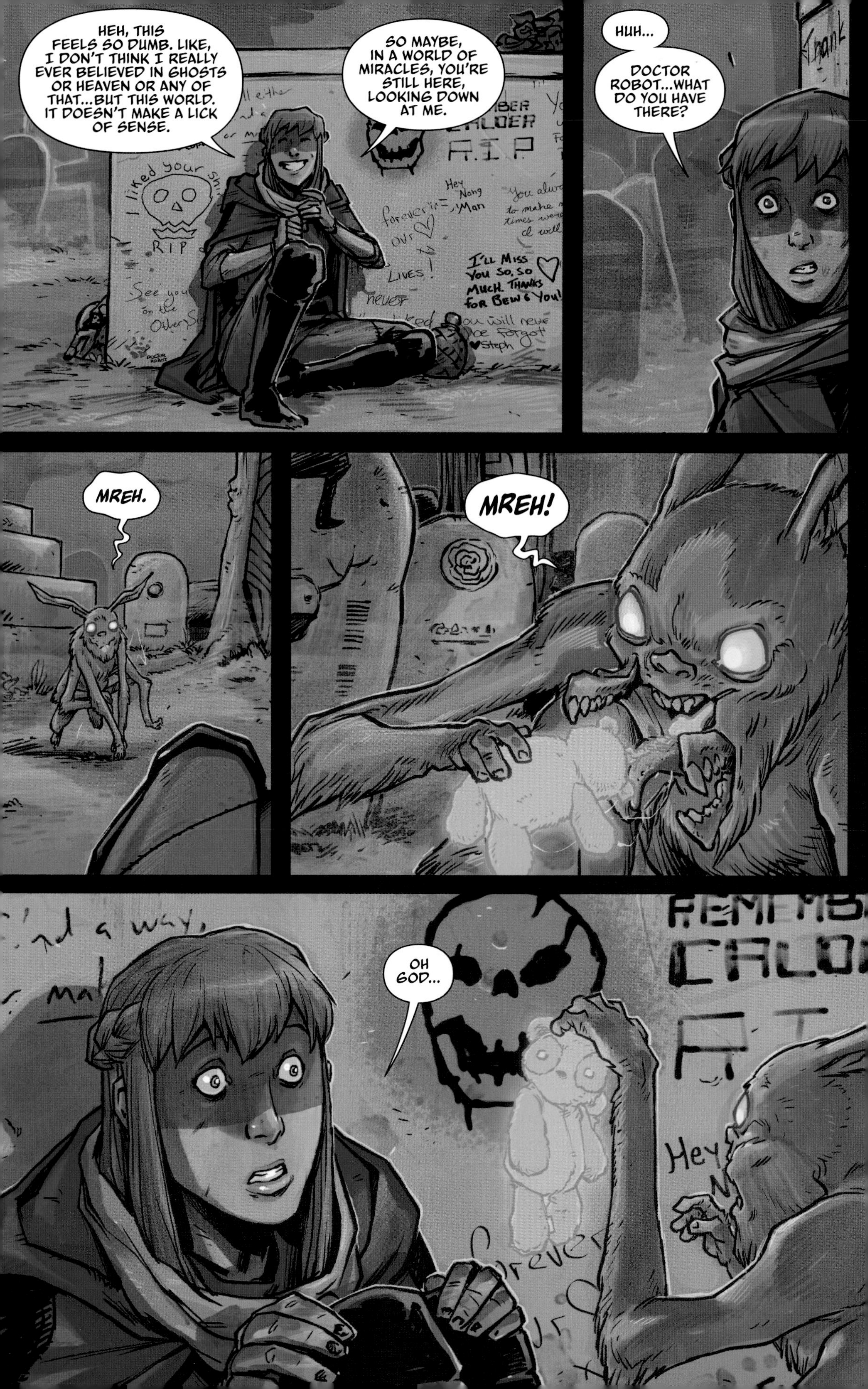
HEH, THIS FEELS SO DUMB. LIKE, I DON'T THINK I REALLY EVER BELIEVED IN GHOSTS OR HEAVEN OR ANY OF THAT...BUT THIS WORLD. IT DOESN'T MAKE A LICK OF SENSE.
SO MAYBE, IN A WORLD OF MIRACLES, YOU'RE STILL HERE, LOOKING DOWN AT ME.
HUH...
DOCTOR ROBOT...WHAT DO YOU HAVE THERE?
MREH.
MREH!
OH GOD...

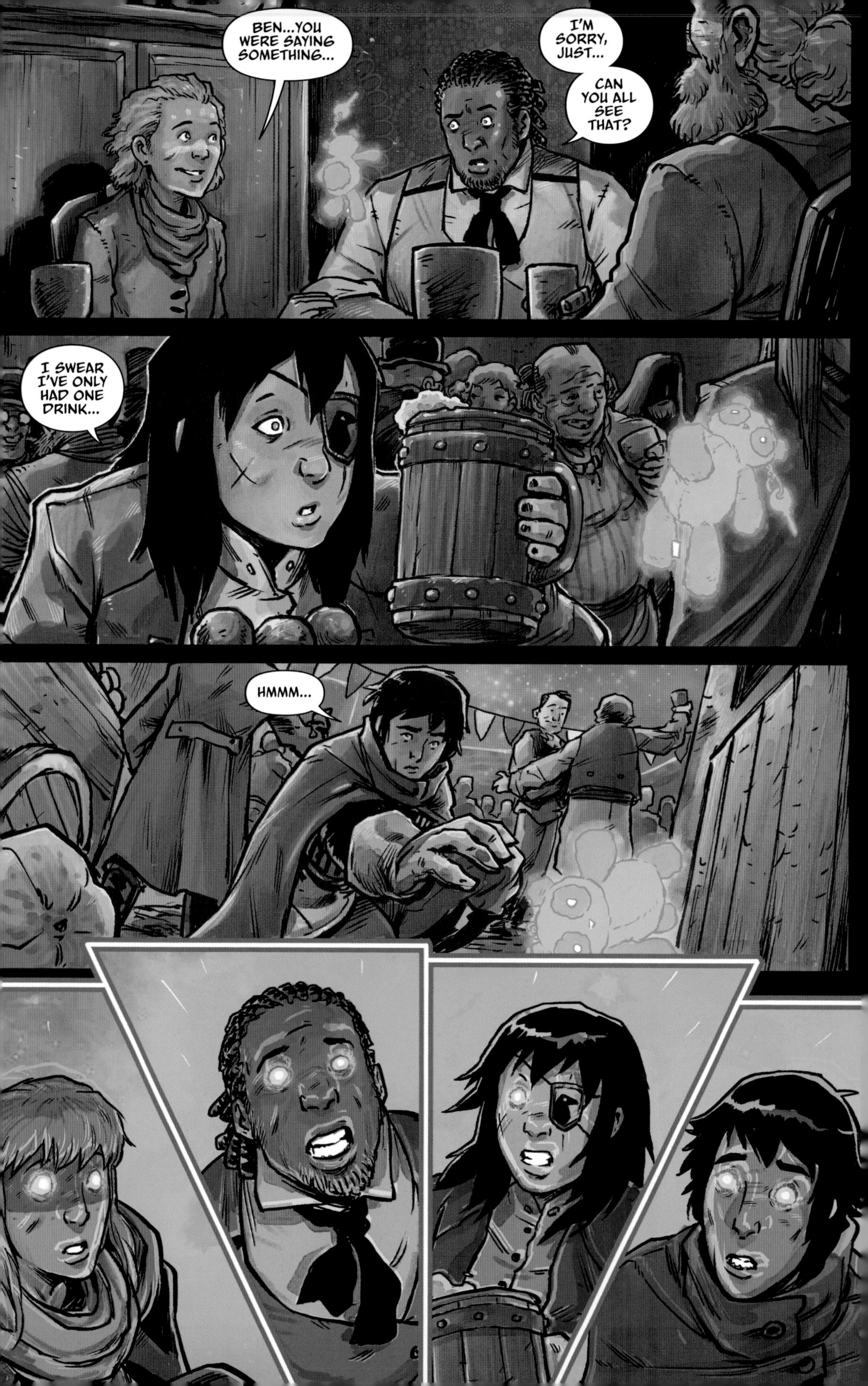
BEN...YOU WERE SAYING SOMETHING...
I'M SORRY, JUST...
CAN YOU ALL SEE THAT?
I SWEAR I'VE ONLY HAD ONE DRINK...
HMMM...

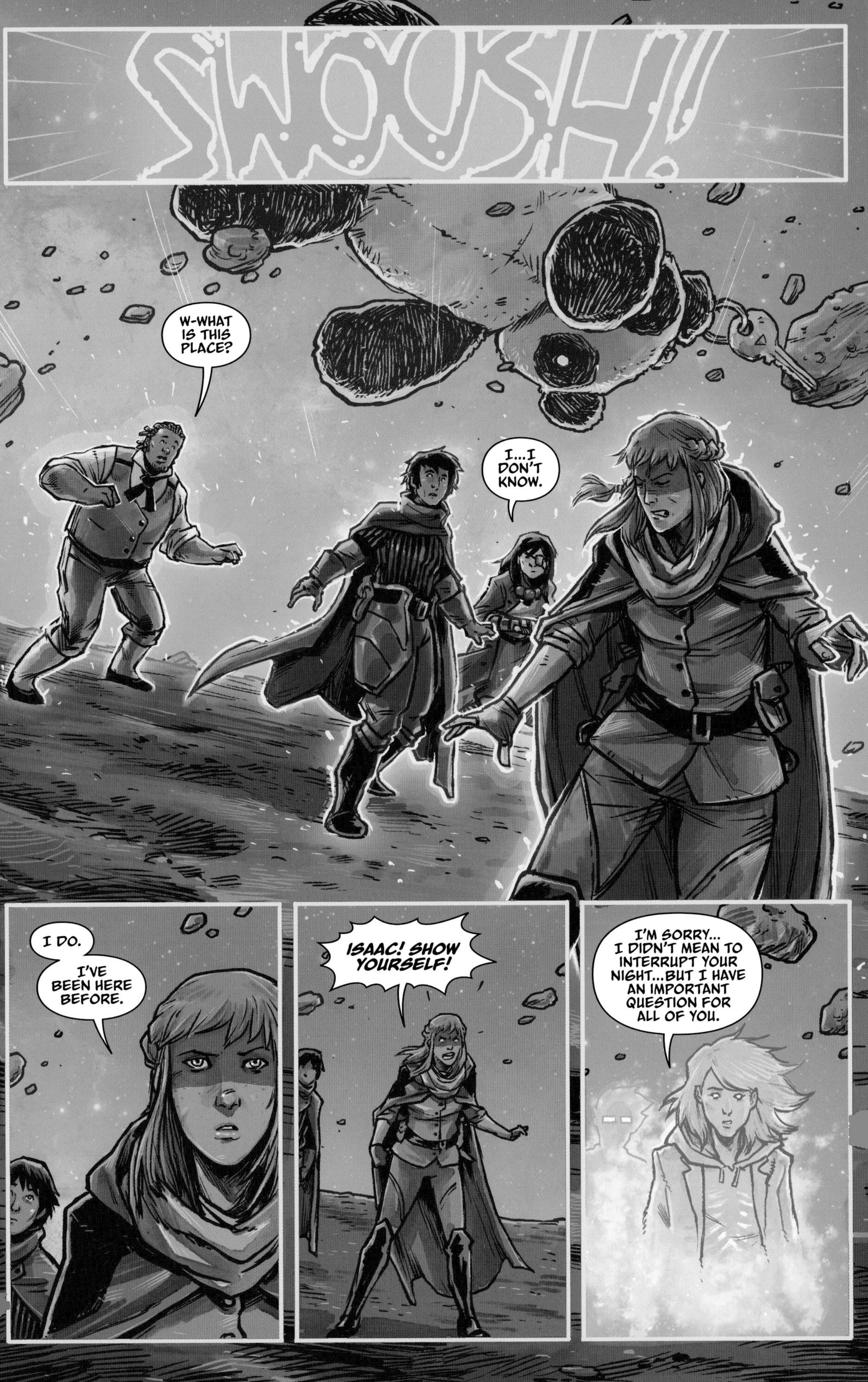
SWOOSH!
W-WHAT IS THIS PLACE?
I...I DON'T KNOW.
I DO.
I'VE BEEN HERE BEFORE.
ISAAC! SHOW YOURSELF!
I'M SORRY... I DIDN'T MEAN TO INTERRUPT YOUR NIGHT...BUT I HAVE AN IMPORTANT QUESTION FOR ALL OF YOU.

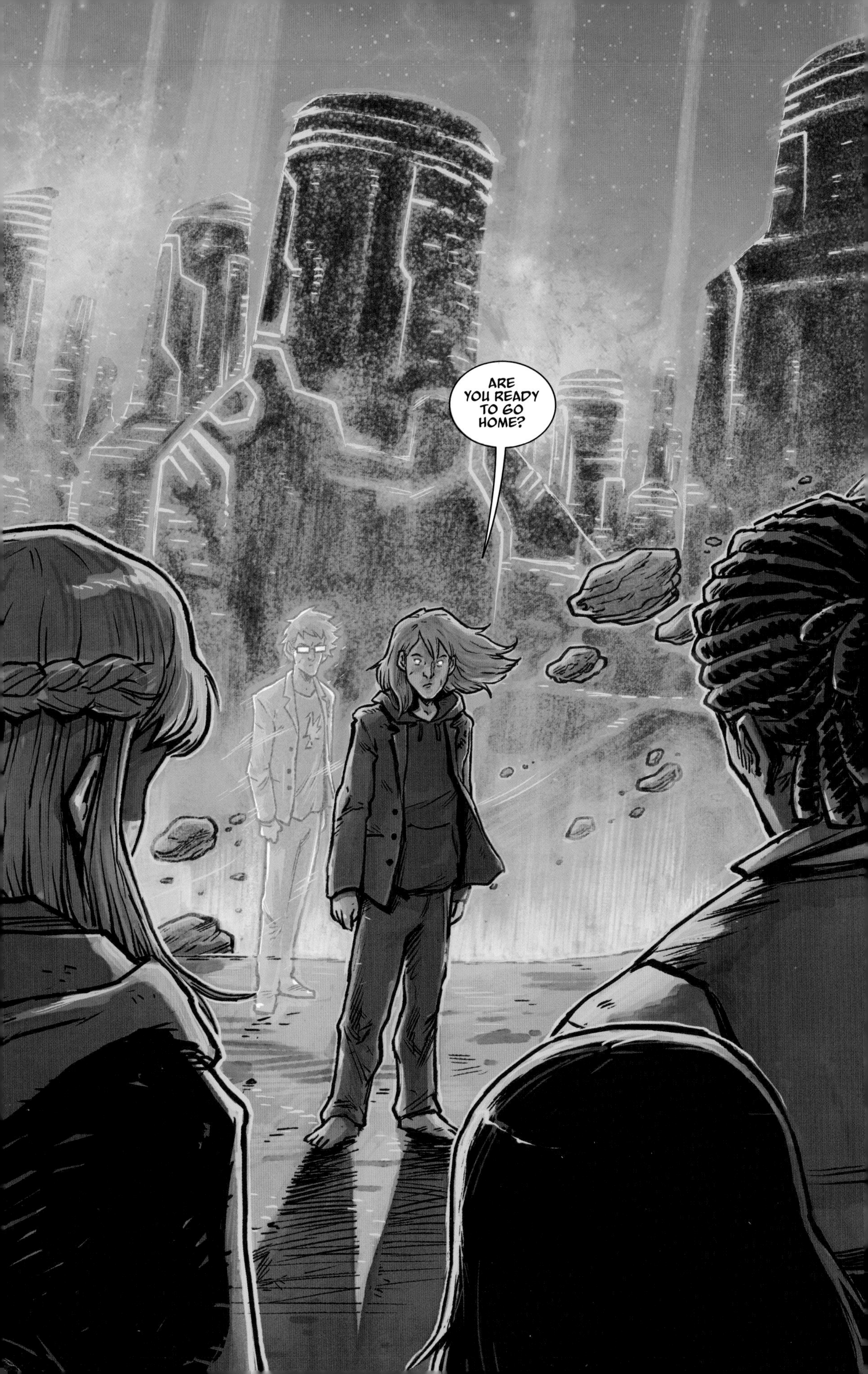
ARE YOU READY TO GO HOME?

CHAPTER TWENTY-SIX

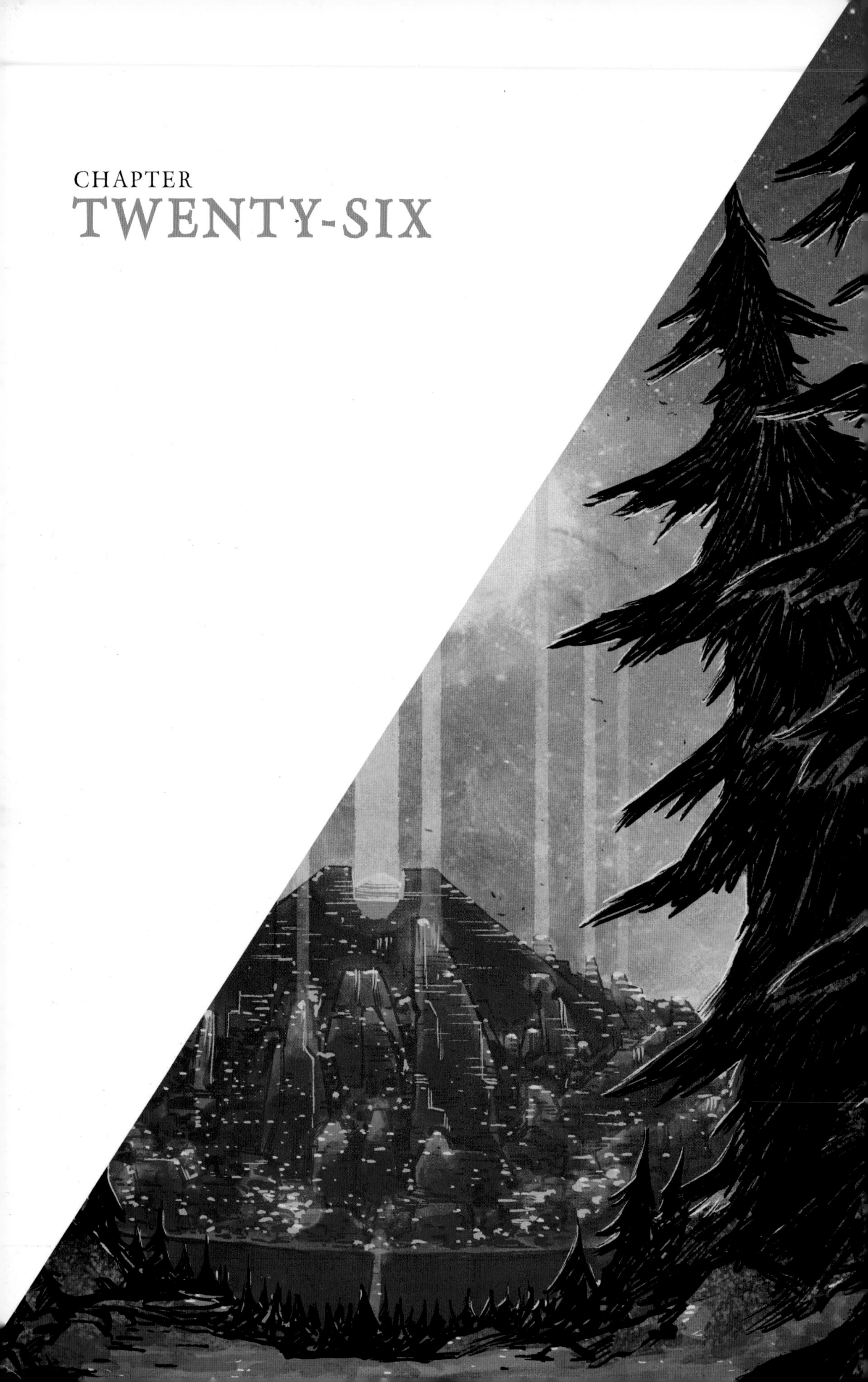

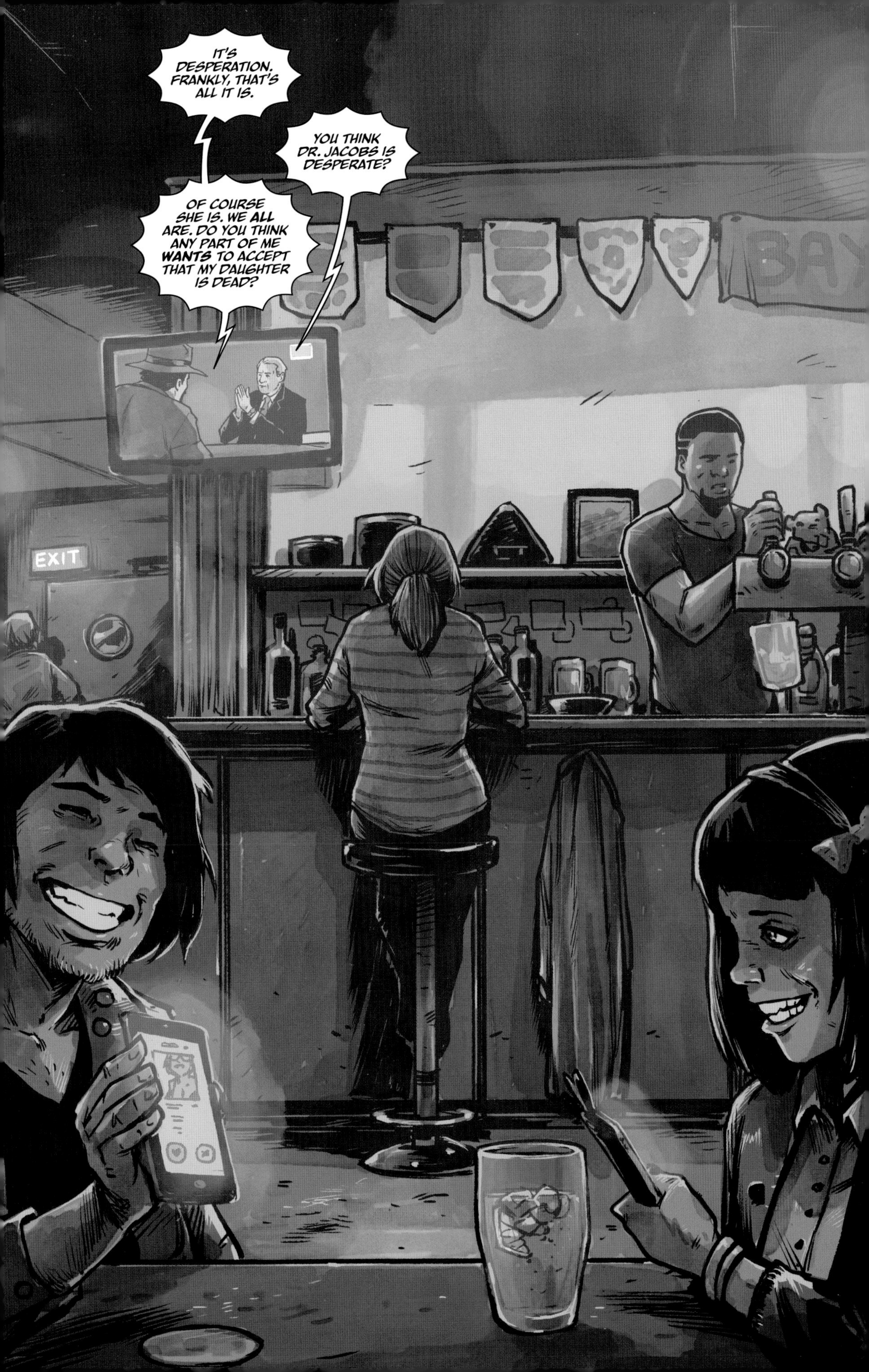
IT'S DESPERATION. FRANKLY, THAT'S ALL IT IS.
YOU THINK DR. JACOBS IS DESPERATE?
OF COURSE SHE IS. WE **ALL** ARE. DO YOU THINK ANY PART OF ME **WANTS** TO ACCEPT THAT MY DAUGHTER IS DEAD?
EXIT

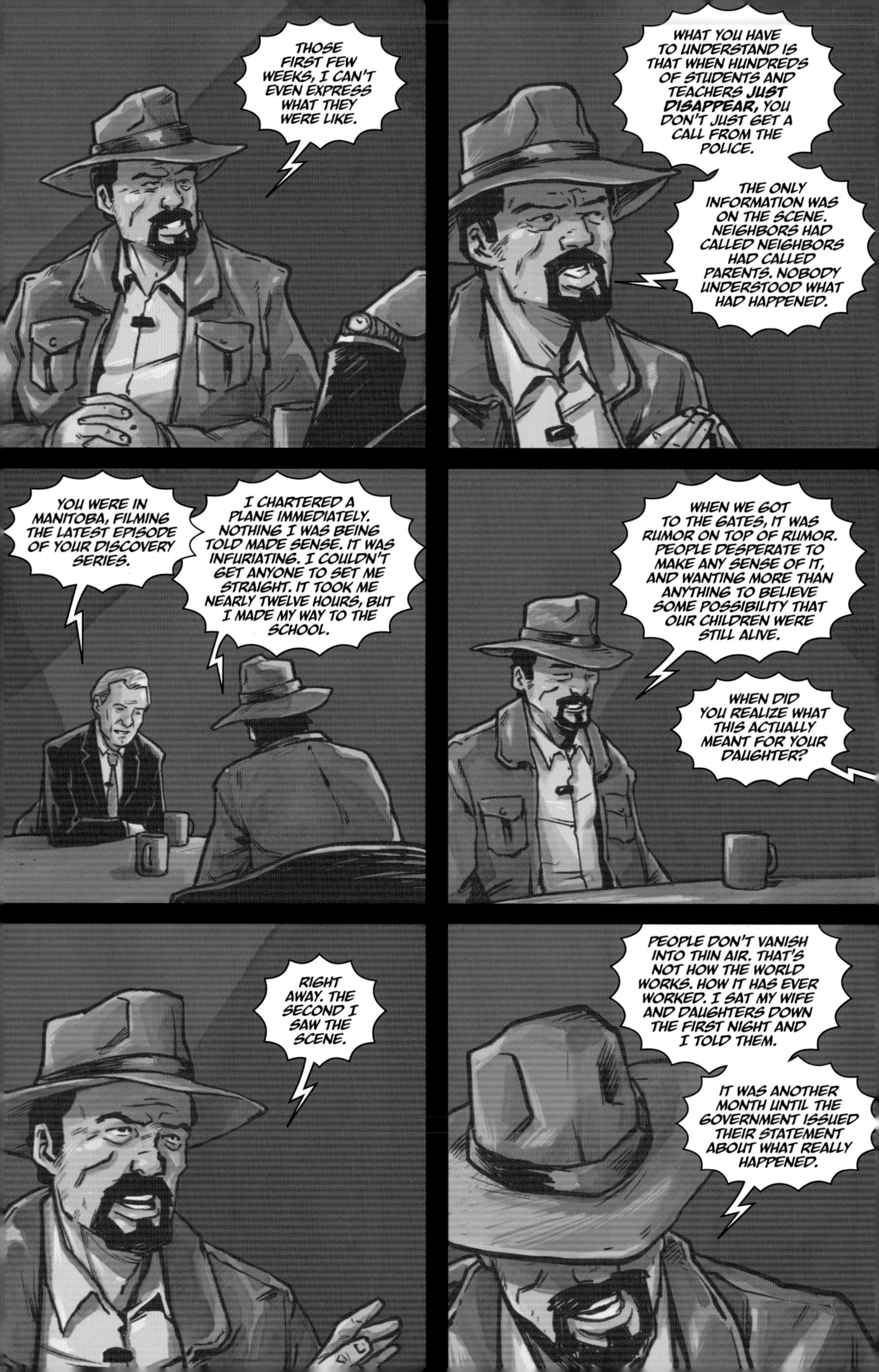
THOSE FIRST FEW WEEKS, I CAN'T EVEN EXPRESS WHAT THEY WERE LIKE.
WHAT YOU HAVE TO UNDERSTAND IS THAT WHEN HUNDREDS OF STUDENTS AND TEACHERS JUST DISAPPEAR, YOU DON'T JUST GET A CALL FROM THE POLICE.
THE ONLY INFORMATION WAS ON THE SCENE. NEIGHBORS HAD CALLED NEIGHBORS HAD CALLED PARENTS. NOBODY UNDERSTOOD WHAT HAD HAPPENED.
YOU WERE IN MANITOBA, FILMING THE LATEST EPISODE OF YOUR DISCOVERY SERIES.
I CHARTERED A PLANE IMMEDIATELY. NOTHING I WAS BEING TOLD MADE SENSE. IT WAS INFURIATING. I COULDN'T GET ANYONE TO SET ME STRAIGHT. IT TOOK ME NEARLY TWELVE HOURS, BUT I MADE MY WAY TO THE SCHOOL.
WHEN WE GOT TO THE GATES, IT WAS RUMOR ON TOP OF RUMOR. PEOPLE DESPERATE TO MAKE ANY SENSE OF IT, AND WANTING MORE THAN ANYTHING TO BELIEVE SOME POSSIBILITY THAT OUR CHILDREN WERE STILL ALIVE.
WHEN DID YOU REALIZE WHAT THIS ACTUALLY MEANT FOR YOUR DAUGHTER?
RIGHT AWAY. THE SECOND I SAW THE SCENE.
PEOPLE DON'T VANISH INTO THIN AIR. THAT'S NOT HOW THE WORLD WORKS. HOW IT HAS EVER WORKED. I SAT MY WIFE AND DAUGHTERS DOWN THE FIRST NIGHT AND I TOLD THEM.
IT WAS ANOTHER MONTH UNTIL THE GOVERNMENT ISSUED THEIR STATEMENT ABOUT WHAT REALLY HAPPENED.

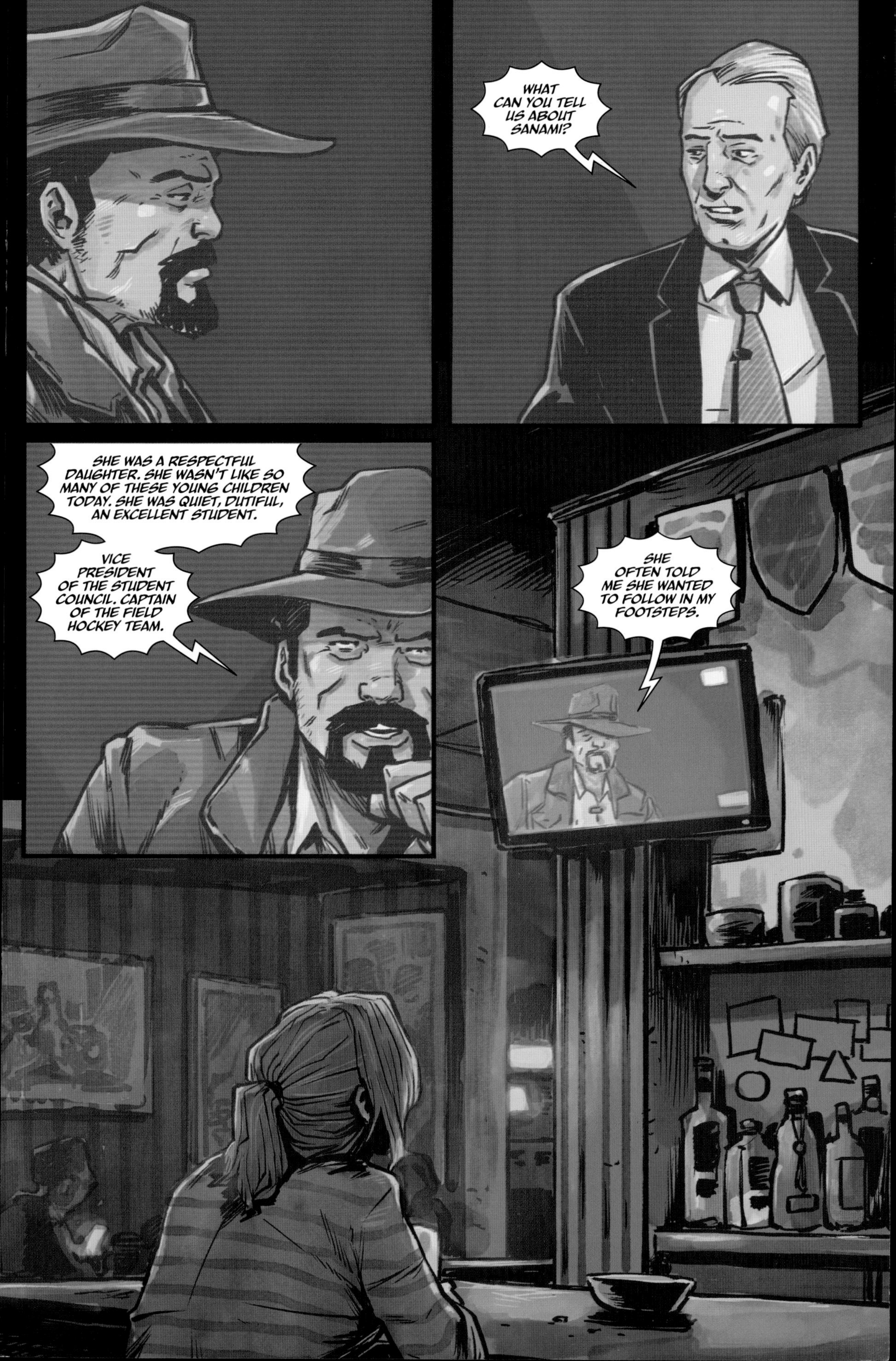
WHAT CAN YOU TELL US ABOUT SANAMI?
SHE WAS A RESPECTFUL DAUGHTER. SHE WASN'T LIKE SO MANY OF THESE YOUNG CHILDREN TODAY. SHE WAS QUIET, DUTIFUL, AN EXCELLENT STUDENT.
VICE PRESIDENT OF THE STUDENT COUNCIL. CAPTAIN OF THE FIELD HOCKEY TEAM.
SHE OFTEN TOLD ME SHE WANTED TO FOLLOW IN MY FOOTSTEPS.

NOW *THERE'S* A LOAD OF BULL.

SORRY?

IT'S NOTHING. JUST CHANGE THE CHANNEL, ALRIGHT?

THE LAST THING I NEED FOR MY SANITY IS TO LISTEN TO ANOTHER WORD THAT COMES OUT OF THAT SMUG JERK'S MOUTH.

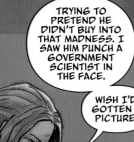

TRYING TO PRETEND HE DIDN'T BUY INTO THAT MADNESS. I SAW HIM PUNCH A GOVERNMENT SCIENTIST IN THE FACE.

WISH I'D GOTTEN A PICTURE.

MARCIA, ISN'T IT GETTING A LITTLE LATE? IT'S PAST ELEVEN P.M.

SOUNDS LIKE IT'S TIME FOR ANOTHER ONE OF THESE HORRIBLE COCKTAILS.

YOU TOLD ME TO CUT YOU--

FORGET WHAT I SAID. I'VE EARNED THIS.

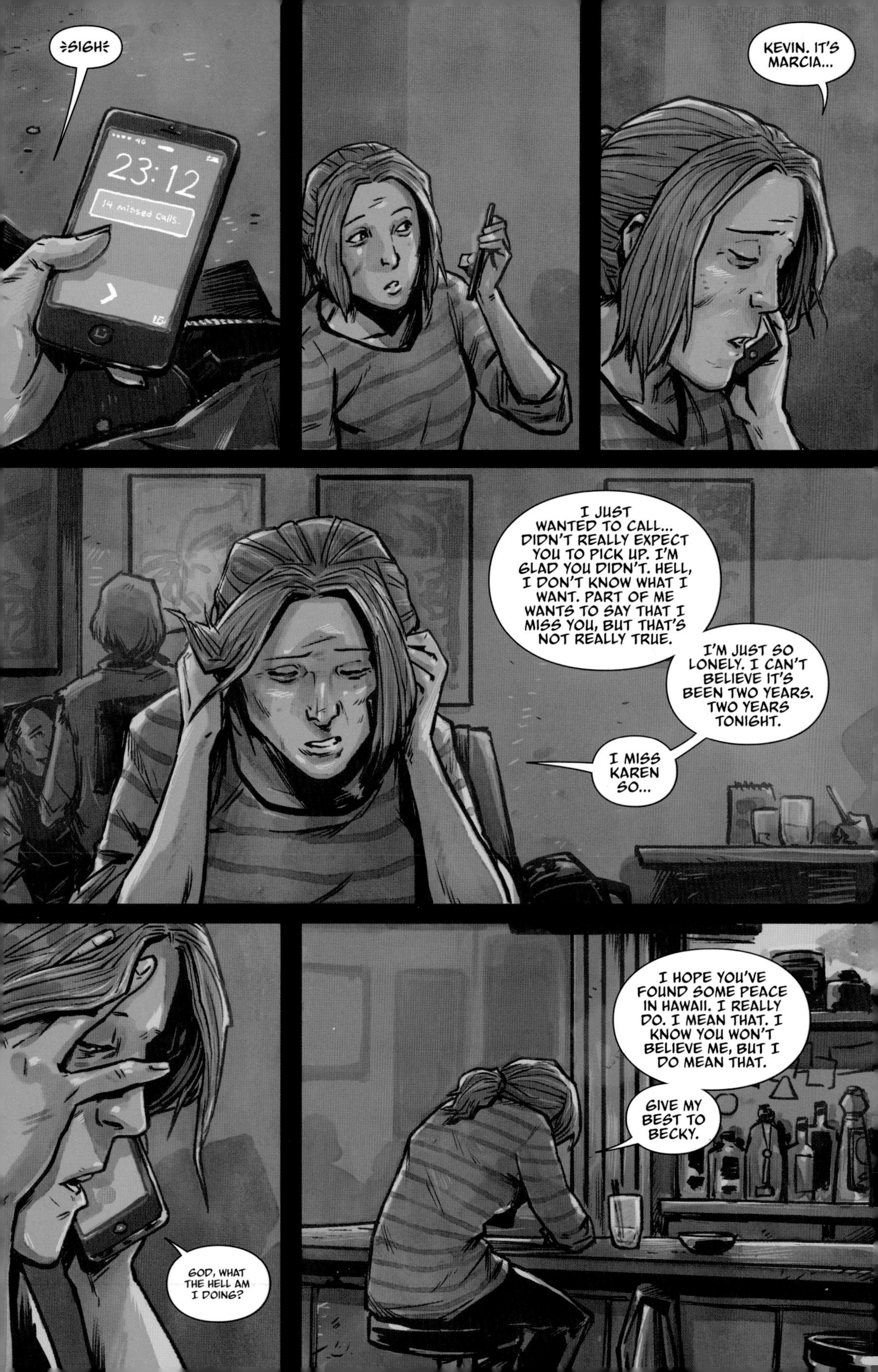

SIGH
23:12
14 missed calls.
KEVIN. IT'S MARCIA...
I JUST WANTED TO CALL... DIDN'T REALLY EXPECT YOU TO PICK UP. I'M GLAD YOU DIDN'T. HELL, I DON'T KNOW WHAT I WANT. PART OF ME WANTS TO SAY THAT I MISS YOU, BUT THAT'S NOT REALLY TRUE.
I'M JUST SO LONELY. I CAN'T BELIEVE IT'S BEEN TWO YEARS. TWO YEARS TONIGHT.
I MISS KAREN SO...
GOD, WHAT THE HELL AM I DOING?
I HOPE YOU'VE FOUND SOME PEACE IN HAWAII. I REALLY DO. I MEAN THAT. I KNOW YOU WON'T BELIEVE ME, BUT I DO MEAN THAT.
GIVE MY BEST TO BECKY.

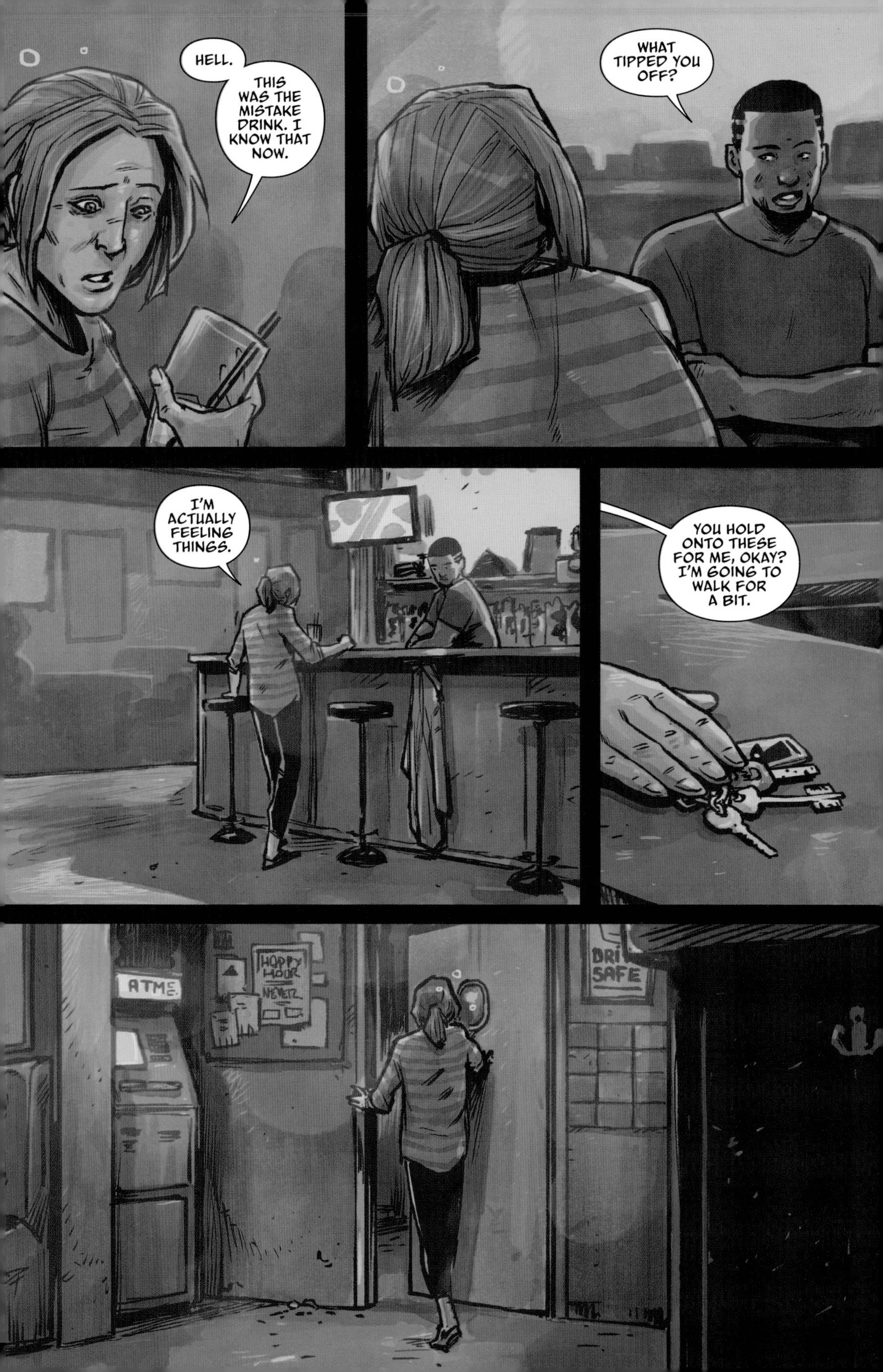
HELL.
THIS WAS THE MISTAKE DRINK. I KNOW THAT NOW.
WHAT TIPPED YOU OFF?
I'M ACTUALLY FEELING THINGS.
YOU HOLD ONTO THESE FOR ME, OKAY? I'M GOING TO WALK FOR A BIT.
ATM
HAPPY HOUR
NEVER
SAFE

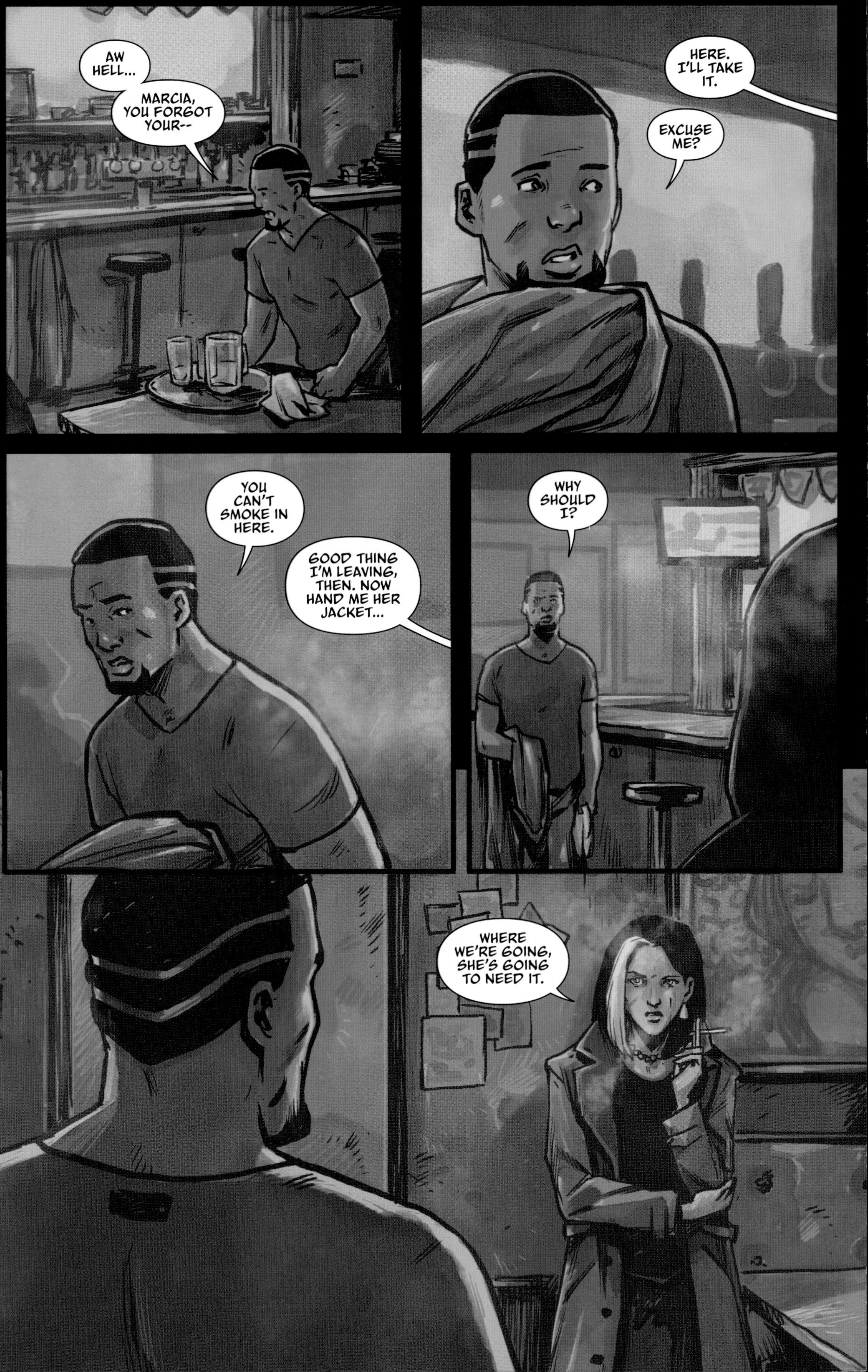
AW HELL...
MARCIA, YOU FORGOT YOUR--
HERE. I'LL TAKE IT.
EXCUSE ME?
YOU CAN'T SMOKE IN HERE.
GOOD THING I'M LEAVING, THEN. NOW HAND ME HER JACKET...
WHY SHOULD I?
WHERE WE'RE GOING, SHE'S GOING TO NEED IT.

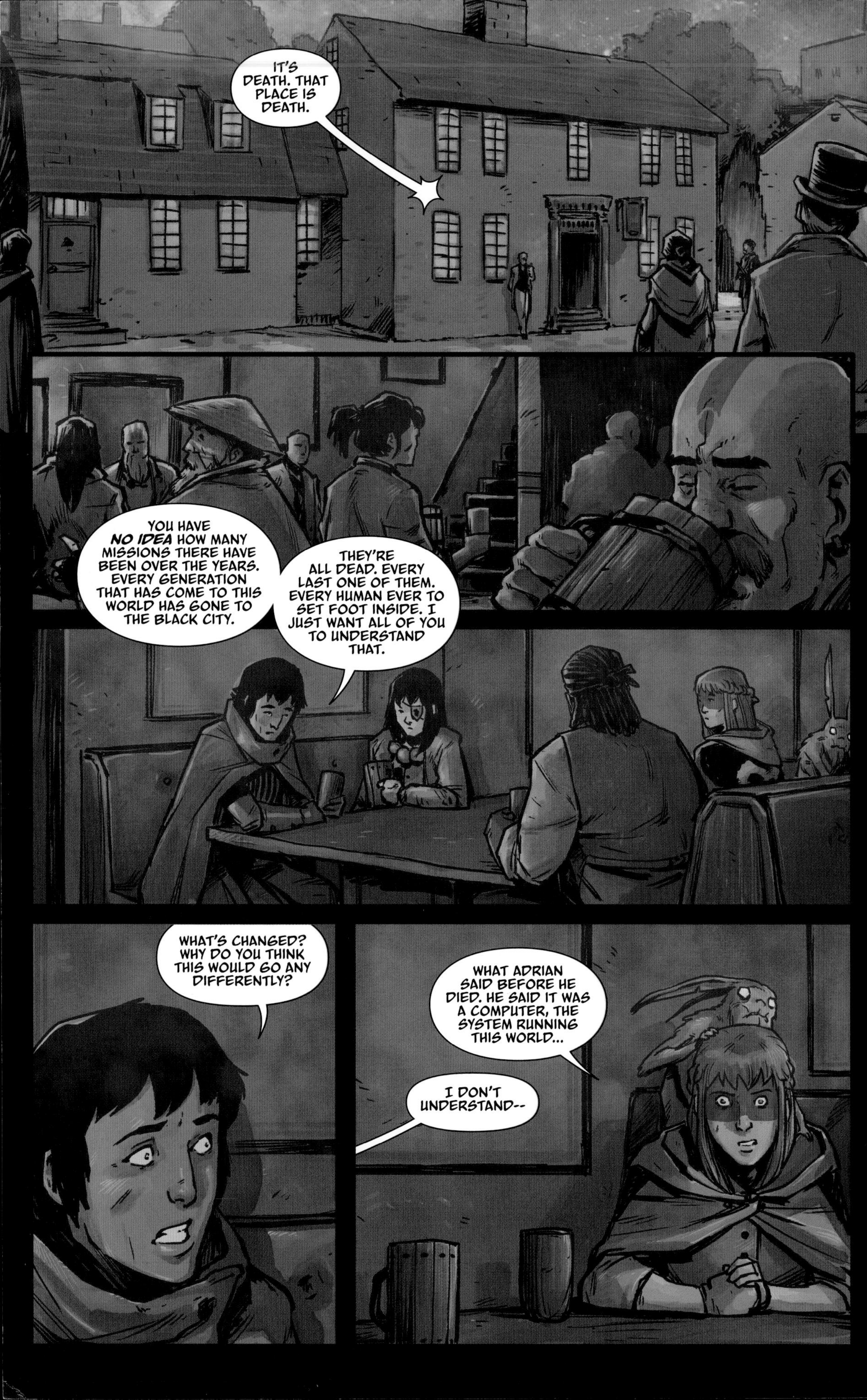
IT'S DEATH. THAT PLACE IS DEATH.
YOU HAVE ***NO IDEA*** HOW MANY MISSIONS THERE HAVE BEEN OVER THE YEARS. EVERY GENERATION THAT HAS COME TO THIS WORLD HAS GONE TO THE BLACK CITY.
THEY'RE ALL DEAD. EVERY LAST ONE OF THEM. EVERY HUMAN EVER TO SET FOOT INSIDE. I JUST WANT ALL OF YOU TO UNDERSTAND THAT.
WHAT'S CHANGED? WHY DO YOU THINK THIS WOULD GO ANY DIFFERENTLY?
WHAT ADRIAN SAID BEFORE HE DIED. HE SAID IT WAS A COMPUTER, THE SYSTEM RUNNING THIS WORLD...
I DON'T UNDERSTAND--

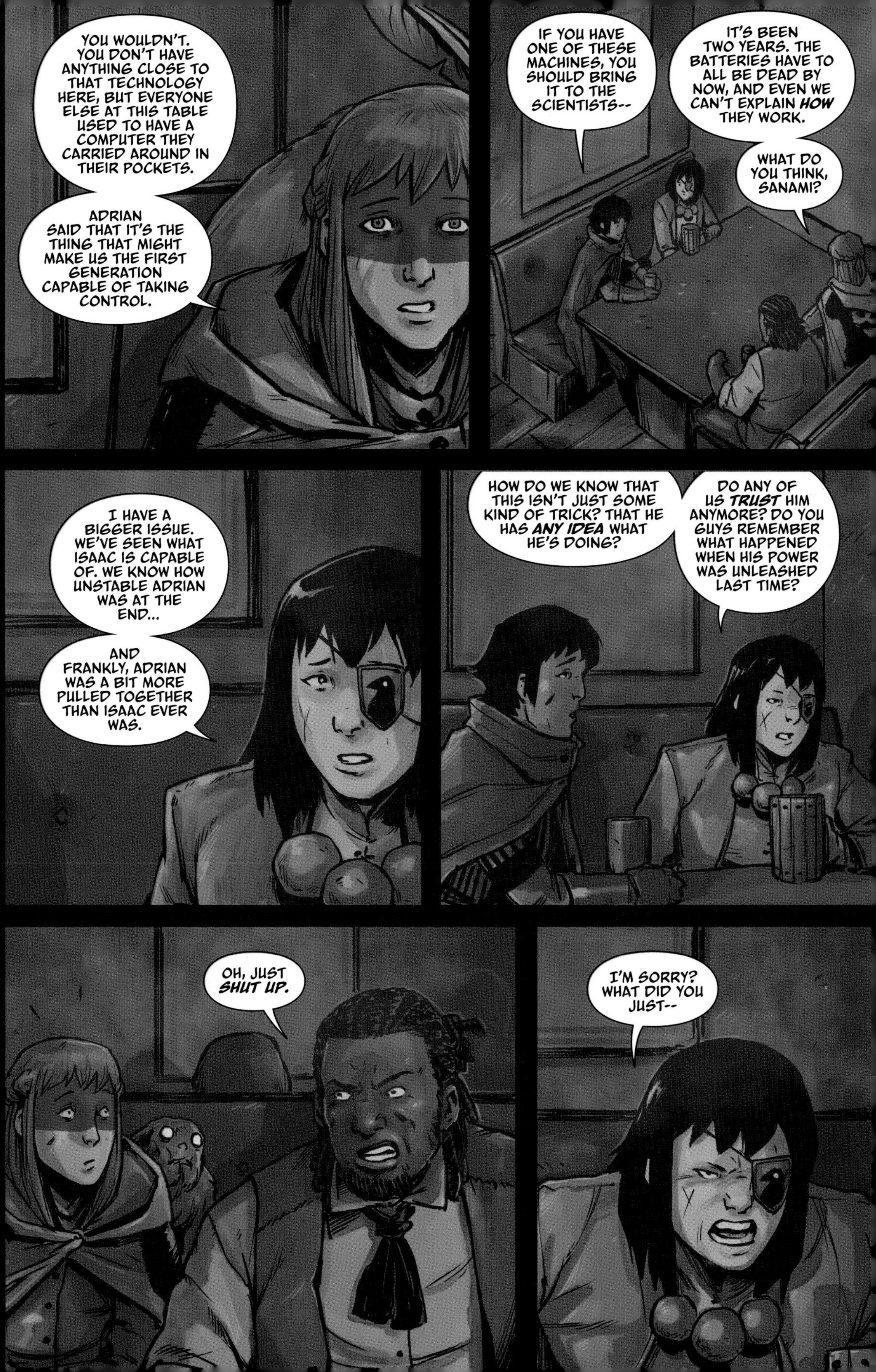

YOU WOULDN'T. YOU DON'T HAVE ANYTHING CLOSE TO THAT TECHNOLOGY HERE, BUT EVERYONE ELSE AT THIS TABLE USED TO HAVE A COMPUTER THEY CARRIED AROUND IN THEIR POCKETS.
ADRIAN SAID THAT IT'S THE THING THAT MIGHT MAKE US THE FIRST GENERATION CAPABLE OF TAKING CONTROL.
IF YOU HAVE ONE OF THESE MACHINES, YOU SHOULD BRING IT TO THE SCIENTISTS--
IT'S BEEN TWO YEARS. THE BATTERIES HAVE TO ALL BE DEAD BY NOW, AND EVEN WE CAN'T EXPLAIN *HOW* THEY WORK.
WHAT DO YOU THINK, SANAMI?
I HAVE A BIGGER ISSUE. WE'VE SEEN WHAT ISAAC IS CAPABLE OF. WE KNOW HOW UNSTABLE ADRIAN WAS AT THE END...
AND FRANKLY, ADRIAN WAS A BIT MORE PULLED TOGETHER THAN ISAAC EVER WAS.
HOW DO WE KNOW THAT THIS ISN'T JUST SOME KIND OF TRICK? THAT HE HAS *ANY IDEA* WHAT HE'S DOING?
DO ANY OF US *TRUST* HIM ANYMORE? DO YOU GUYS REMEMBER WHAT HAPPENED WHEN HIS POWER WAS UNLEASHED LAST TIME?
OH, JUST *SHUT UP.*
I'M SORRY? WHAT DID YOU JUST--

I'M JUST GOING TO SPEED THINGS UP BY LAYING DOWN THE TRUTH.

WE'RE AFRAID. OF COURSE WE'RE AFRAID. WE'D BE INSANE NOT TO BE.

BUT TWO YEARS AGO, WE SET OUT INTO THE FOREST TO FIND A WAY HOME, AND WE NEVER FINISHED THAT TRIP. SOMEWHERE ALONG THE WAY, WE STOPPED LOOKING FOR ANSWERS BECAUSE WE KNEW THE COST WOULD BE TOO MUCH.

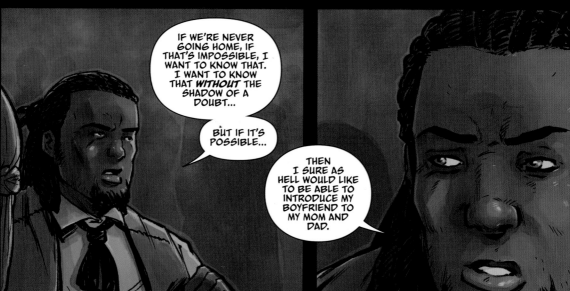

IF WE'RE NEVER GOING HOME, IF THAT'S IMPOSSIBLE, I WANT TO KNOW THAT. I WANT TO KNOW THAT *WITHOUT* THE SHADOW OF A DOUBT...

BUT IF IT'S POSSIBLE...

THEN I SURE AS HELL WOULD LIKE TO BE ABLE TO INTRODUCE MY BOYFRIEND TO MY MOM AND DAD.

YOU CAN ALL FIGHT ME ABOUT IT, YOU CAN LASH OUT. BUT I'M DONE BEING QUIET, I'M DONE BEING SPOKEN OVER. I'M GOING.

AND I KNOW EACH OF YOU WELL ENOUGH TO KNOW THAT YOU'VE ALREADY PACKED YOUR BAGS.

SAY YOUR GOODBYES. WE'LL MEET AT THE DRAGON PEN IN THREE HOURS.

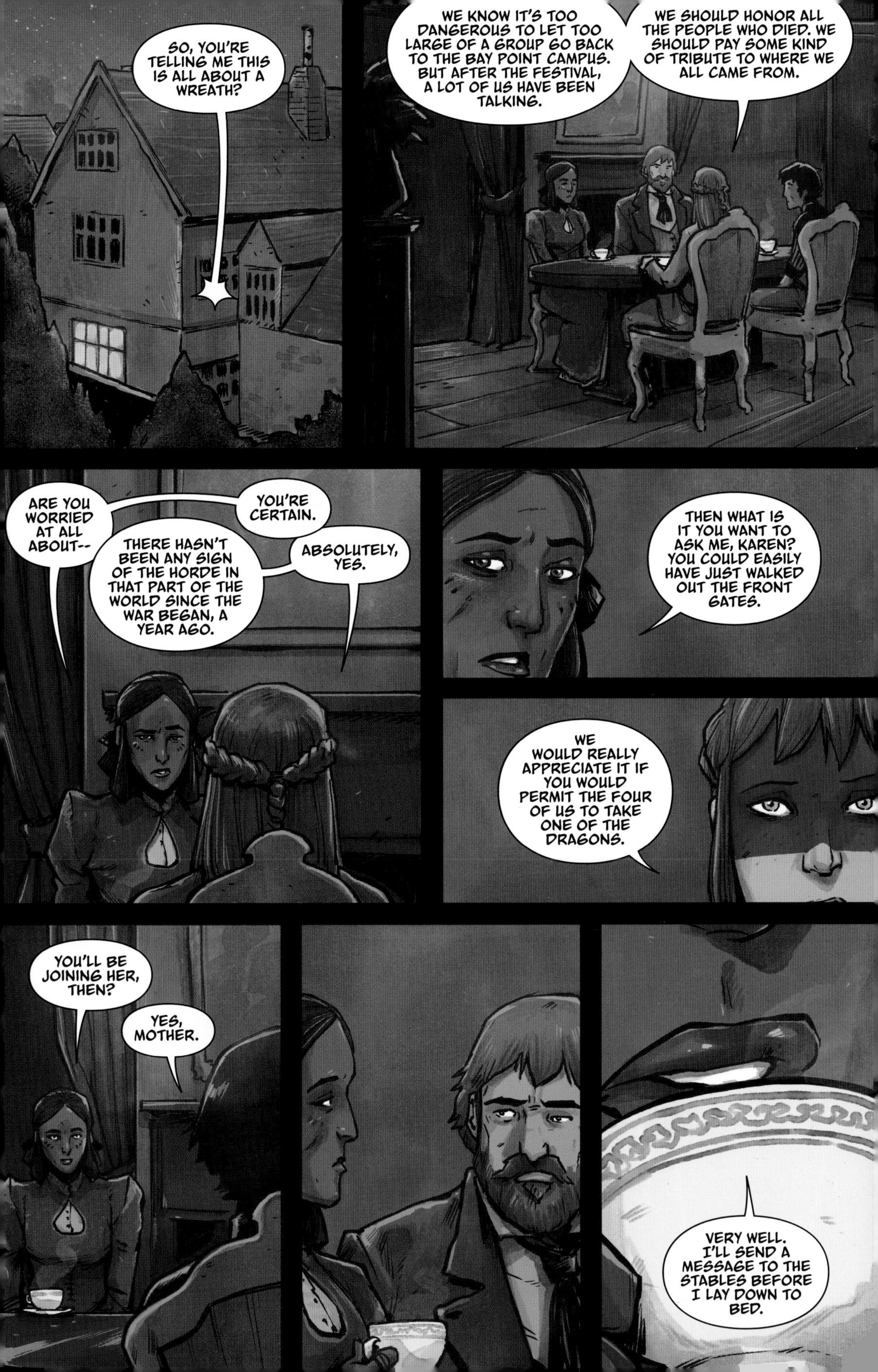
SO, YOU'RE TELLING ME THIS IS ALL ABOUT A WREATH?
WE KNOW IT'S TOO DANGEROUS TO LET TOO LARGE OF A GROUP GO BACK TO THE BAY POINT CAMPUS. BUT AFTER THE FESTIVAL, A LOT OF US HAVE BEEN TALKING.
WE SHOULD HONOR ALL THE PEOPLE WHO DIED. WE SHOULD PAY SOME KIND OF TRIBUTE TO WHERE WE ALL CAME FROM.
ARE YOU WORRIED AT ALL ABOUT--
YOU'RE CERTAIN.
THERE HASN'T BEEN ANY SIGN OF THE HORDE IN THAT PART OF THE WORLD SINCE THE WAR BEGAN, A YEAR AGO.
ABSOLUTELY, YES.
THEN WHAT IS IT YOU WANT TO ASK ME, KAREN? YOU COULD EASILY HAVE JUST WALKED OUT THE FRONT GATES.
WE WOULD REALLY APPRECIATE IT IF YOU WOULD PERMIT THE FOUR OF US TO TAKE ONE OF THE DRAGONS.
YOU'LL BE JOINING HER, THEN?
YES, MOTHER.
VERY WELL. I'LL SEND A MESSAGE TO THE STABLES BEFORE I LAY DOWN TO BED.

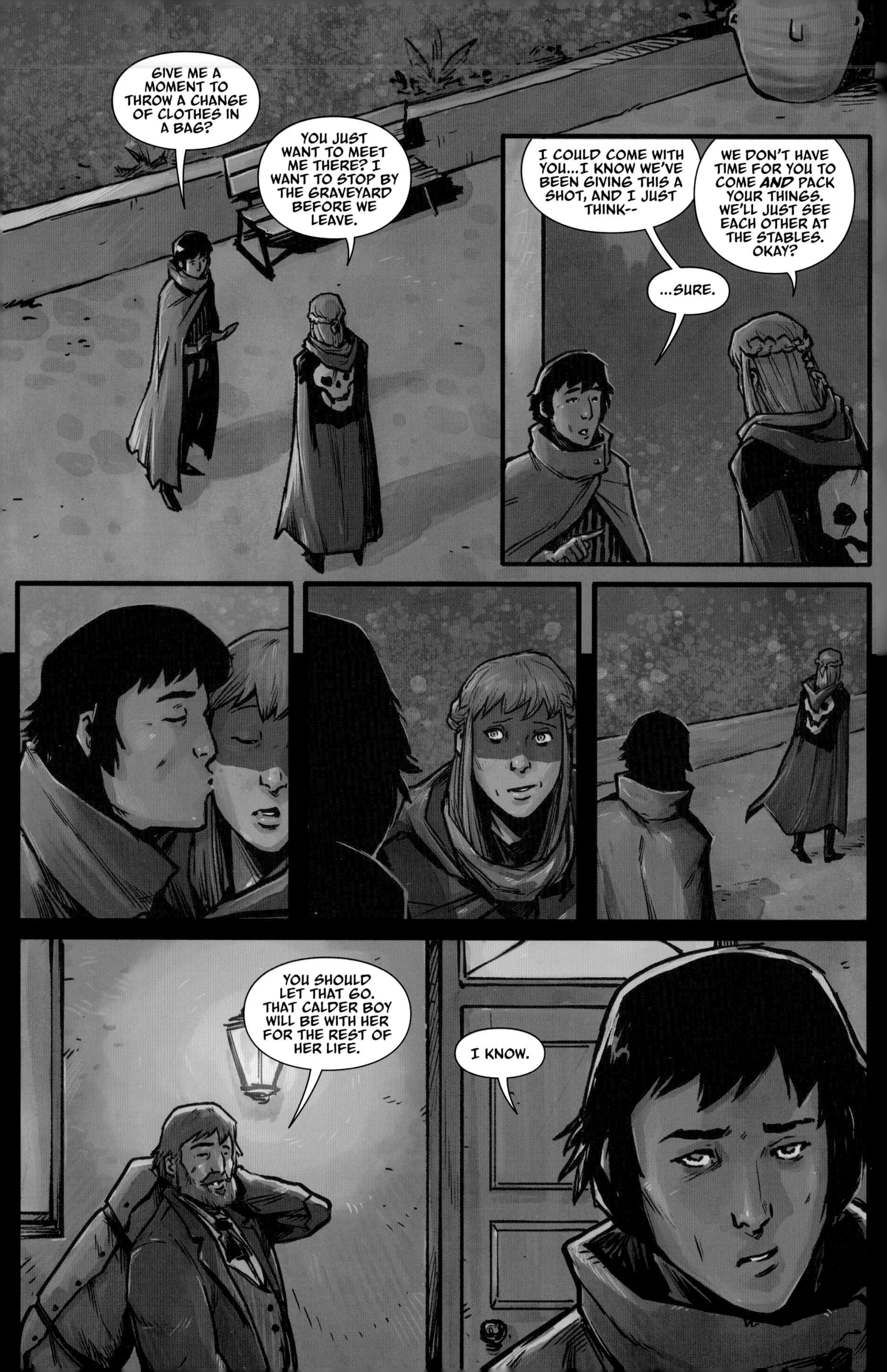
GIVE ME A MOMENT TO THROW A CHANGE OF CLOTHES IN A BAG?
YOU JUST WANT TO MEET ME THERE? I WANT TO STOP BY THE GRAVEYARD BEFORE WE LEAVE.
I COULD COME WITH YOU...I KNOW WE'VE BEEN GIVING THIS A SHOT, AND I JUST THINK--
WE DON'T HAVE TIME FOR YOU TO COME AND PACK YOUR THINGS. WE'LL JUST SEE EACH OTHER AT THE STABLES. OKAY?
...SURE.
YOU SHOULD LET THAT GO. THAT CALDER BOY WILL BE WITH HER FOR THE REST OF HER LIFE.
I KNOW.

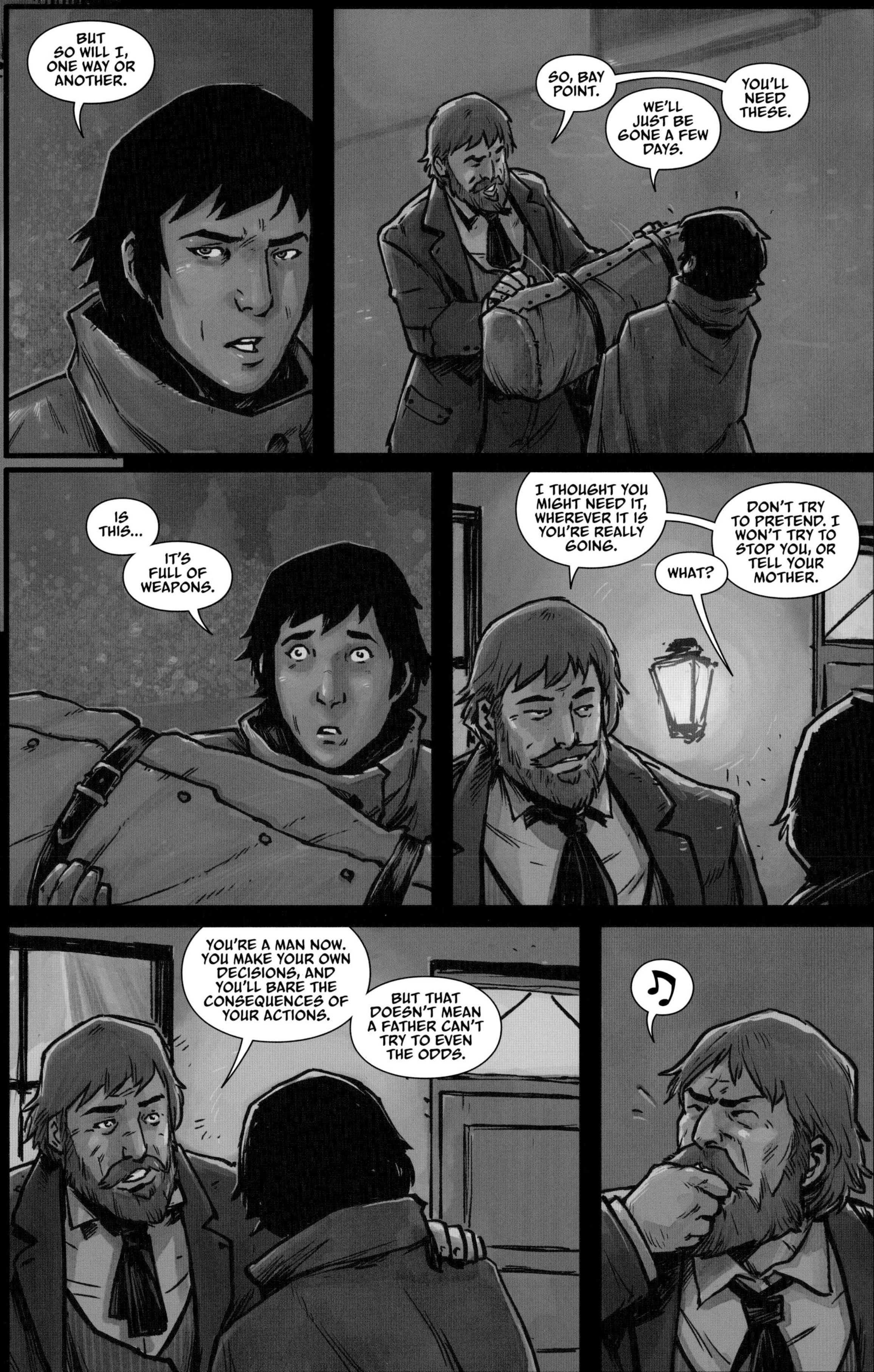
BUT SO WILL I, ONE WAY OR ANOTHER.
SO, BAY POINT.
WE'LL JUST BE GONE A FEW DAYS.
YOU'LL NEED THESE.
IS THIS...
IT'S FULL OF WEAPONS.
I THOUGHT YOU MIGHT NEED IT, WHEREVER IT IS YOU'RE REALLY GOING.
WHAT?
DON'T TRY TO PRETEND. I WON'T TRY TO STOP YOU, OR TELL YOUR MOTHER.
YOU'RE A MAN NOW. YOU MAKE YOUR OWN DECISIONS, AND YOU'LL BARE THE CONSEQUENCES OF YOUR ACTIONS.
BUT THAT DOESN'T MEAN A FATHER CAN'T TRY TO EVEN THE ODDS.
♪

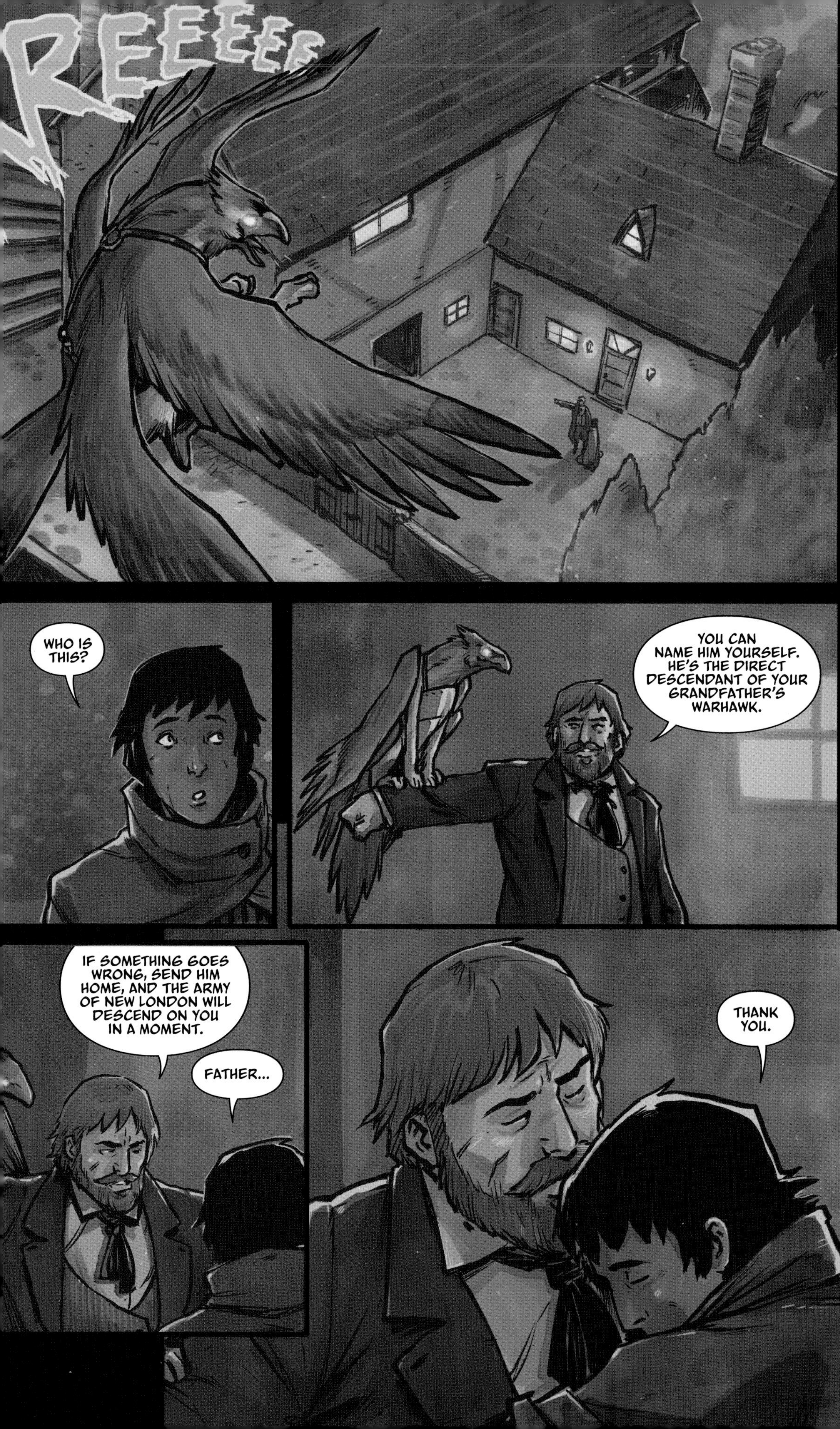
REEEEE
WHO IS THIS?
YOU CAN NAME HIM YOURSELF. HE'S THE DIRECT DESCENDANT OF YOUR GRANDFATHER'S WARHAWK.
IF SOMETHING GOES WRONG, SEND HIM HOME, AND THE ARMY OF NEW LONDON WILL DESCEND ON YOU IN A MOMENT.
FATHER...
THANK YOU.

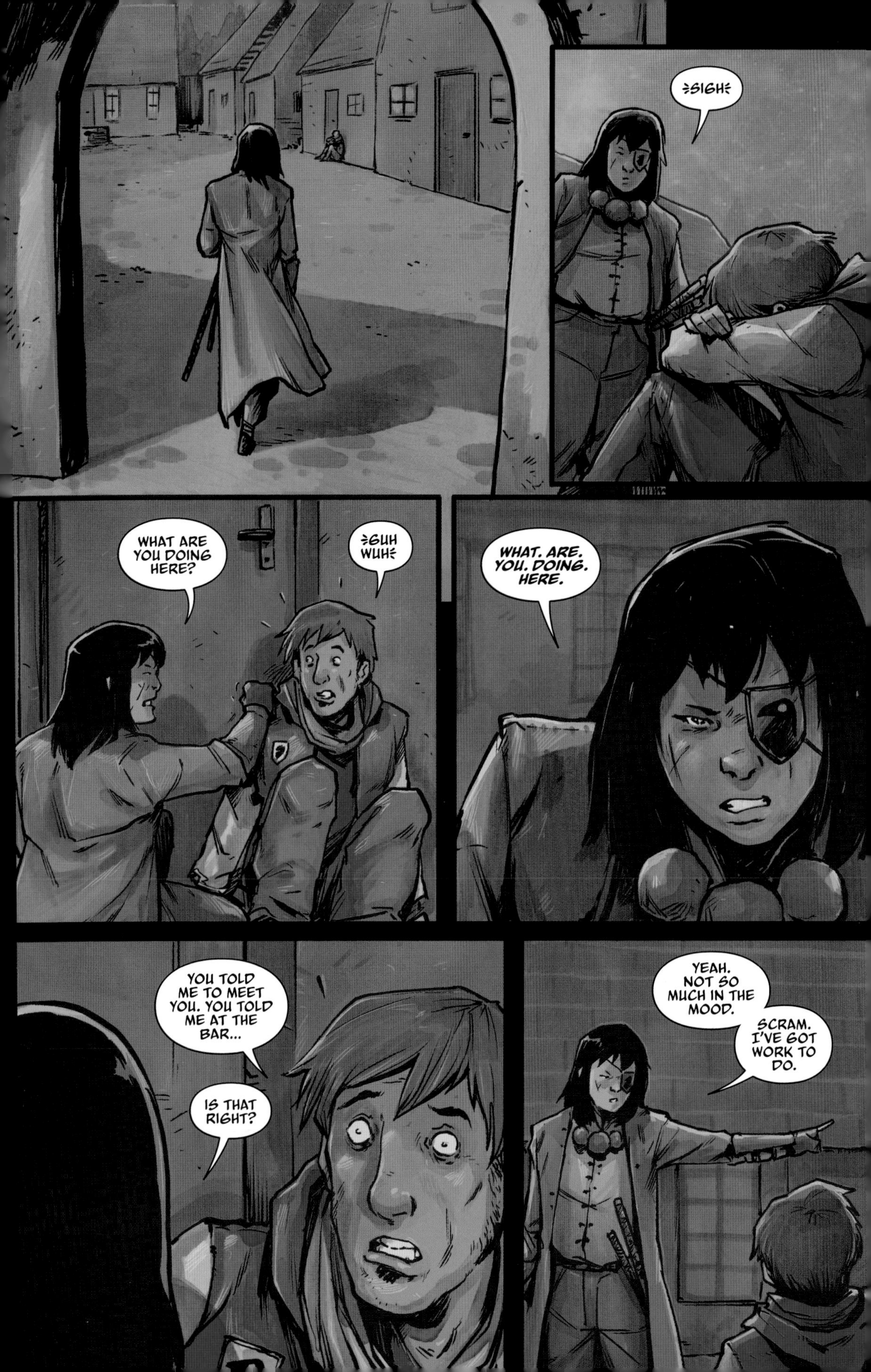

≶SIGH≷
WHAT ARE YOU DOING HERE?
≶GUH WUH≷
WHAT. ARE. YOU. DOING. HERE.
YOU TOLD ME TO MEET YOU. YOU TOLD ME AT THE BAR...
IS THAT RIGHT?
YEAH. NOT SO MUCH IN THE MOOD.
SCRAM. I'VE GOT WORK TO DO.

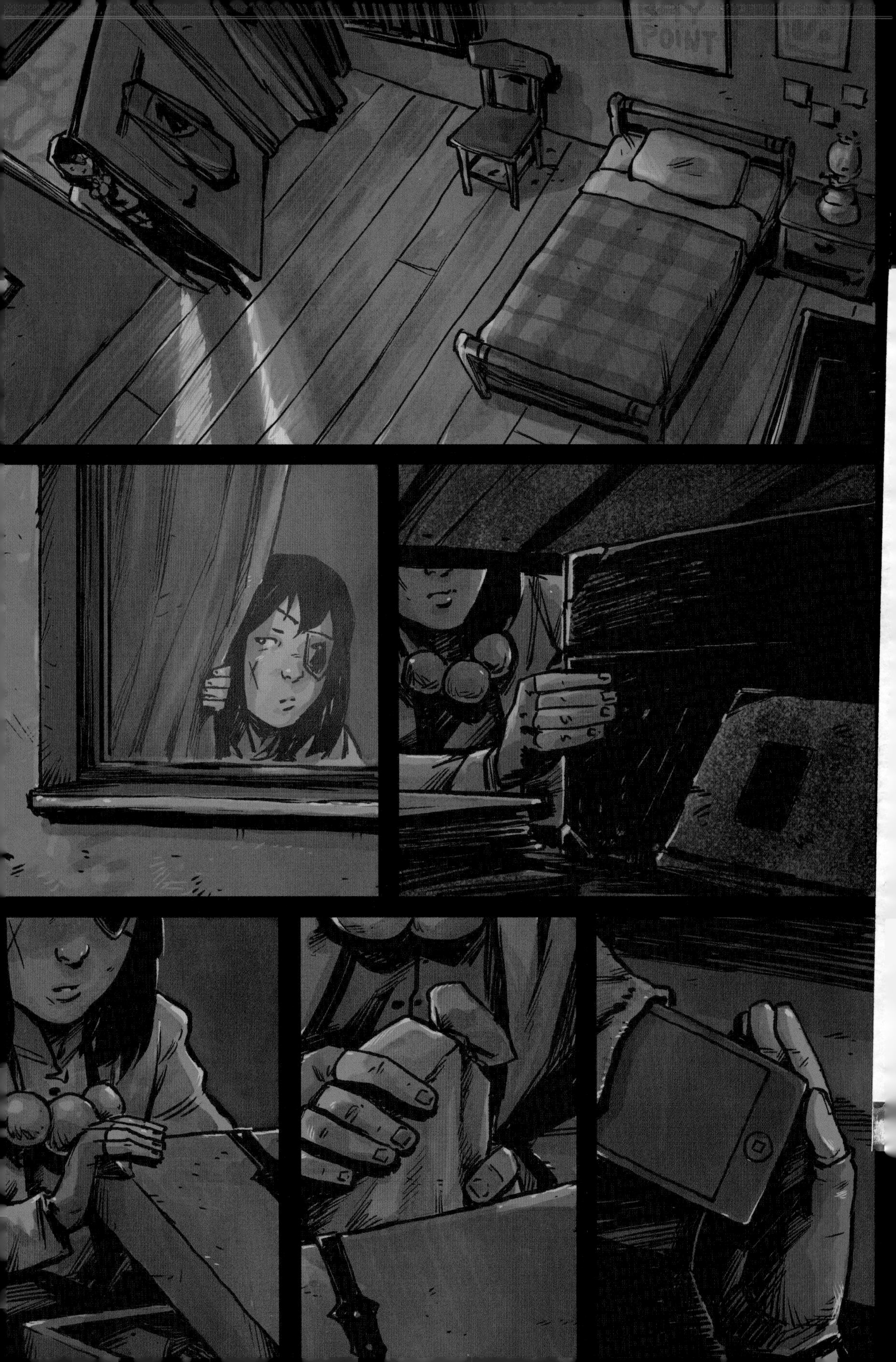
POINT

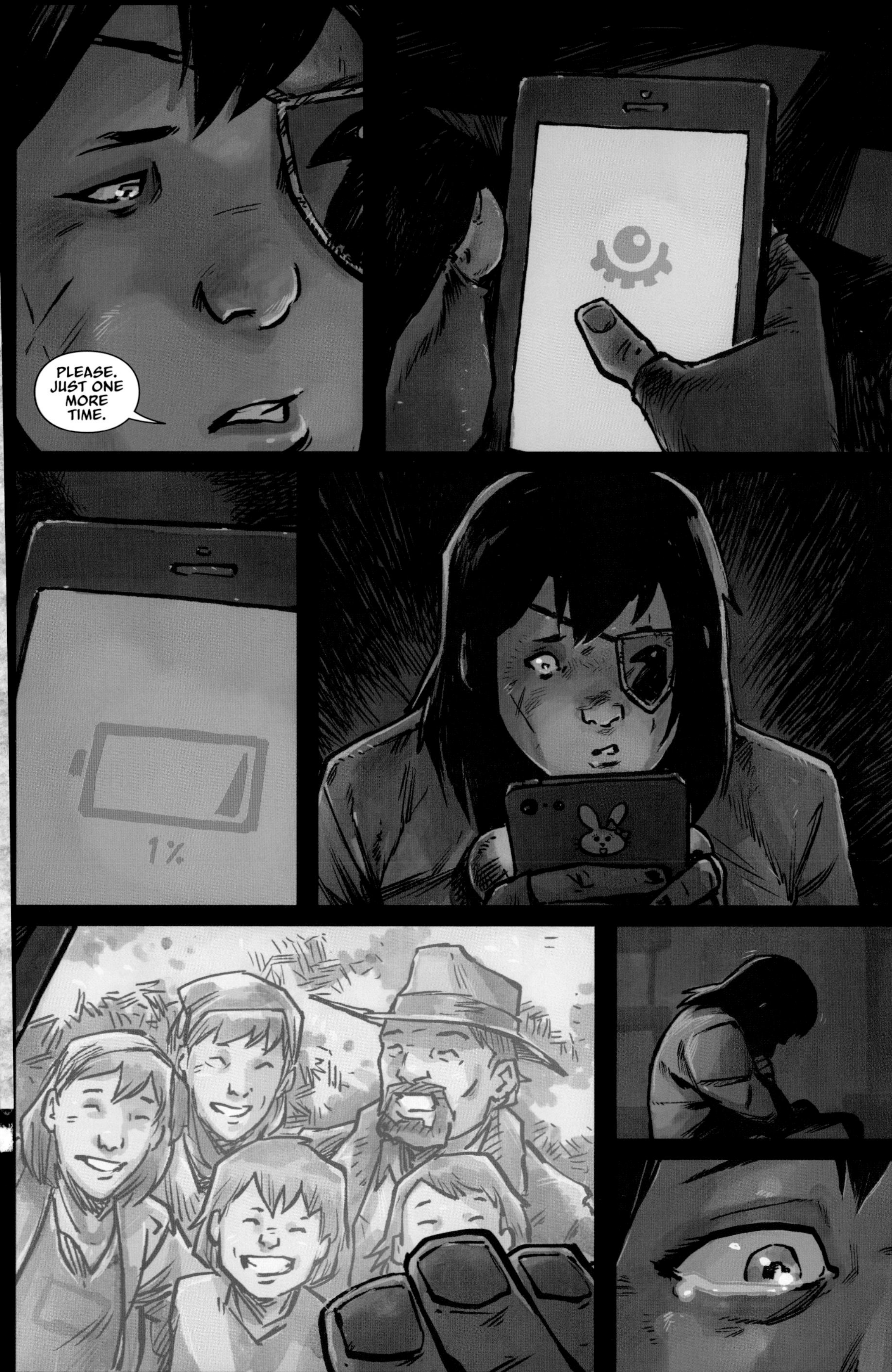
PLEASE. JUST ONE MORE TIME.
1%

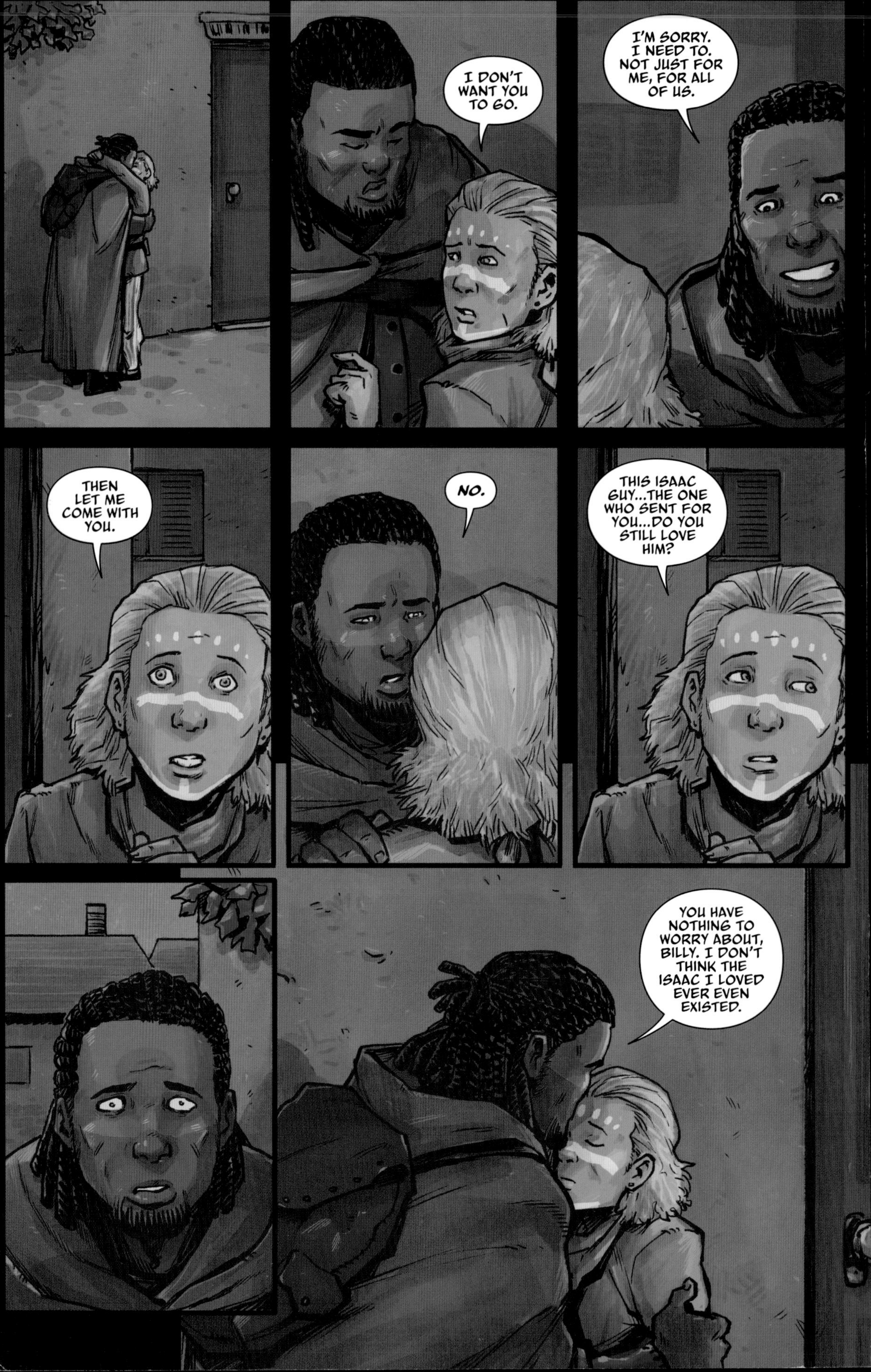
I DON'T WANT YOU TO GO.
I'M SORRY. I NEED TO. NOT JUST FOR ME, FOR ALL OF US.
THEN LET ME COME WITH YOU.
NO.
THIS ISAAC GUY...THE ONE WHO SENT FOR YOU...DO YOU STILL LOVE HIM?
YOU HAVE NOTHING TO WORRY ABOUT, BILLY. I DON'T THINK THE ISAAC I LOVED EVER EVEN EXISTED.

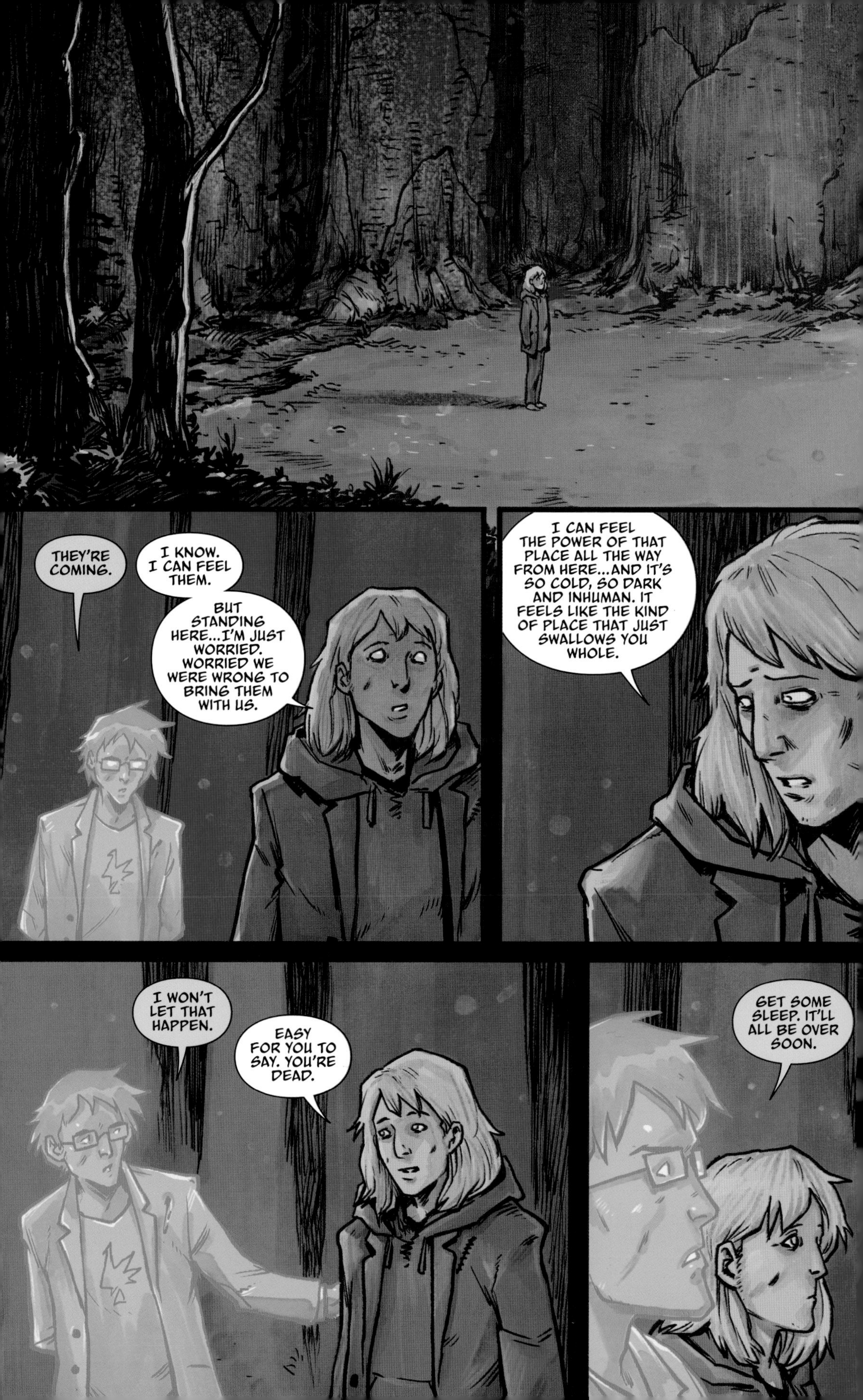
THEY'RE COMING.
I KNOW. I CAN FEEL THEM.
BUT STANDING HERE...I'M JUST WORRIED. WORRIED WE WERE WRONG TO BRING THEM WITH US.
I CAN FEEL THE POWER OF THAT PLACE ALL THE WAY FROM HERE...AND IT'S SO COLD, SO DARK AND INHUMAN. IT FEELS LIKE THE KIND OF PLACE THAT JUST SWALLOWS YOU WHOLE.
I WON'T LET THAT HAPPEN.
EASY FOR YOU TO SAY. YOU'RE DEAD.
GET SOME SLEEP. IT'LL ALL BE OVER SOON.

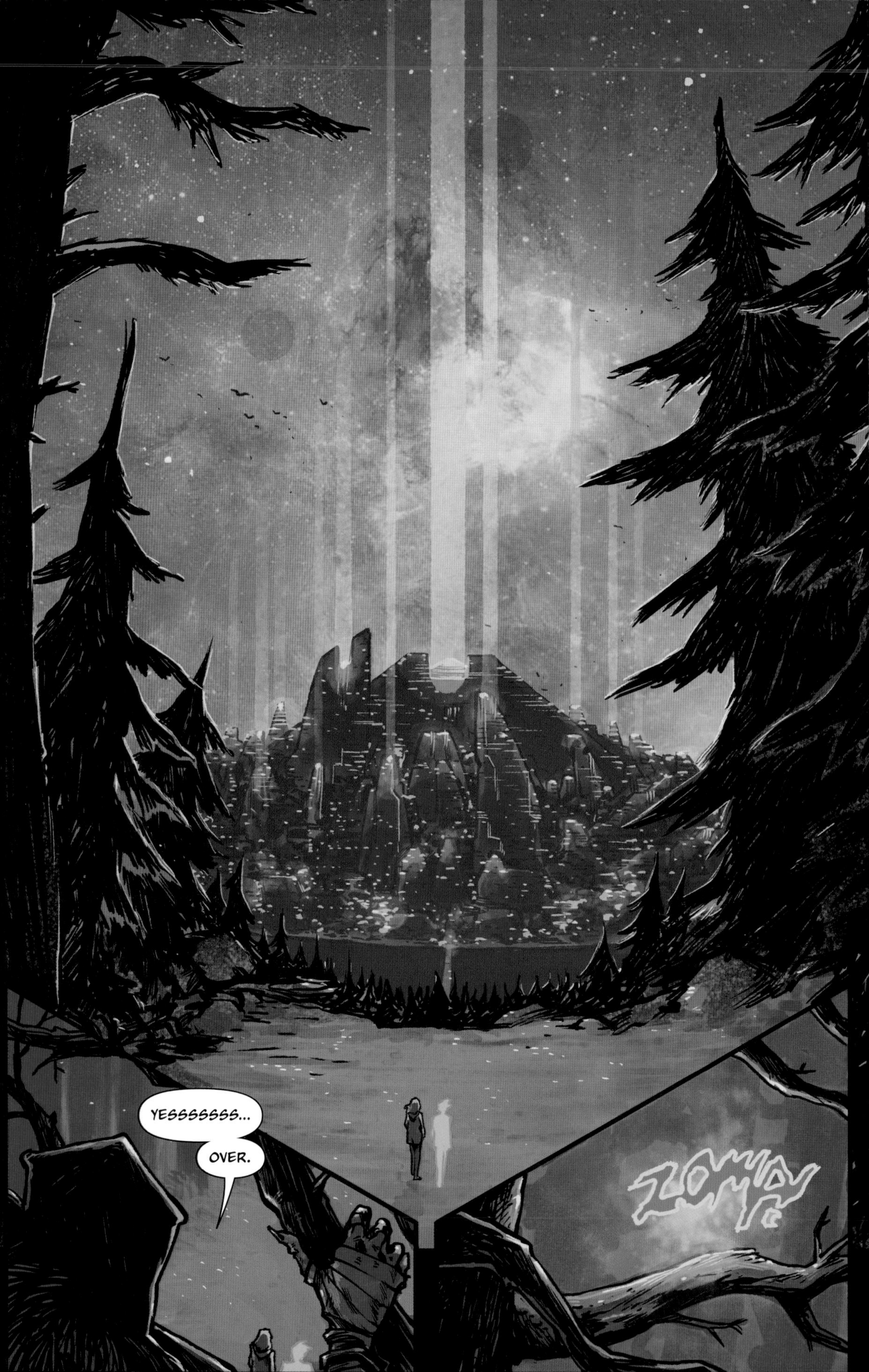
YESSSSSSS...
OVER.

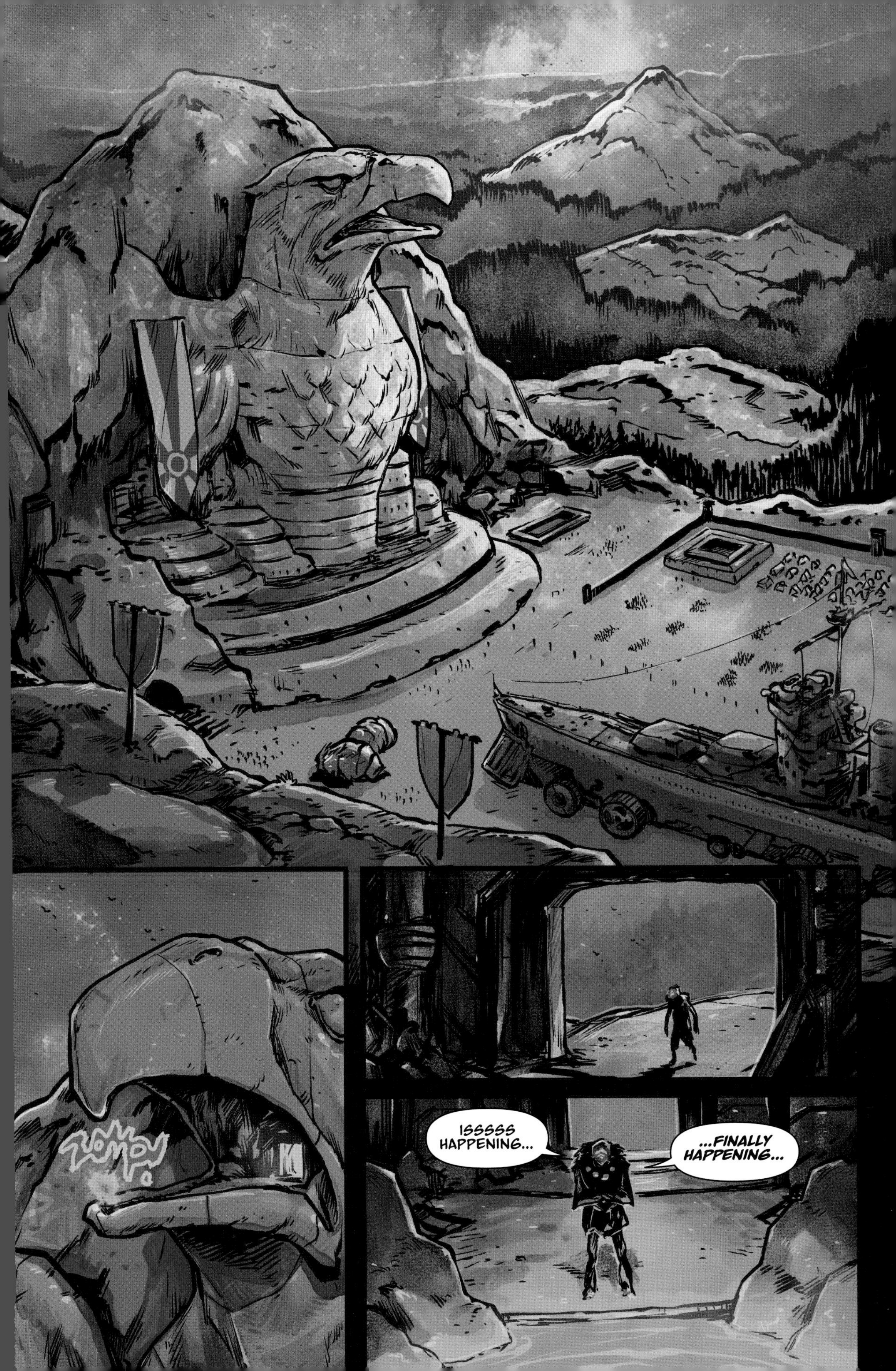
ISSSSS HAPPENING...
...FINALLY HAPPENING...

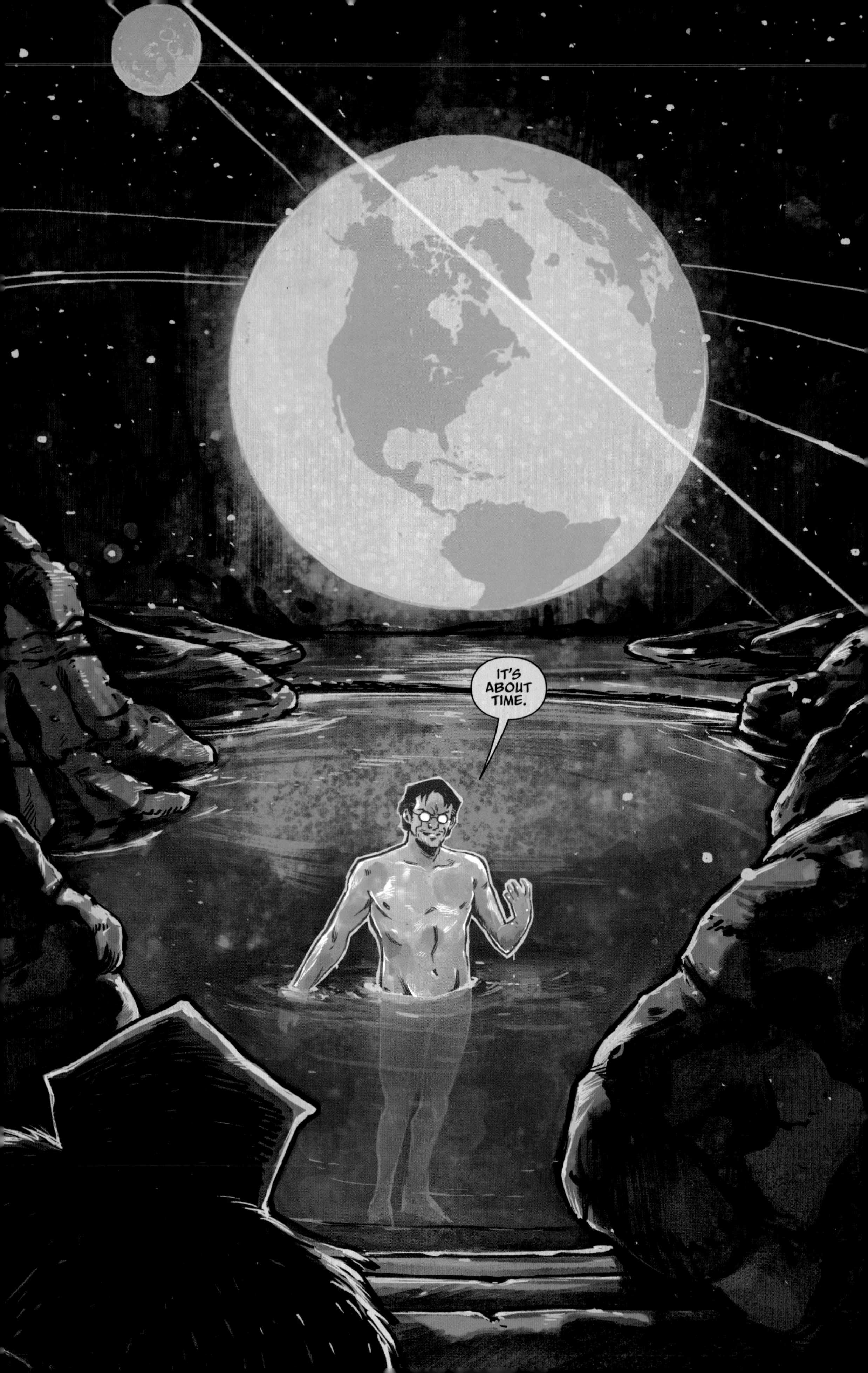
IT'S ABOUT TIME.

CHAPTER
TWENTY-SEVEN

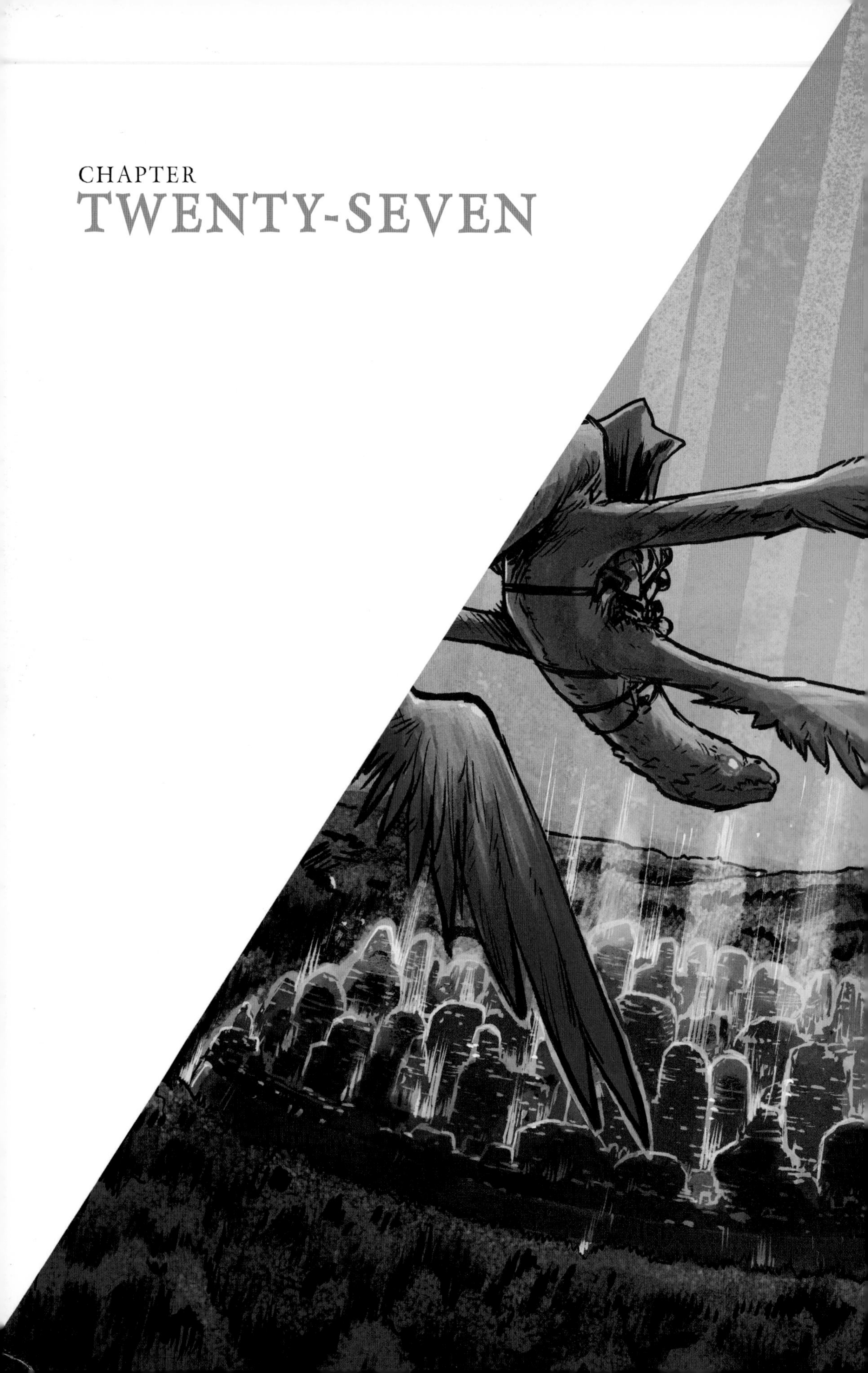

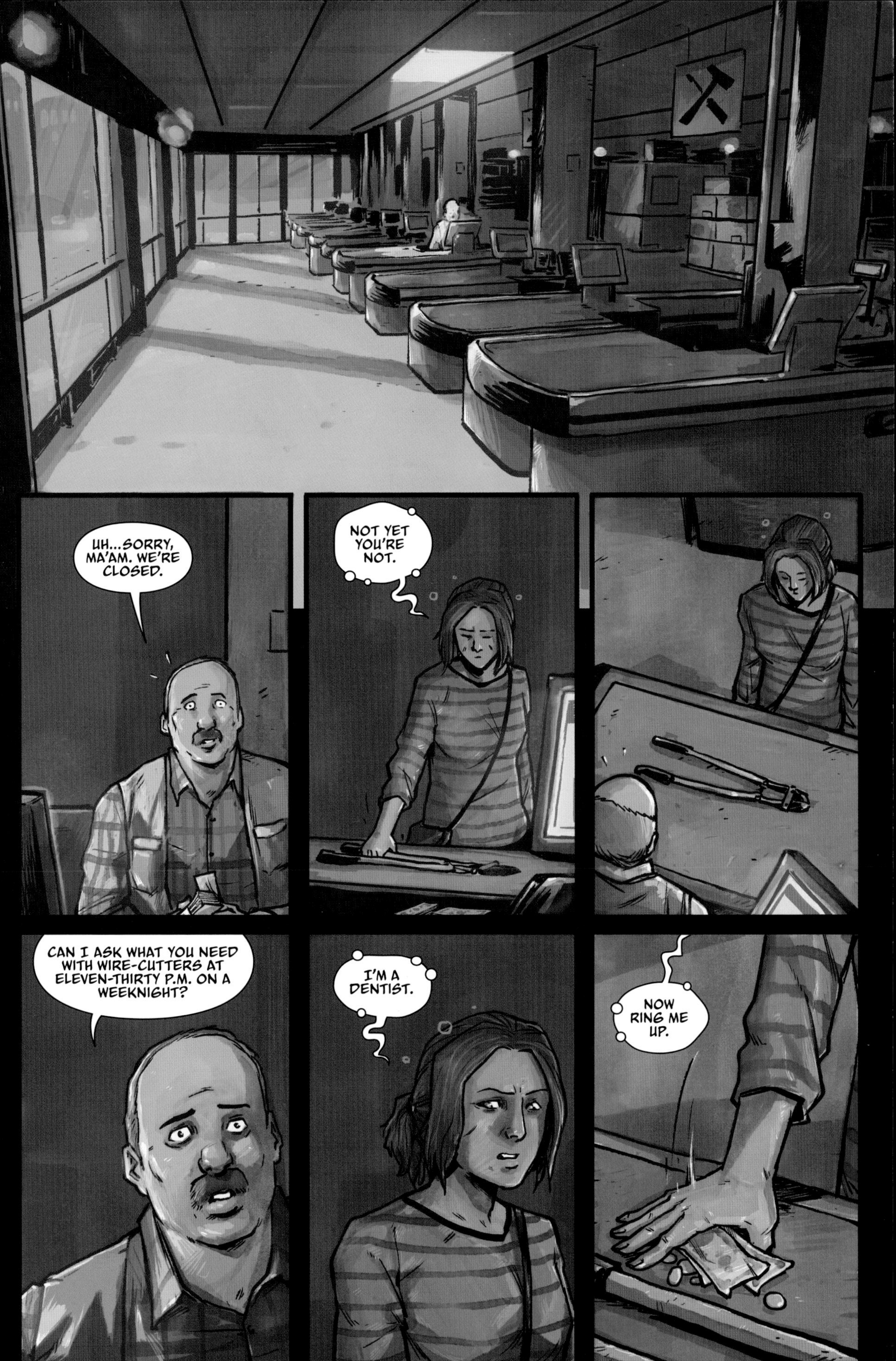
UH...SORRY, MA'AM. WE'RE CLOSED.
NOT YET YOU'RE NOT.
CAN I ASK WHAT YOU NEED WITH WIRE-CUTTERS AT ELEVEN-THIRTY P.M. ON A WEEKNIGHT?
I'M A DENTIST.
NOW RING ME UP.

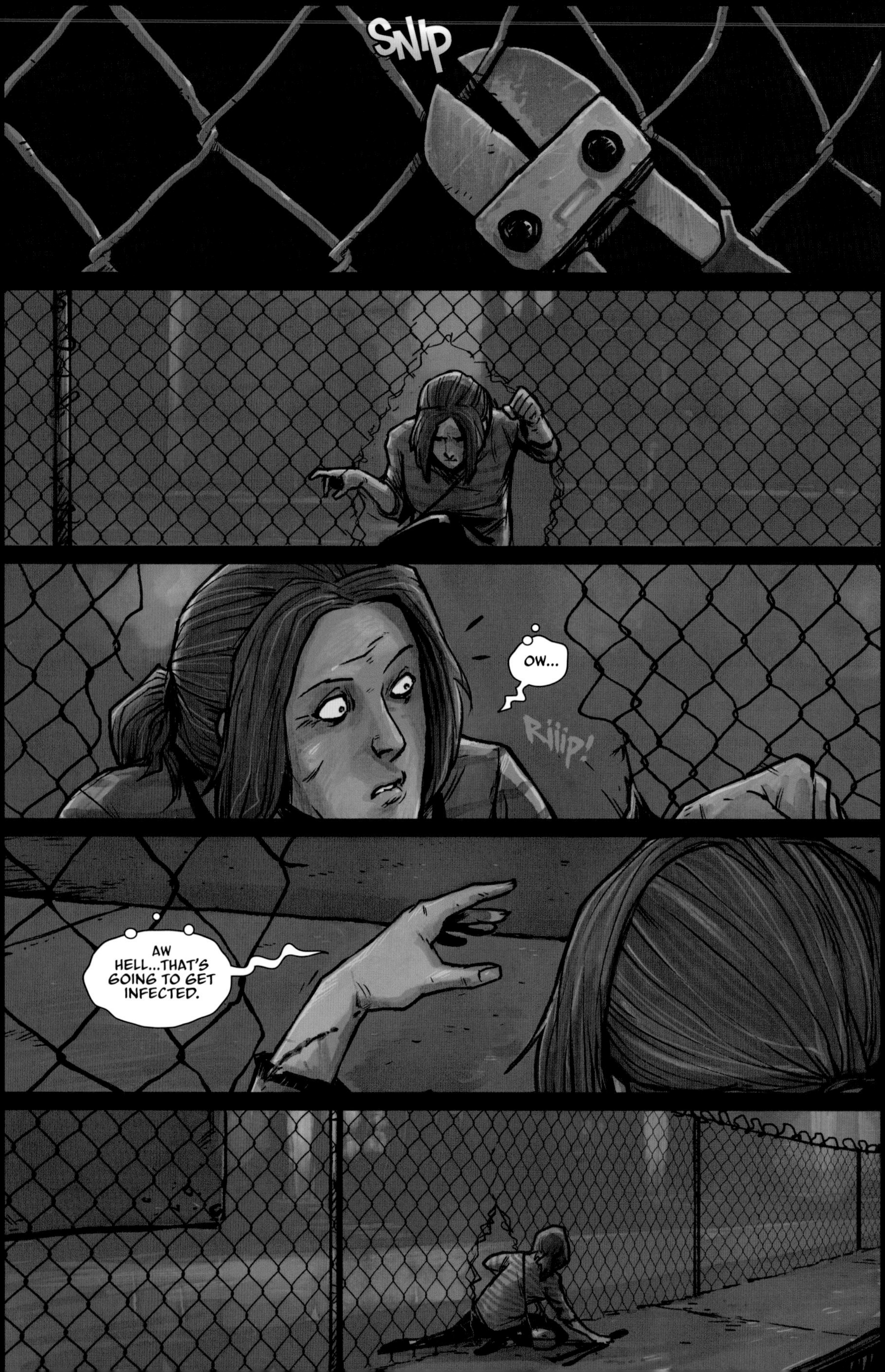
SNIP
OW...
Riiip!
AW HELL...THAT'S GOING TO GET INFECTED.

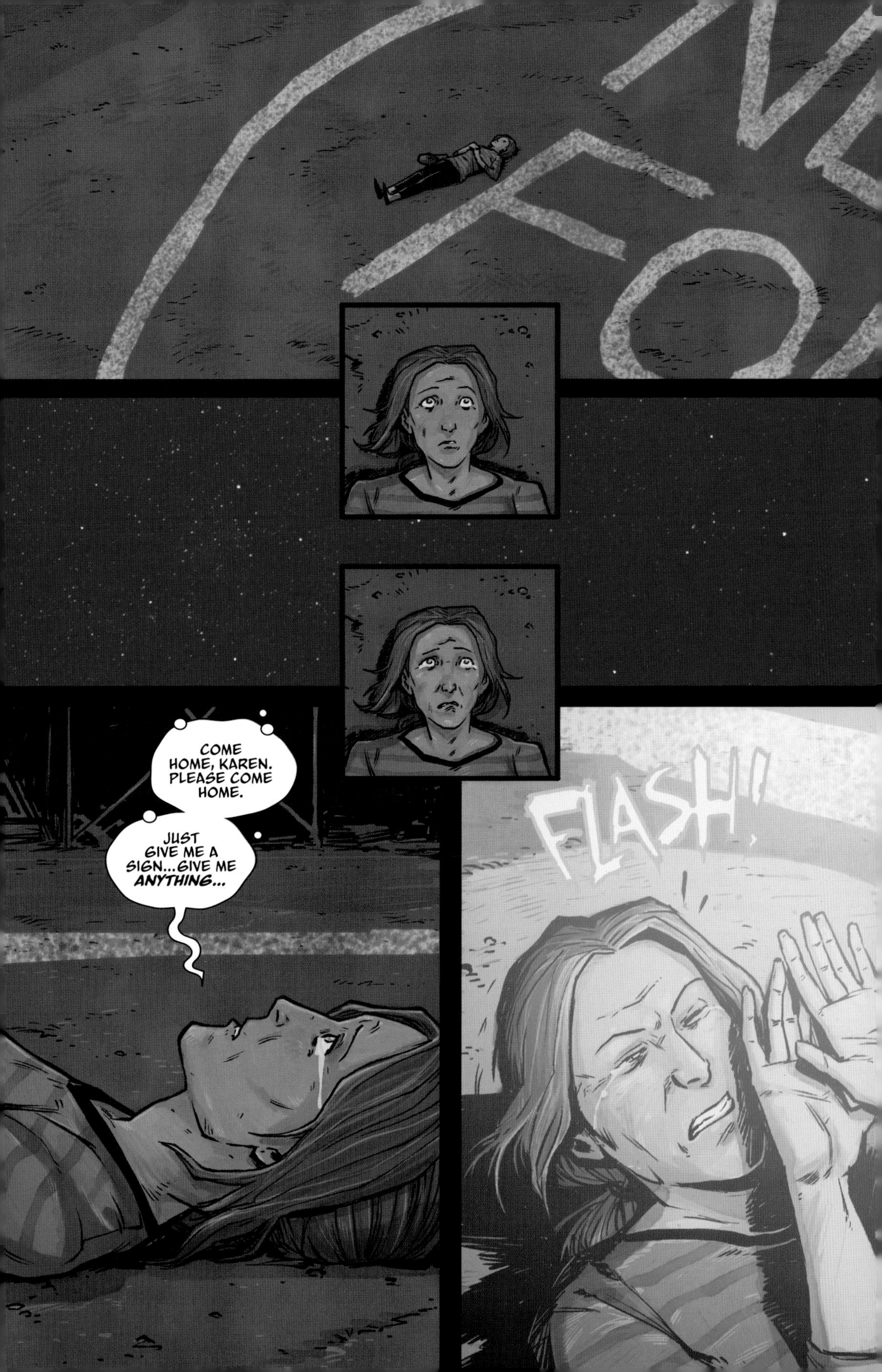
COME HOME, KAREN. PLEASE COME HOME.
JUST GIVE ME A SIGN...GIVE ME *ANYTHING...*
FLASH!

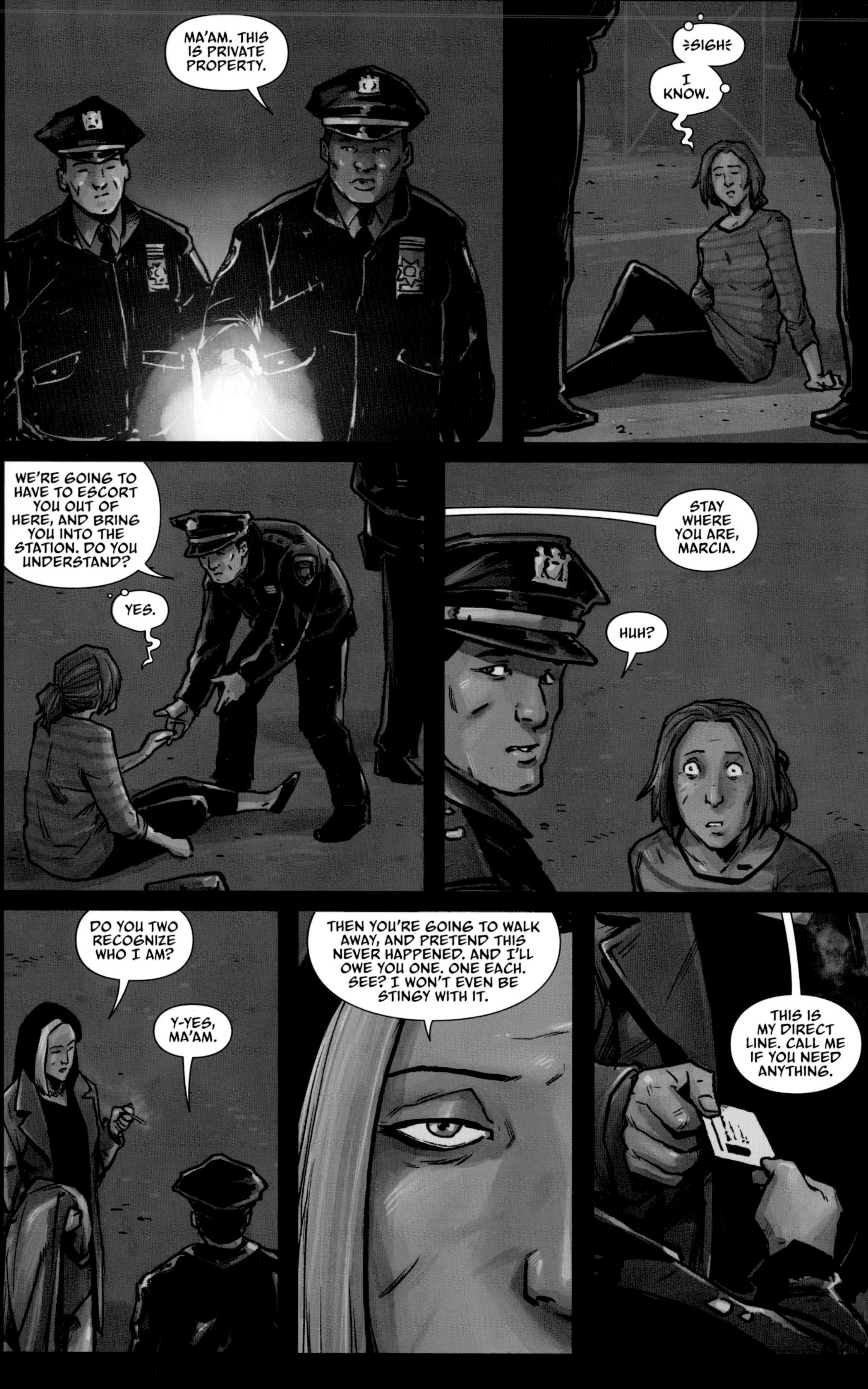

MA'AM. THIS IS PRIVATE PROPERTY.
SIGH
I KNOW.
WE'RE GOING TO HAVE TO ESCORT YOU OUT OF HERE, AND BRING YOU INTO THE STATION. DO YOU UNDERSTAND?
YES.
STAY WHERE YOU ARE, MARCIA.
HUH?
DO YOU TWO RECOGNIZE WHO I AM?
Y-YES, MA'AM.
THEN YOU'RE GOING TO WALK AWAY, AND PRETEND THIS NEVER HAPPENED. AND I'LL OWE YOU ONE. ONE EACH. SEE? I WON'T EVEN BE STINGY WITH IT.
THIS IS MY DIRECT LINE. CALL ME IF YOU NEED ANYTHING.

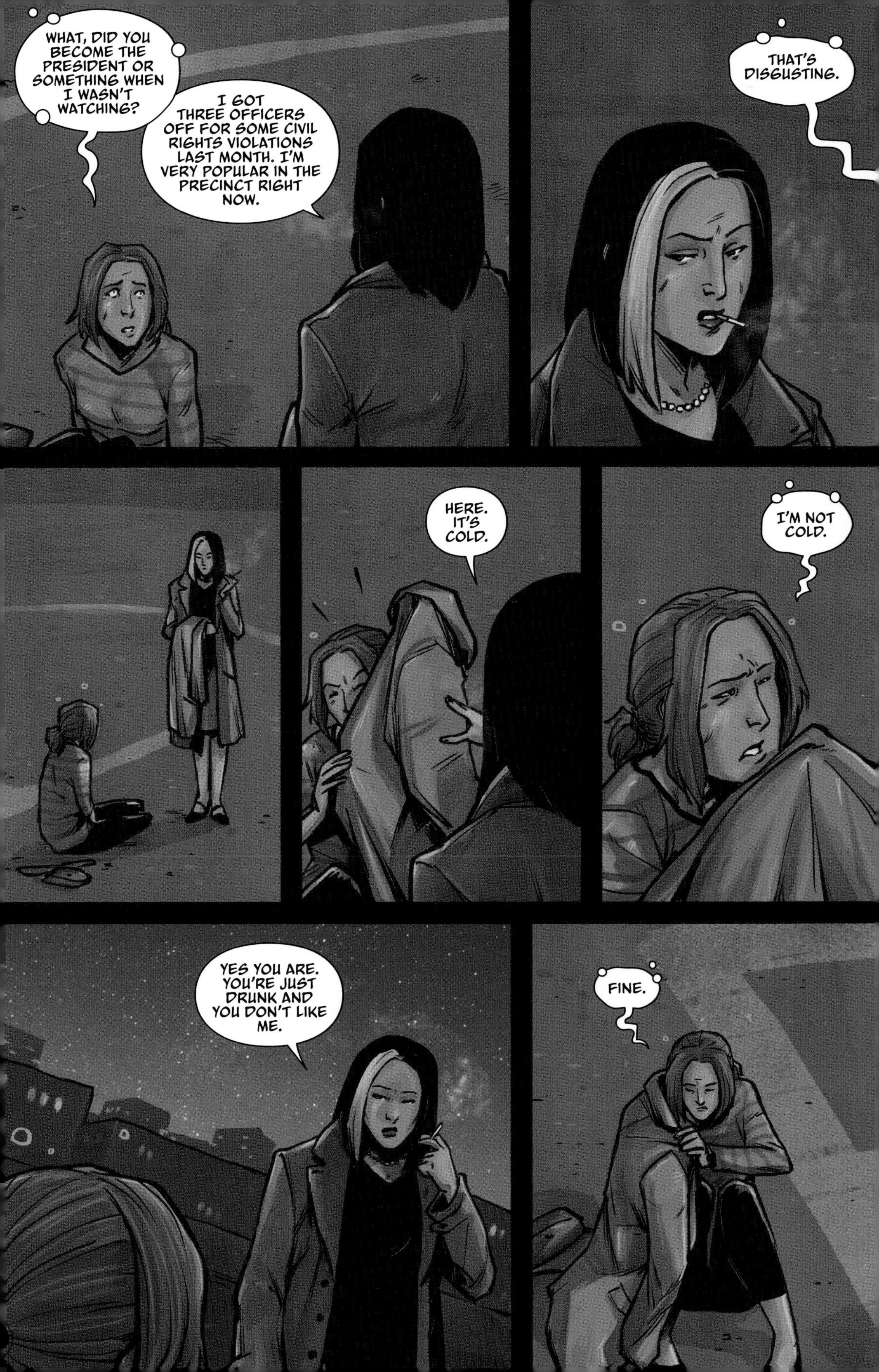
WHAT, DID YOU BECOME THE PRESIDENT OR SOMETHING WHEN I WASN'T WATCHING?
I GOT THREE OFFICERS OFF FOR SOME CIVIL RIGHTS VIOLATIONS LAST MONTH. I'M VERY POPULAR IN THE PRECINCT RIGHT NOW.
THAT'S DISGUSTING.
HERE. IT'S COLD.
I'M NOT COLD.
YES YOU ARE. YOU'RE JUST DRUNK AND YOU DON'T LIKE ME.
FINE.

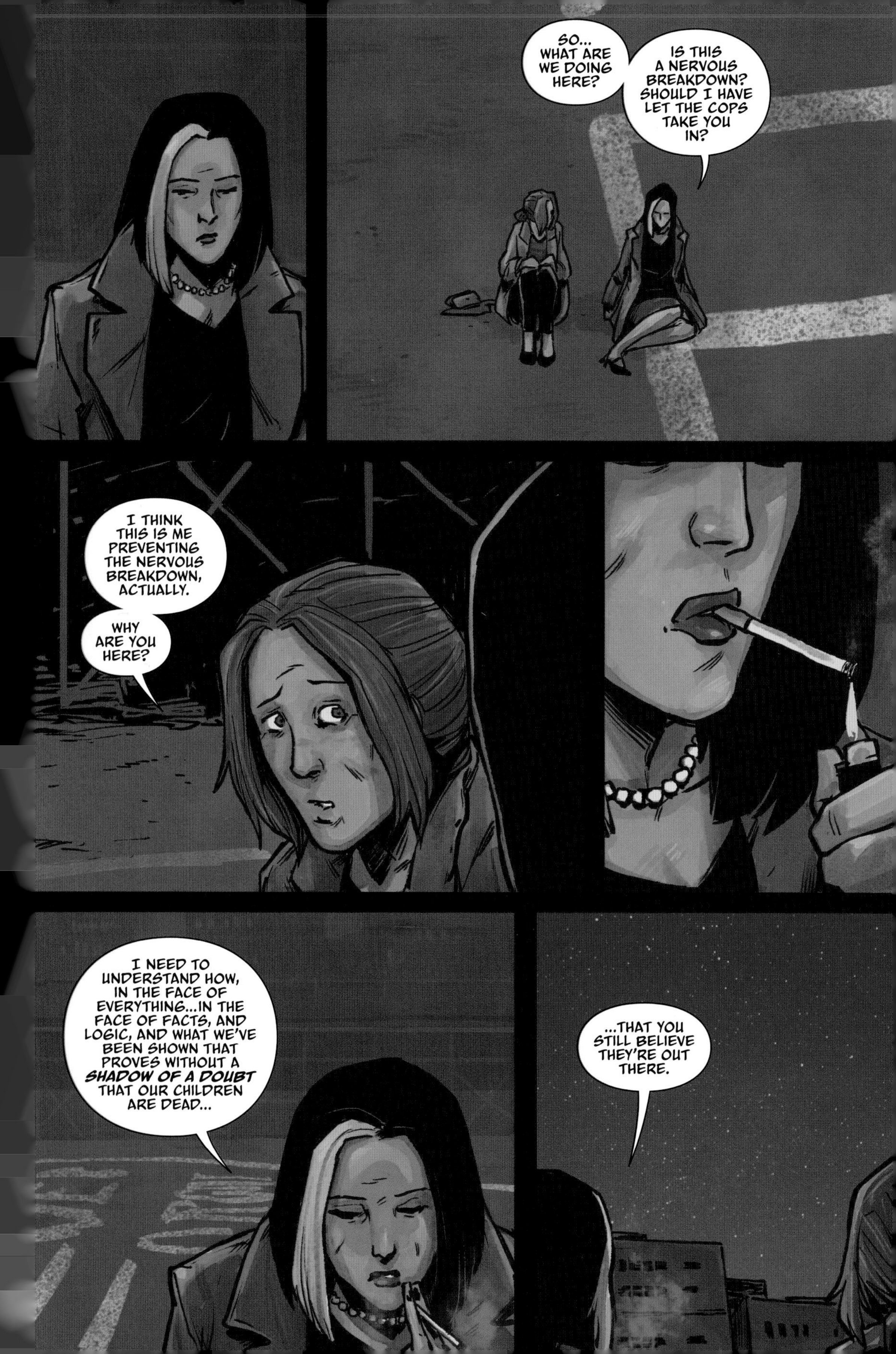
SO... WHAT ARE WE DOING HERE?
IS THIS A NERVOUS BREAKDOWN? SHOULD I HAVE LET THE COPS TAKE YOU IN?
I THINK THIS IS ME PREVENTING THE NERVOUS BREAKDOWN, ACTUALLY.
WHY ARE YOU HERE?
I NEED TO UNDERSTAND HOW, IN THE FACE OF EVERYTHING...IN THE FACE OF FACTS, AND LOGIC, AND WHAT WE'VE BEEN SHOWN THAT PROVES WITHOUT A SHADOW OF A DOUBT THAT OUR CHILDREN ARE DEAD...
...THAT YOU STILL BELIEVE THEY'RE OUT THERE.

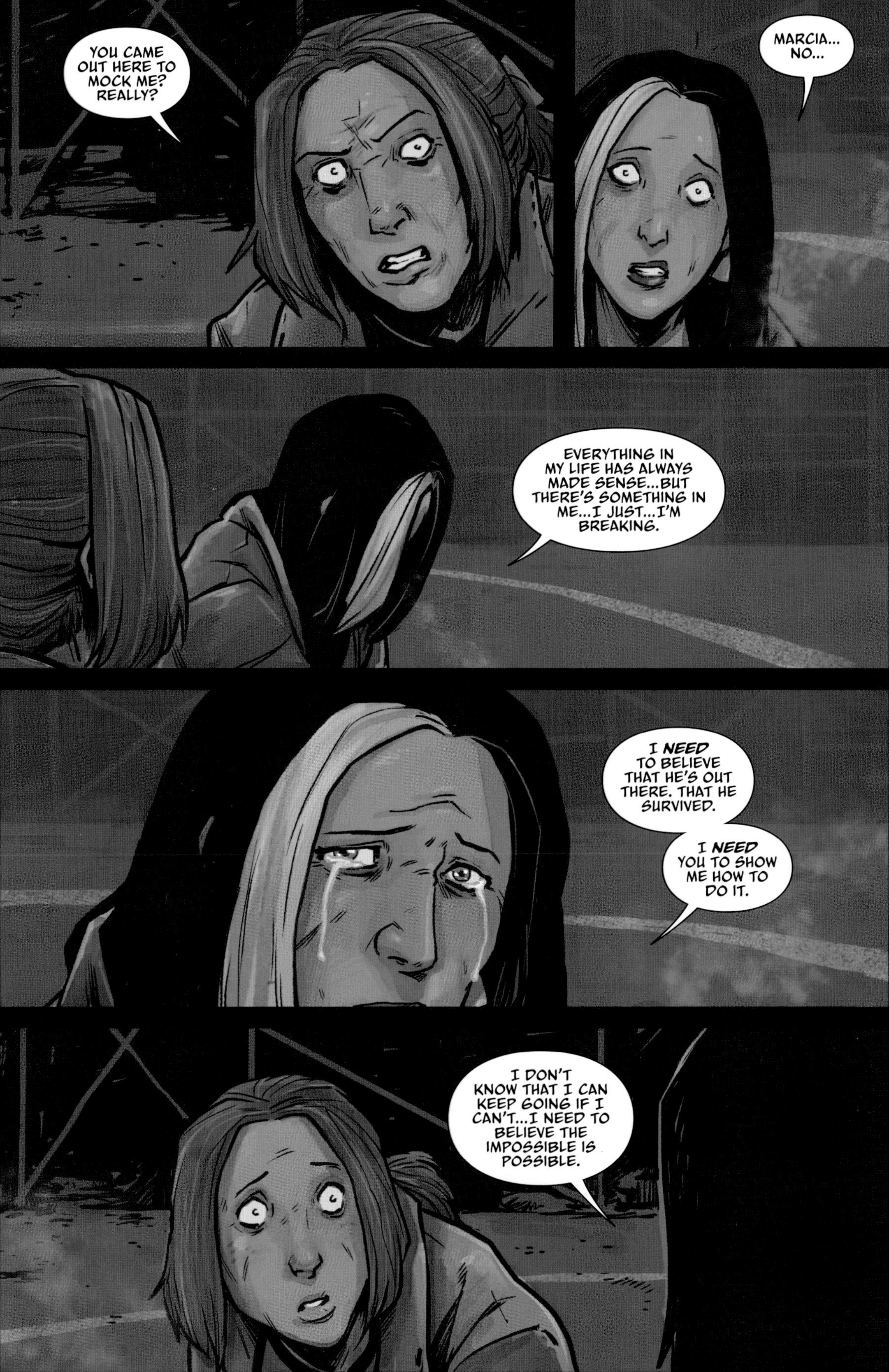
YOU CAME OUT HERE TO MOCK ME? REALLY?
MARCIA... NO...
EVERYTHING IN MY LIFE HAS ALWAYS MADE SENSE...BUT THERE'S SOMETHING IN ME...I JUST...I'M BREAKING.
I *NEED* TO BELIEVE THAT HE'S OUT THERE. THAT HE SURVIVED.
I *NEED* YOU TO SHOW ME HOW TO DO IT.
I DON'T KNOW THAT I CAN KEEP GOING IF I CAN'T...I NEED TO BELIEVE THE IMPOSSIBLE IS POSSIBLE.

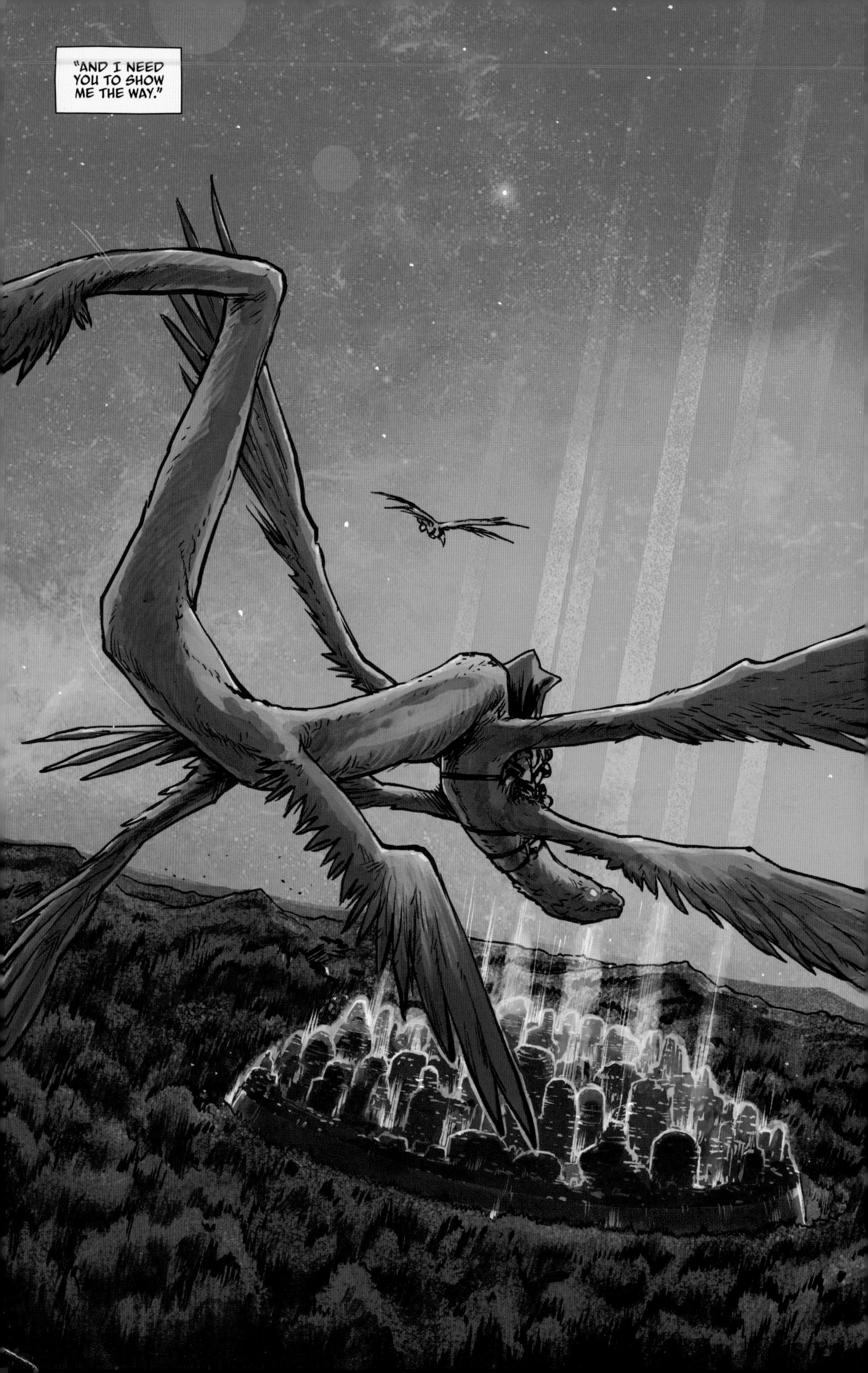
"AND I NEED YOU TO SHOW ME THE WAY."

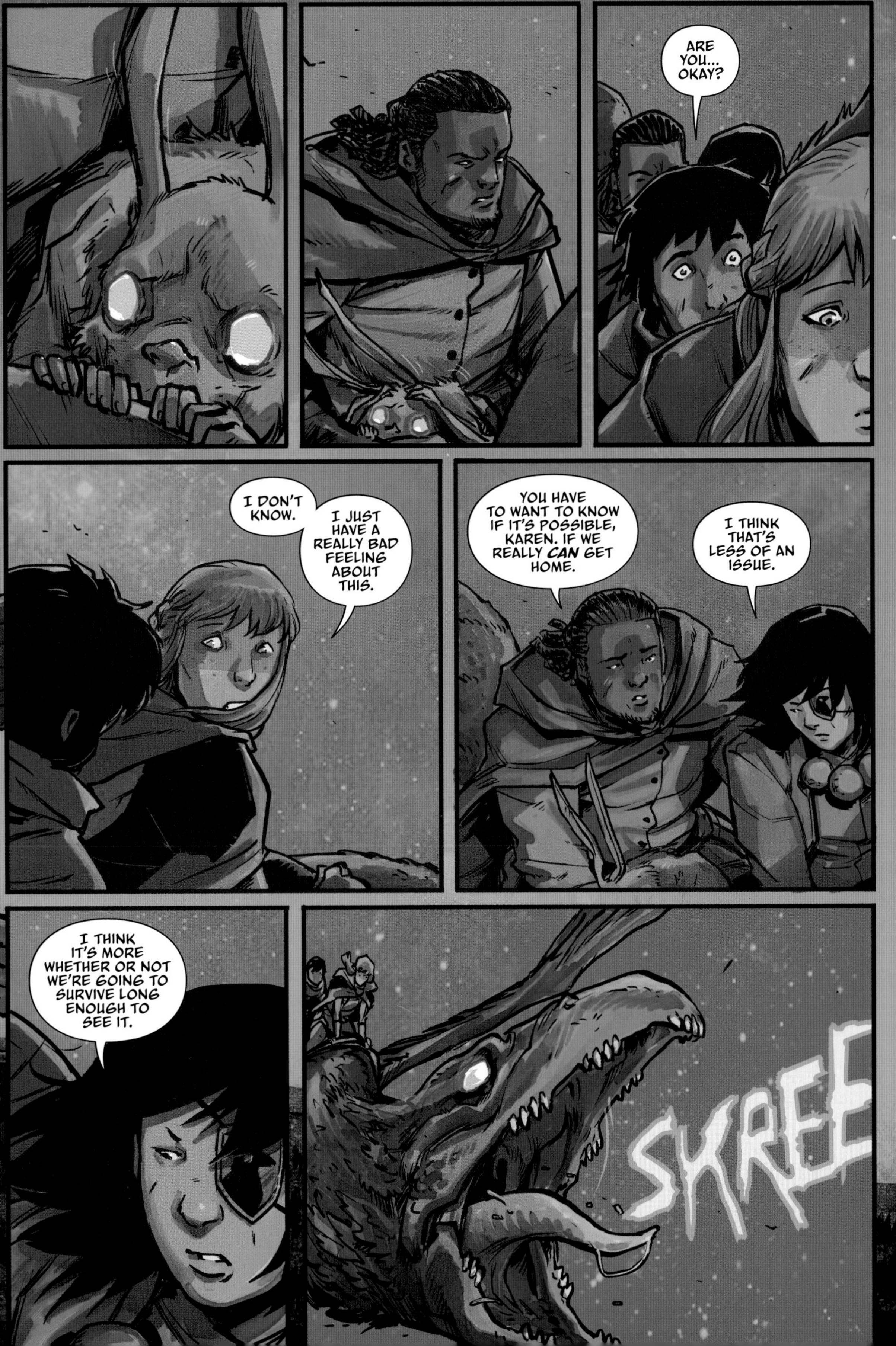
ARE YOU... OKAY?
I DON'T KNOW.
I JUST HAVE A REALLY BAD FEELING ABOUT THIS.
YOU HAVE TO WANT TO KNOW IF IT'S POSSIBLE, KAREN. IF WE REALLY CAN GET HOME.
I THINK THAT'S LESS OF AN ISSUE.
I THINK IT'S MORE WHETHER OR NOT WE'RE GOING TO SURVIVE LONG ENOUGH TO SEE IT.
SKREE

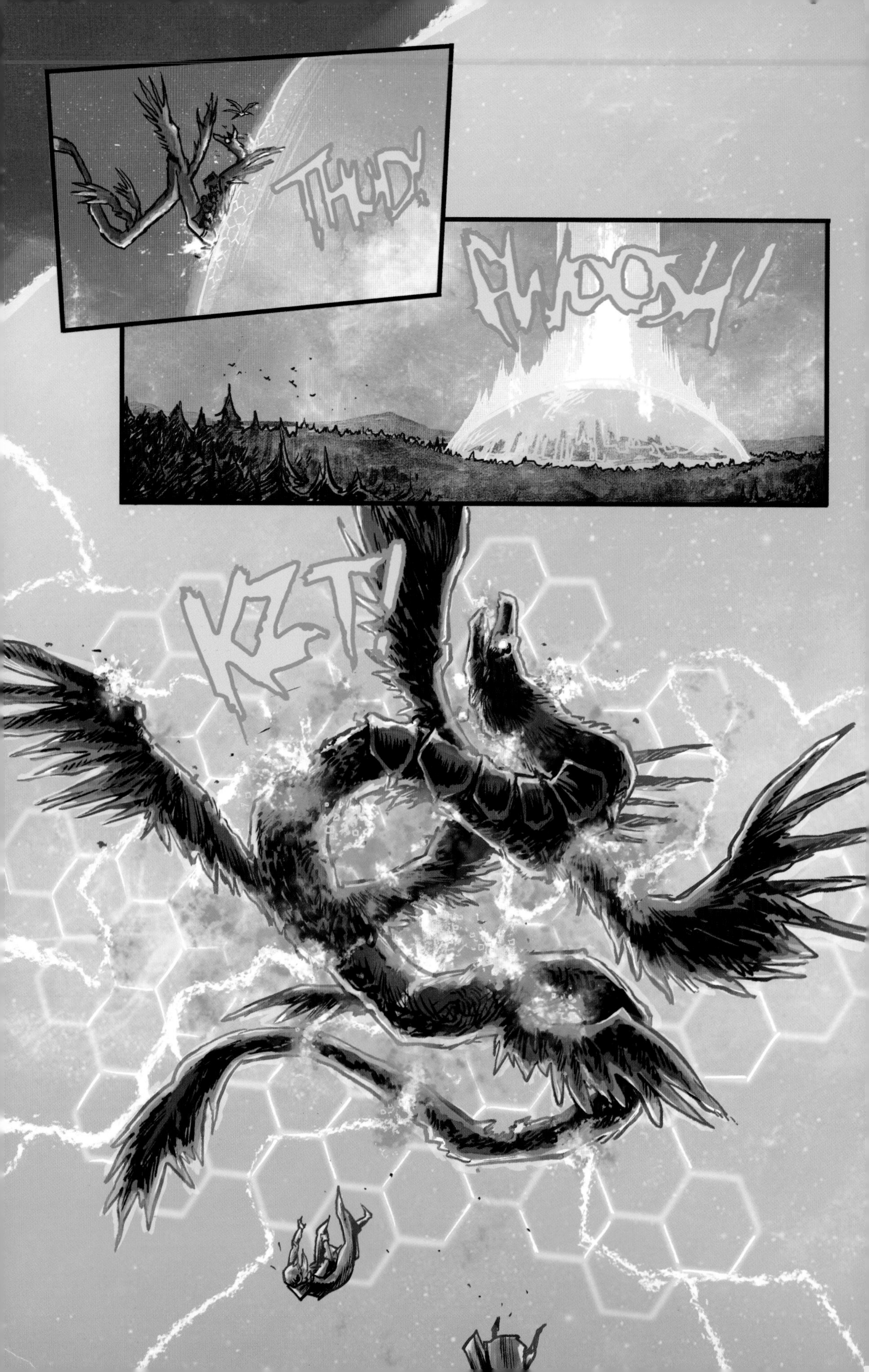
THUD!
FWOOSH!
KZZT!

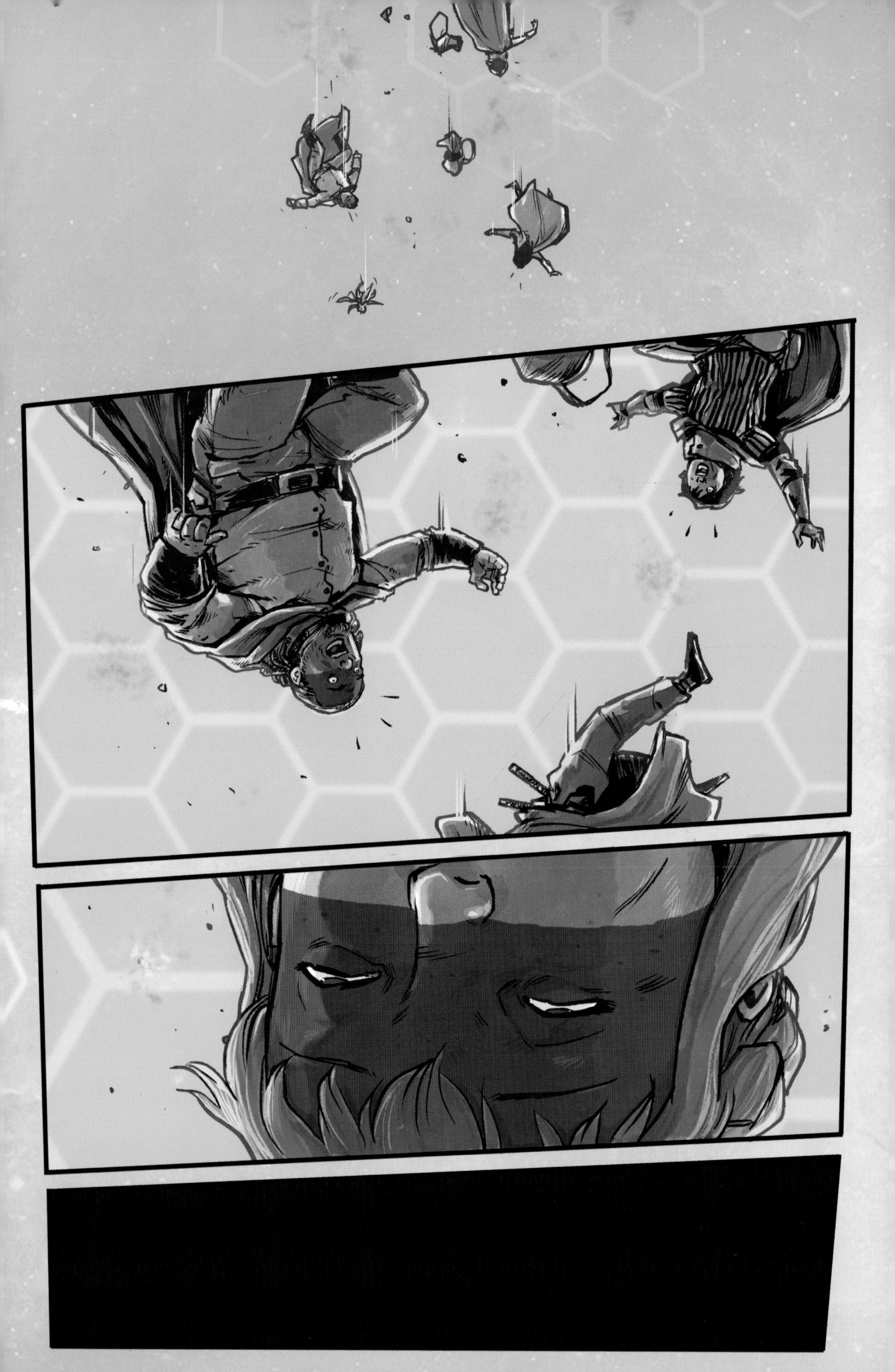

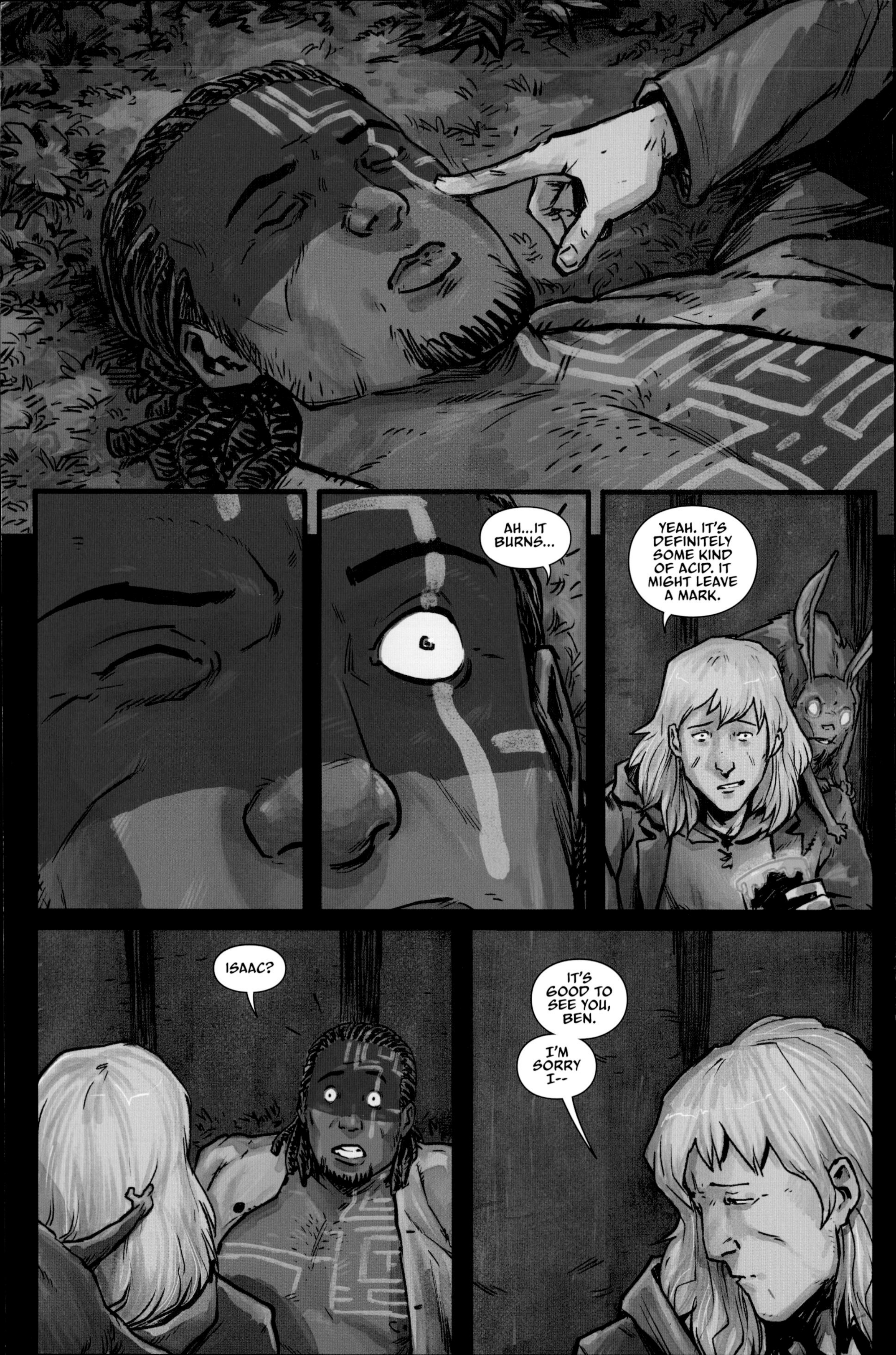
AH...IT BURNS...
YEAH. IT'S DEFINITELY SOME KIND OF ACID. IT MIGHT LEAVE A MARK.
ISAAC?
IT'S GOOD TO SEE YOU, BEN.
I'M SORRY I--

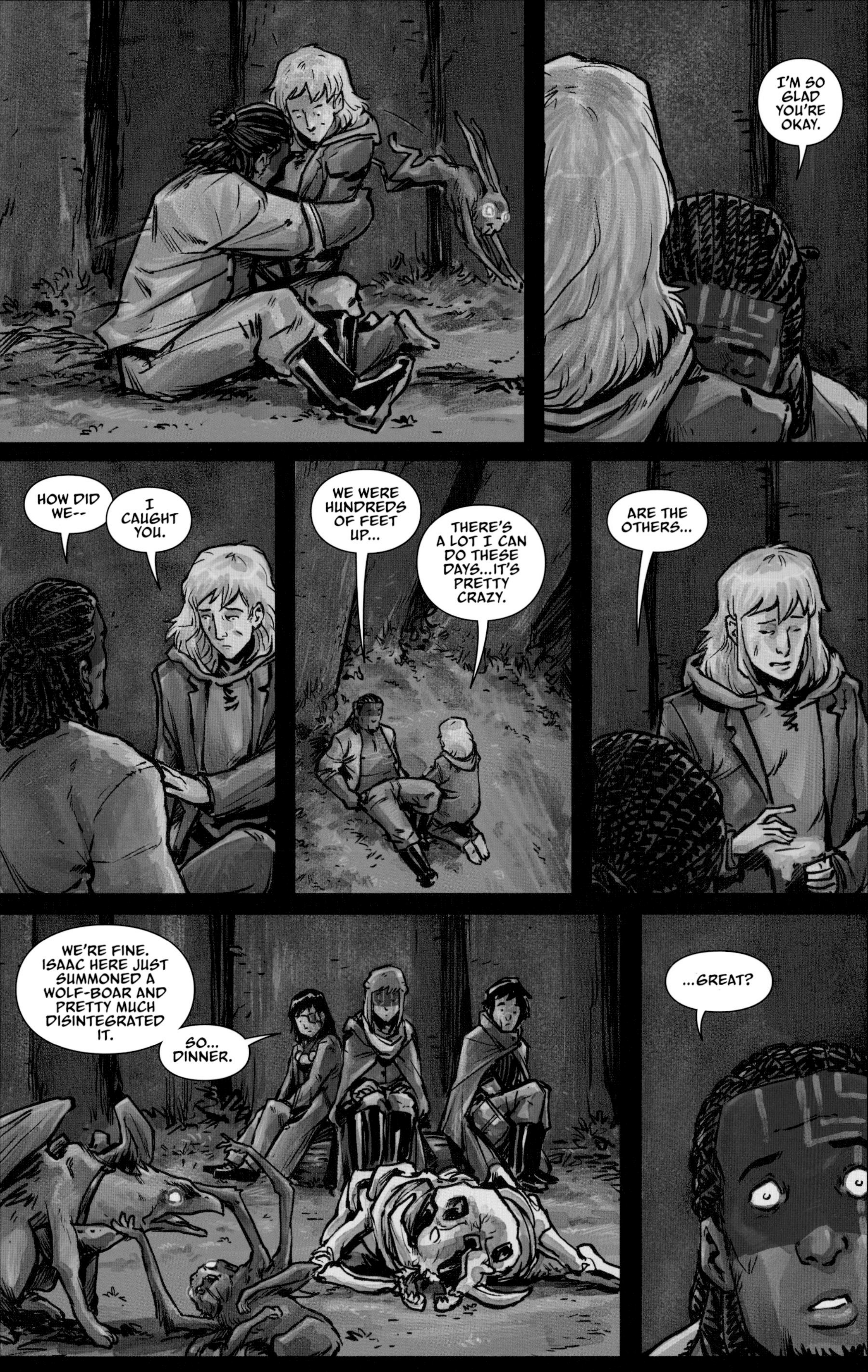
I'M SO GLAD YOU'RE OKAY.
HOW DID WE--
I CAUGHT YOU.
WE WERE HUNDREDS OF FEET UP...
THERE'S A LOT I CAN DO THESE DAYS...IT'S PRETTY CRAZY.
ARE THE OTHERS...
WE'RE FINE. ISAAC HERE JUST SUMMONED A WOLF-BOAR AND PRETTY MUCH DISINTEGRATED IT.
SO... DINNER.
...GREAT?

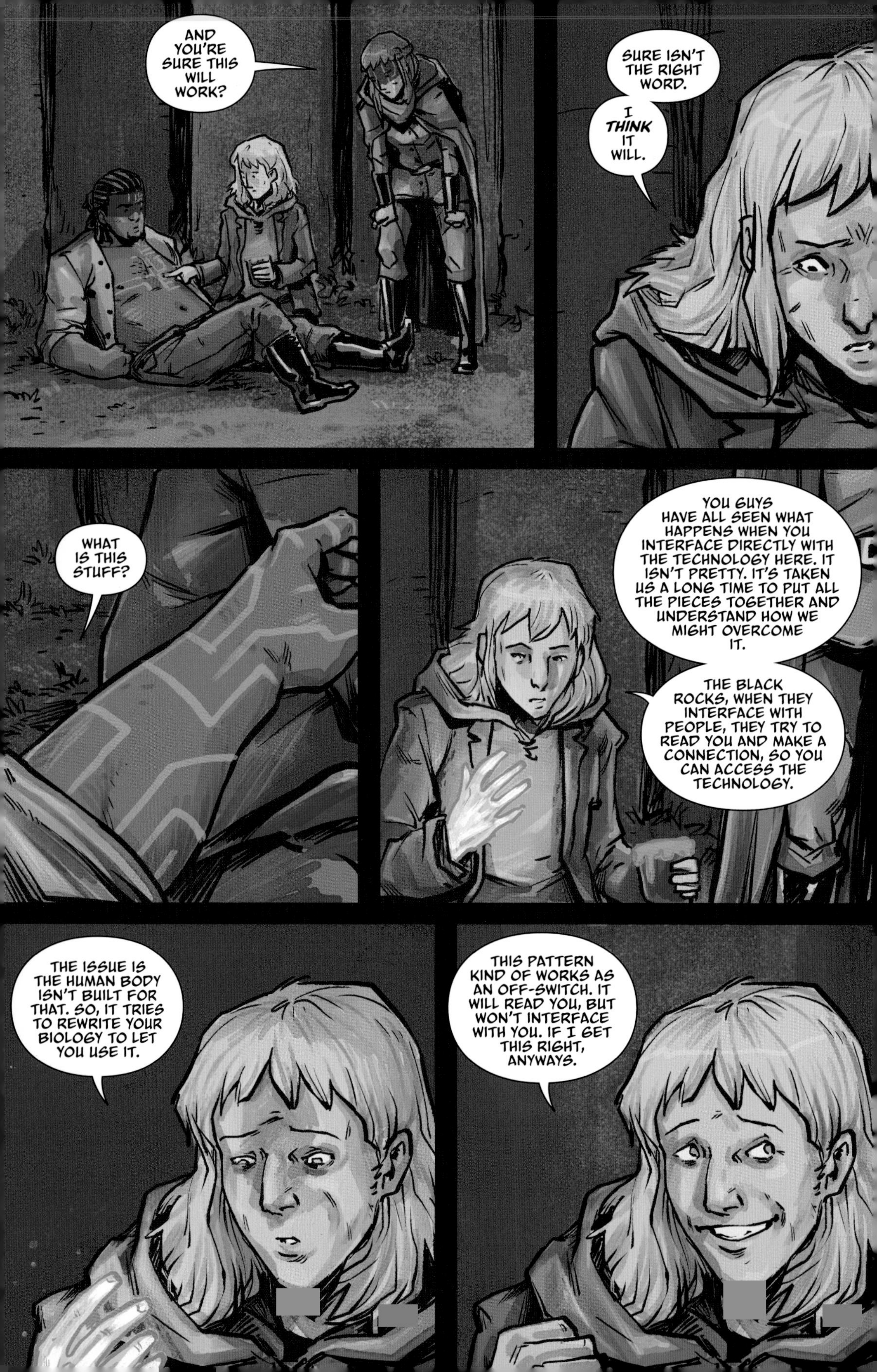
AND YOU'RE SURE THIS WILL WORK?
SURE ISN'T THE RIGHT WORD.
I *THINK* IT WILL.
WHAT IS THIS STUFF?
YOU GUYS HAVE ALL SEEN WHAT HAPPENS WHEN YOU INTERFACE DIRECTLY WITH THE TECHNOLOGY HERE. IT ISN'T PRETTY. IT'S TAKEN US A LONG TIME TO PUT ALL THE PIECES TOGETHER AND UNDERSTAND HOW WE MIGHT OVERCOME IT.
THE BLACK ROCKS, WHEN THEY INTERFACE WITH PEOPLE, THEY TRY TO READ YOU AND MAKE A CONNECTION, SO YOU CAN ACCESS THE TECHNOLOGY.
THE ISSUE IS THE HUMAN BODY ISN'T BUILT FOR THAT. SO, IT TRIES TO REWRITE YOUR BIOLOGY TO LET YOU USE IT.
THIS PATTERN KIND OF WORKS AS AN OFF-SWITCH. IT WILL READ YOU, BUT WON'T INTERFACE WITH YOU. IF I GET THIS RIGHT, ANYWAYS.

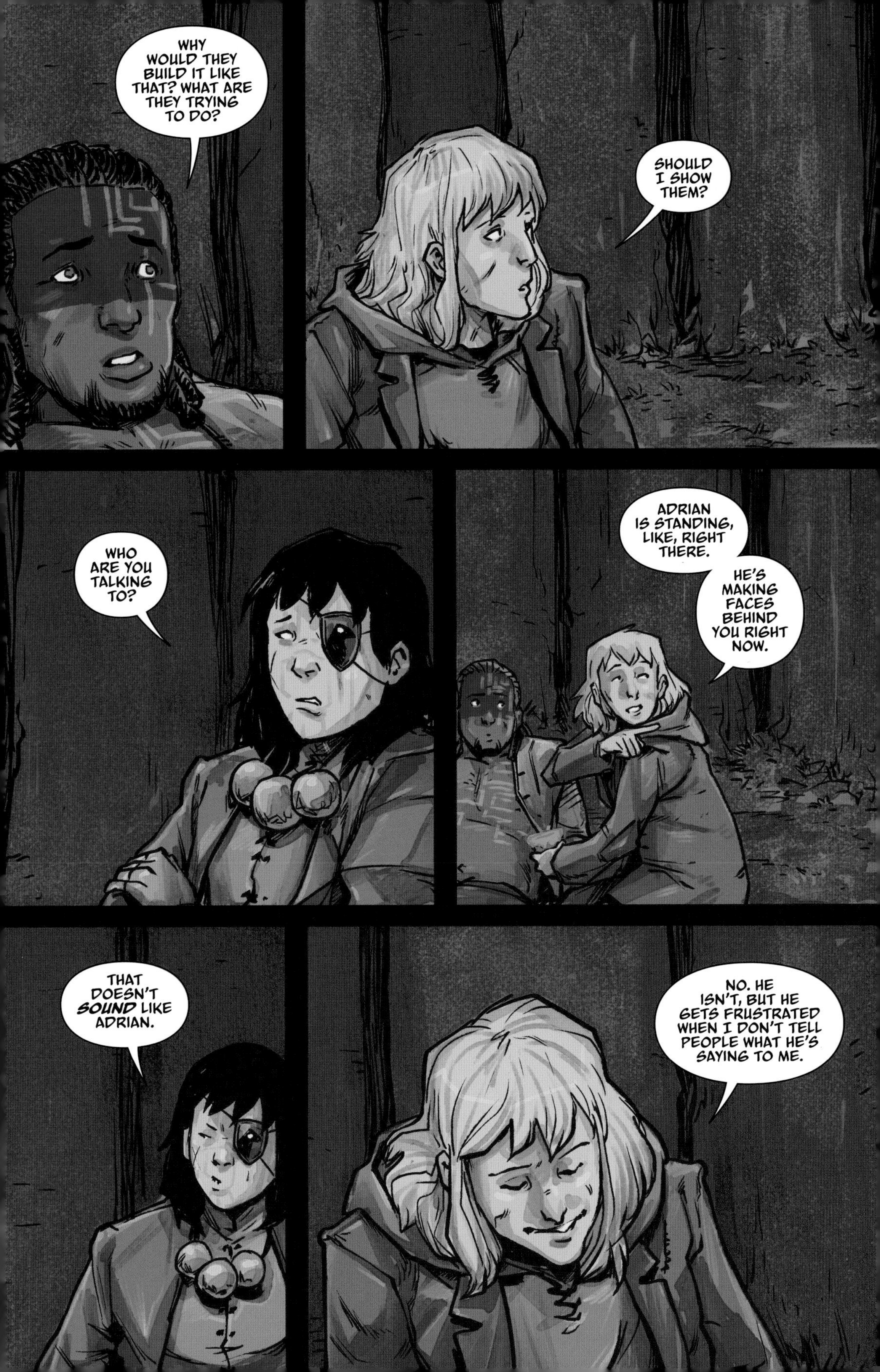
WHY WOULD THEY BUILD IT LIKE THAT? WHAT ARE THEY TRYING TO DO?
SHOULD I SHOW THEM?
WHO ARE YOU TALKING TO?
ADRIAN IS STANDING, LIKE, RIGHT THERE.
HE'S MAKING FACES BEHIND YOU RIGHT NOW.
THAT DOESN'T *SOUND* LIKE ADRIAN.
NO. HE ISN'T, BUT HE GETS FRUSTRATED WHEN I DON'T TELL PEOPLE WHAT HE'S SAYING TO ME.

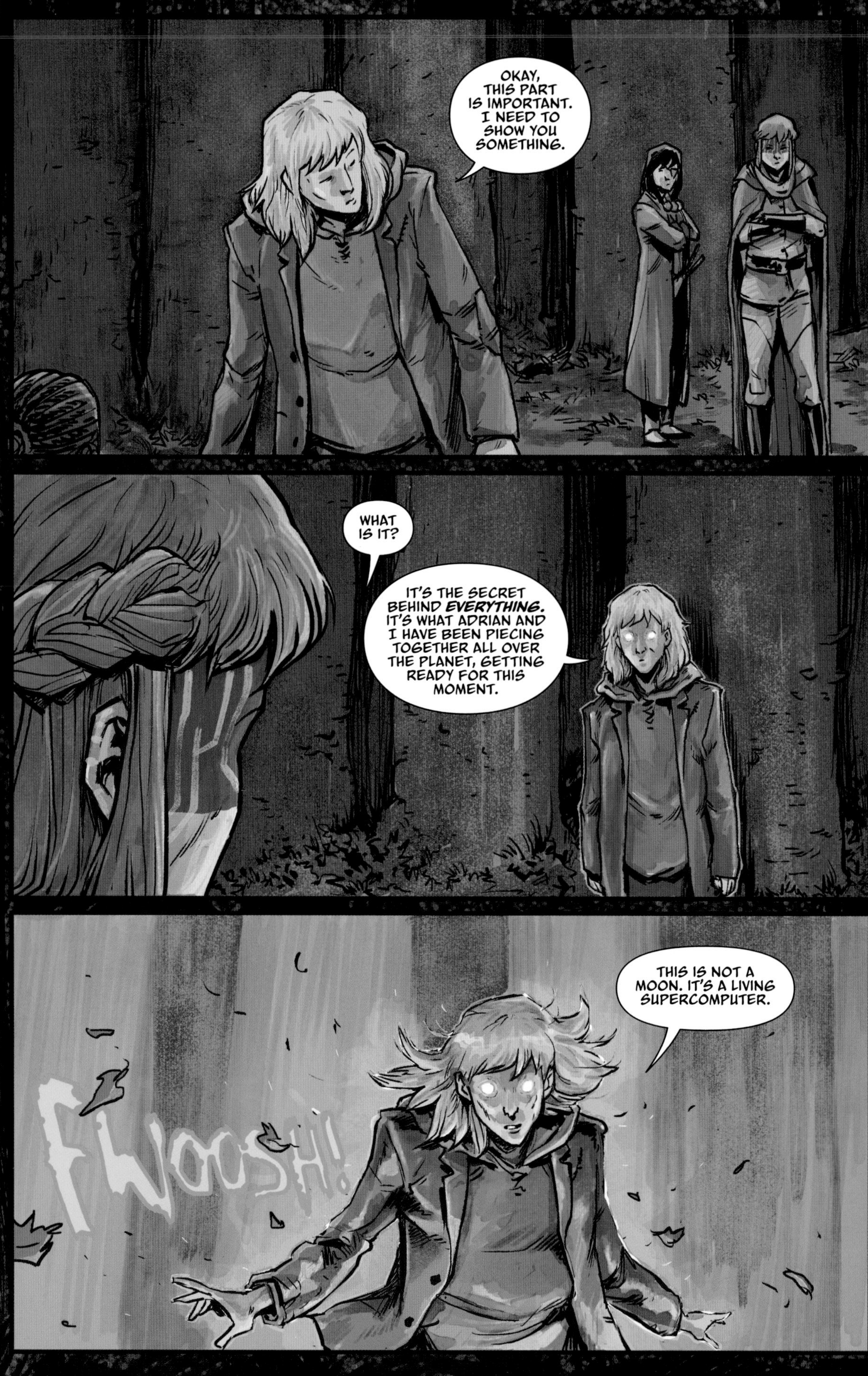
OKAY, THIS PART IS IMPORTANT. I NEED TO SHOW YOU SOMETHING.
WHAT IS IT?
IT'S THE SECRET BEHIND **EVERYTHING.** IT'S WHAT ADRIAN AND I HAVE BEEN PIECING TOGETHER ALL OVER THE PLANET, GETTING READY FOR THIS MOMENT.
THIS IS NOT A MOON. IT'S A LIVING SUPERCOMPUTER.
FWOOSH!

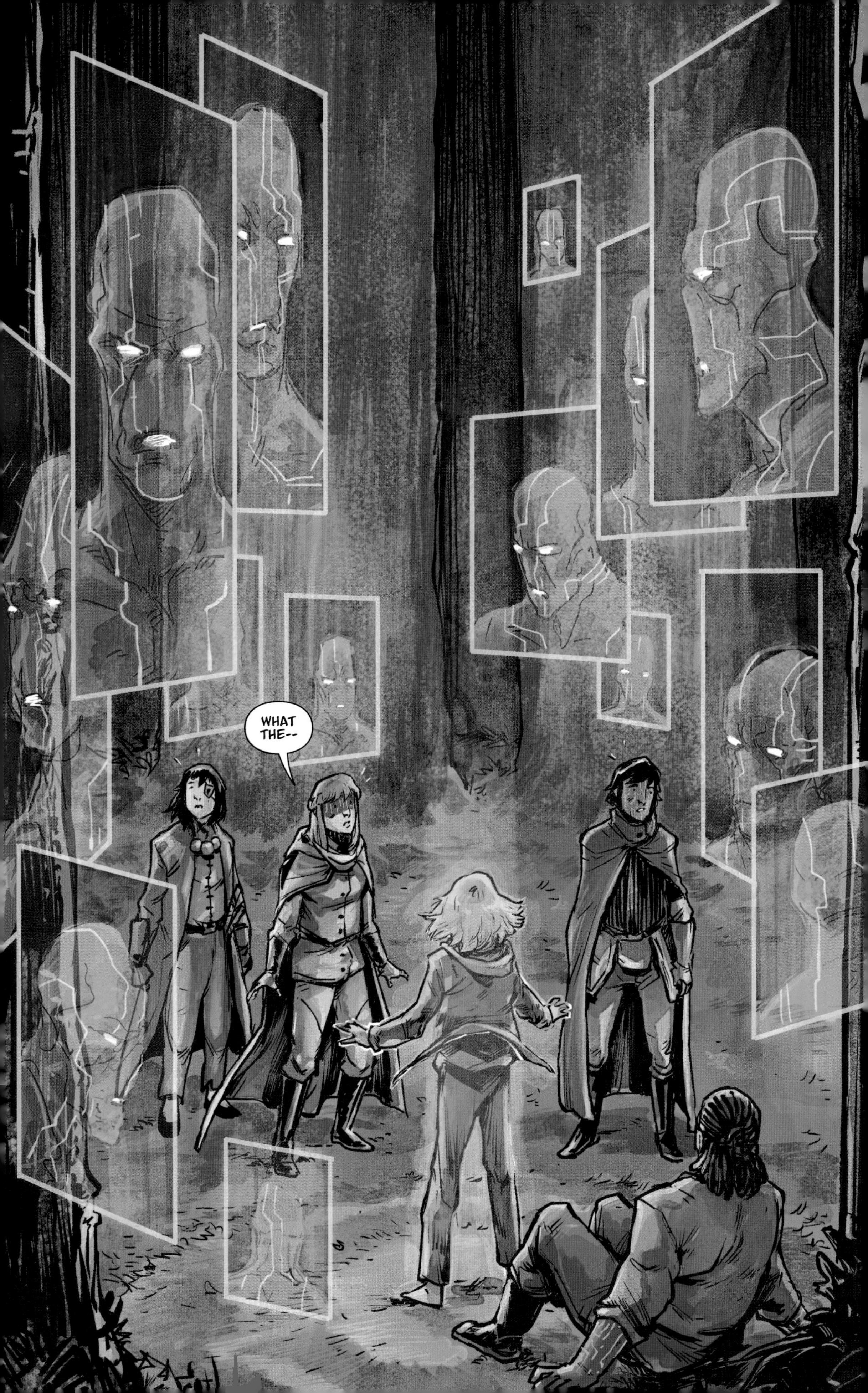
WHAT THE--

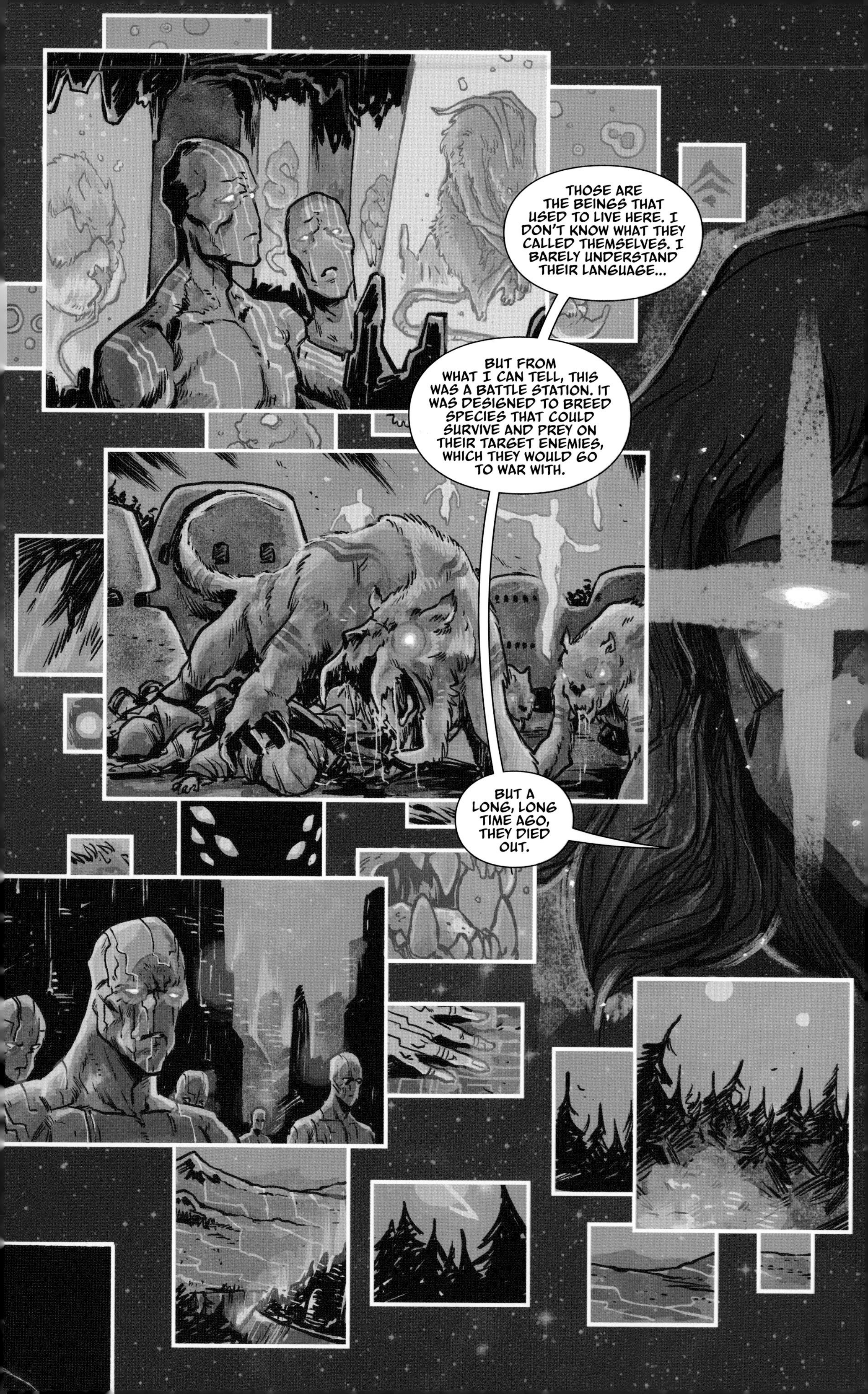
THOSE ARE THE BEINGS THAT USED TO LIVE HERE. I DON'T KNOW WHAT THEY CALLED THEMSELVES. I BARELY UNDERSTAND THEIR LANGUAGE...
BUT FROM WHAT I CAN TELL, THIS WAS A BATTLE STATION. IT WAS DESIGNED TO BREED SPECIES THAT COULD SURVIVE AND PREY ON THEIR TARGET ENEMIES, WHICH THEY WOULD GO TO WAR WITH.
BUT A LONG, LONG TIME AGO, THEY DIED OUT.

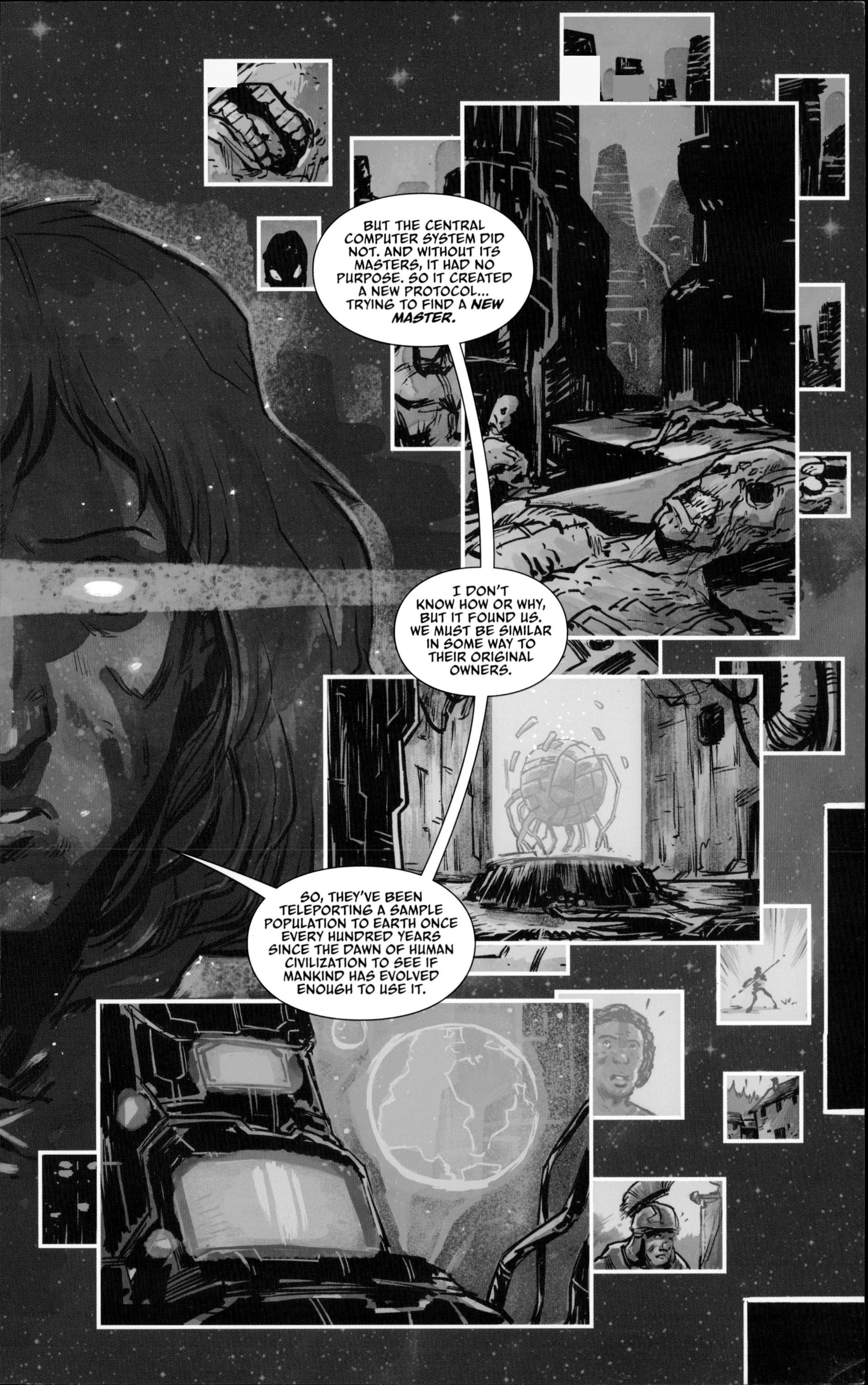
BUT THE CENTRAL COMPUTER SYSTEM DID NOT. AND WITHOUT ITS MASTERS, IT HAD NO PURPOSE. SO IT CREATED A NEW PROTOCOL... TRYING TO FIND A *NEW MASTER.*
I DON'T KNOW HOW OR WHY, BUT IT FOUND US. WE MUST BE SIMILAR IN SOME WAY TO THEIR ORIGINAL OWNERS.
SO, THEY'VE BEEN TELEPORTING A SAMPLE POPULATION TO EARTH ONCE EVERY HUNDRED YEARS SINCE THE DAWN OF HUMAN CIVILIZATION TO SEE IF MANKIND HAS EVOLVED ENOUGH TO USE IT.

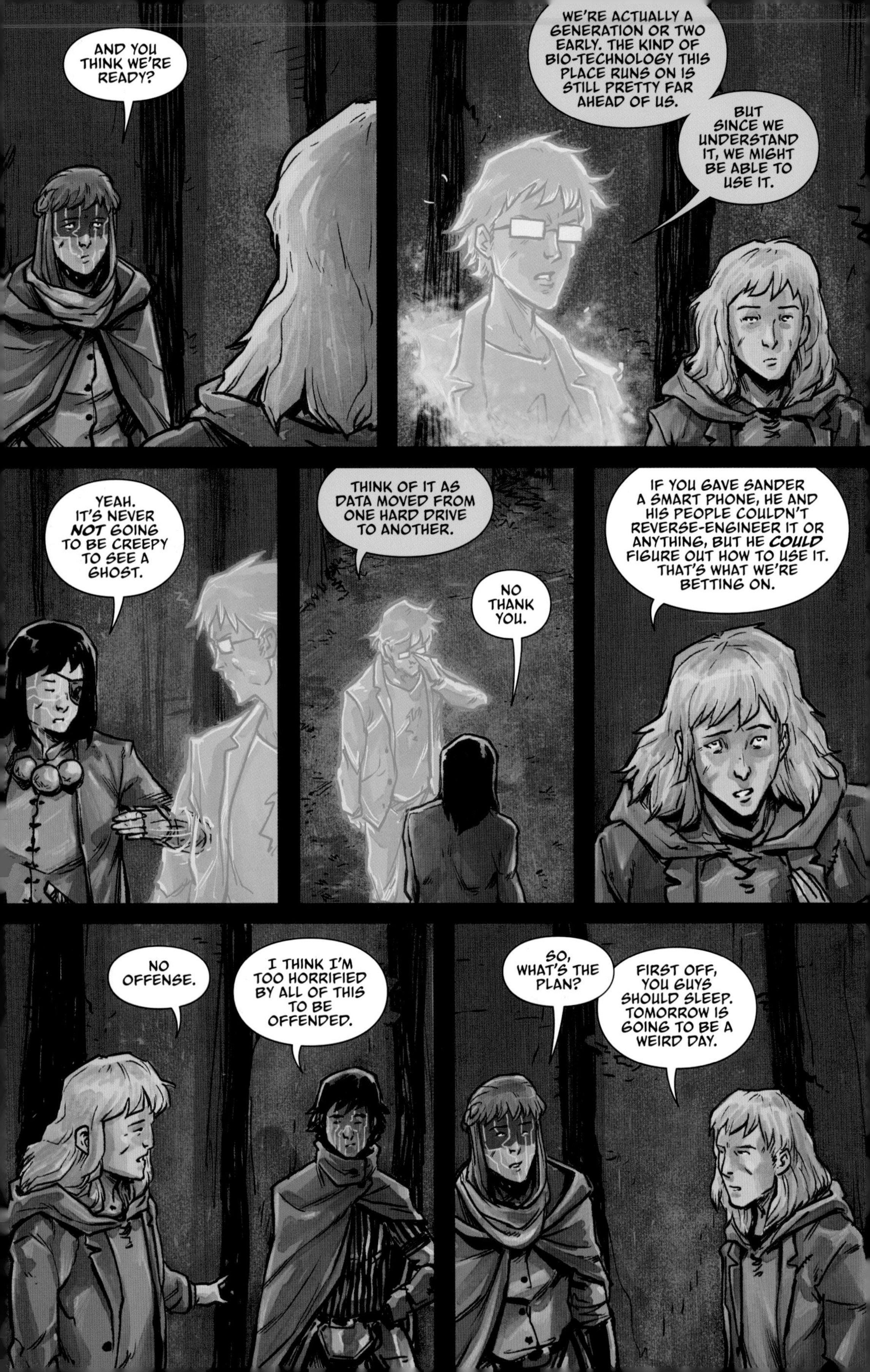
AND YOU THINK WE'RE READY?
WE'RE ACTUALLY A GENERATION OR TWO EARLY. THE KIND OF BIO-TECHNOLOGY THIS PLACE RUNS ON IS STILL PRETTY FAR AHEAD OF US.
BUT SINCE WE UNDERSTAND IT, WE MIGHT BE ABLE TO USE IT.
YEAH. IT'S NEVER *NOT* GOING TO BE CREEPY TO SEE A GHOST.
THINK OF IT AS DATA MOVED FROM ONE HARD DRIVE TO ANOTHER.
NO THANK YOU.
IF YOU GAVE SANDER A SMART PHONE, HE AND HIS PEOPLE COULDN'T REVERSE-ENGINEER IT OR ANYTHING, BUT HE *COULD* FIGURE OUT HOW TO USE IT. THAT'S WHAT WE'RE BETTING ON.
NO OFFENSE.
I THINK I'M TOO HORRIFIED BY ALL OF THIS TO BE OFFENDED.
SO, WHAT'S THE PLAN?
FIRST OFF, YOU GUYS SHOULD SLEEP. TOMORROW IS GOING TO BE A WEIRD DAY.

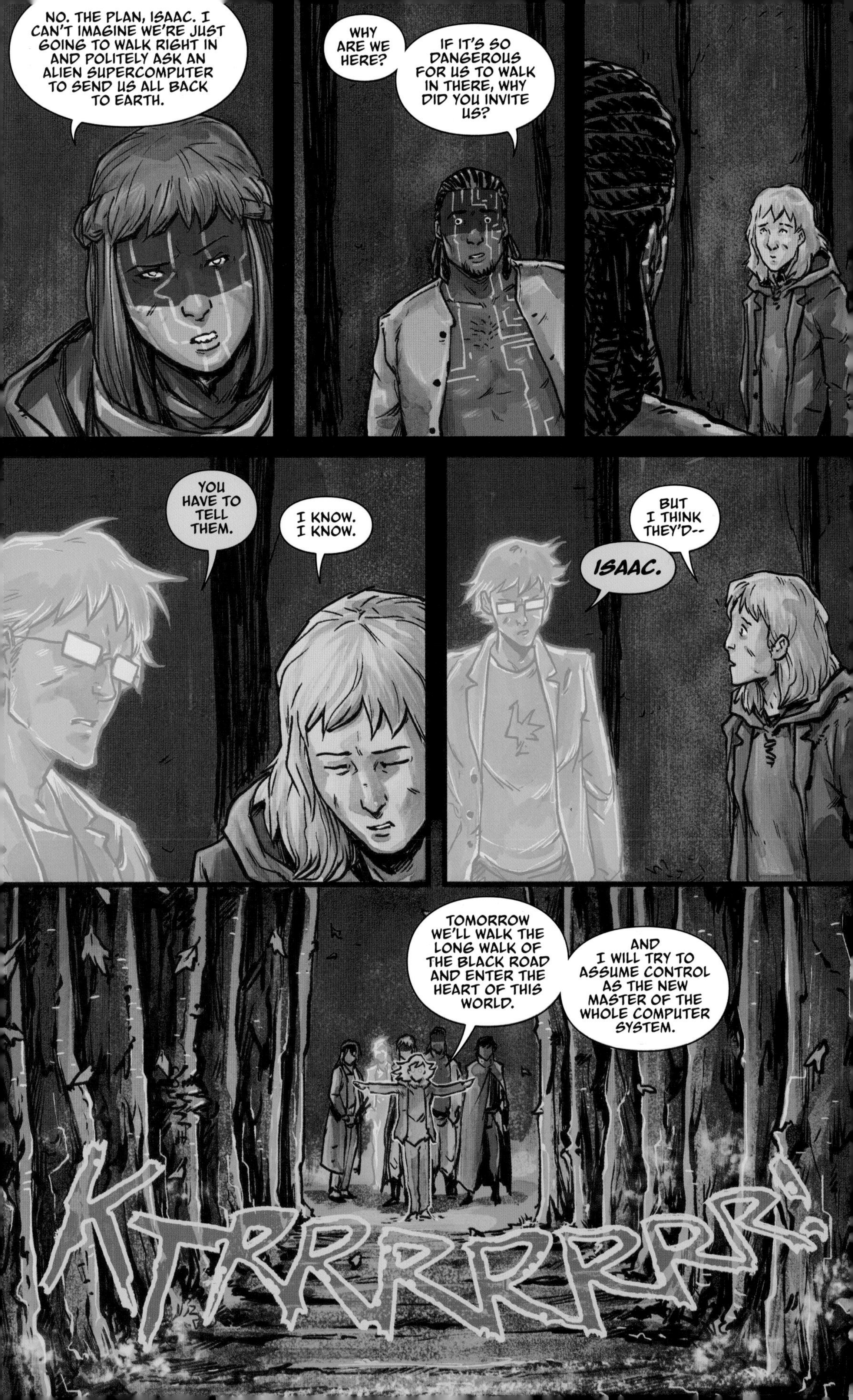

NO. THE PLAN, ISAAC. I CAN'T IMAGINE WE'RE JUST GOING TO WALK RIGHT IN AND POLITELY ASK AN ALIEN SUPERCOMPUTER TO SEND US ALL BACK TO EARTH.
WHY ARE WE HERE?
IF IT'S SO DANGEROUS FOR US TO WALK IN THERE, WHY DID YOU INVITE US?
YOU HAVE TO TELL THEM.
I KNOW. I KNOW.
BUT I THINK THEY'D--
ISAAC.
TOMORROW WE'LL WALK THE LONG WALK OF THE BLACK ROAD AND ENTER THE HEART OF THIS WORLD.
AND I WILL TRY TO ASSUME CONTROL AS THE NEW MASTER OF THE WHOLE COMPUTER SYSTEM.
KTRRRRRRK!

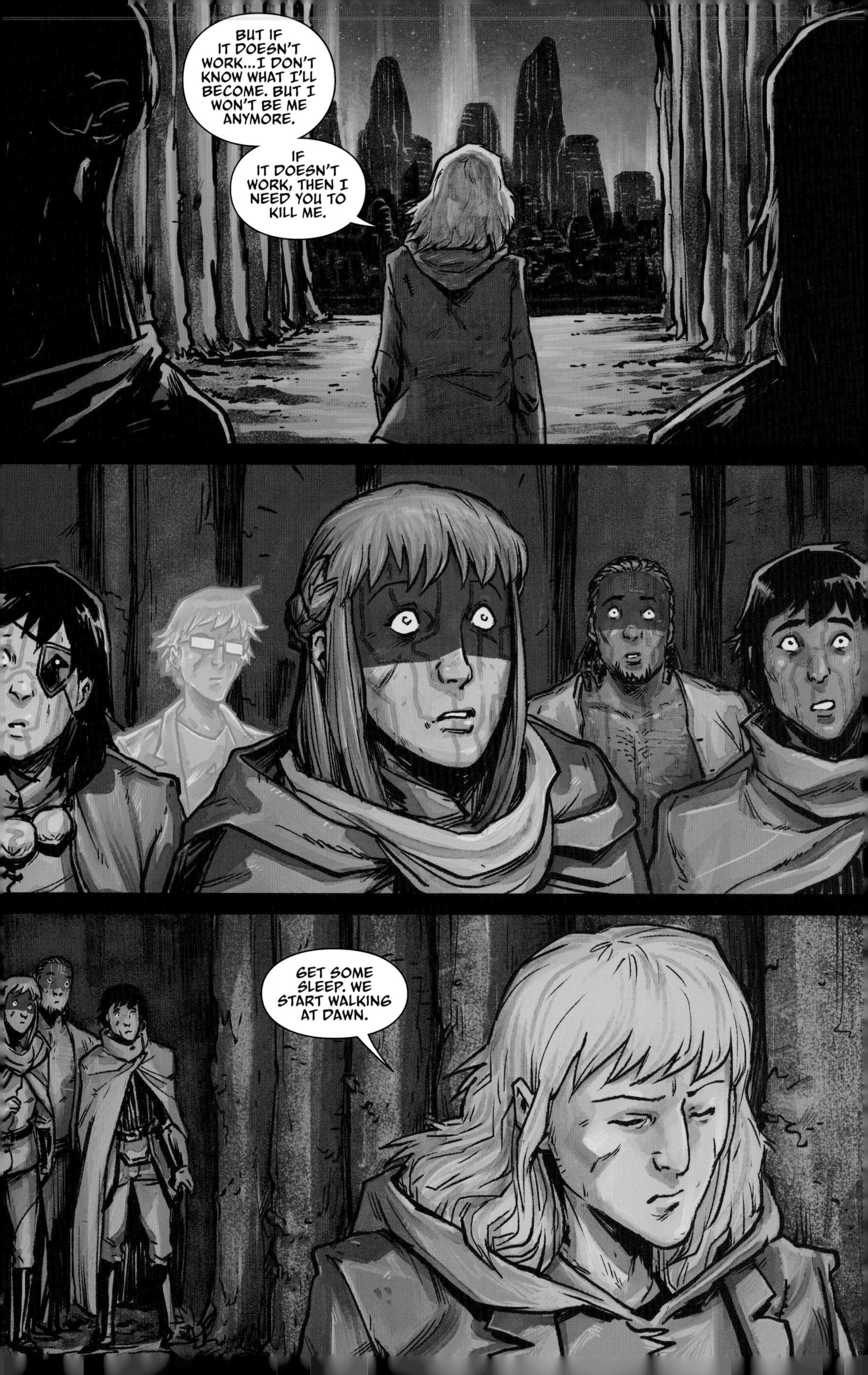
BUT IF IT DOESN'T WORK...I DON'T KNOW WHAT I'LL BECOME. BUT I WON'T BE ME ANYMORE.
IF IT DOESN'T WORK, THEN I NEED YOU TO KILL ME.
GET SOME SLEEP. WE START WALKING AT DAWN.

CHAPTER
TWENTY-EIGHT

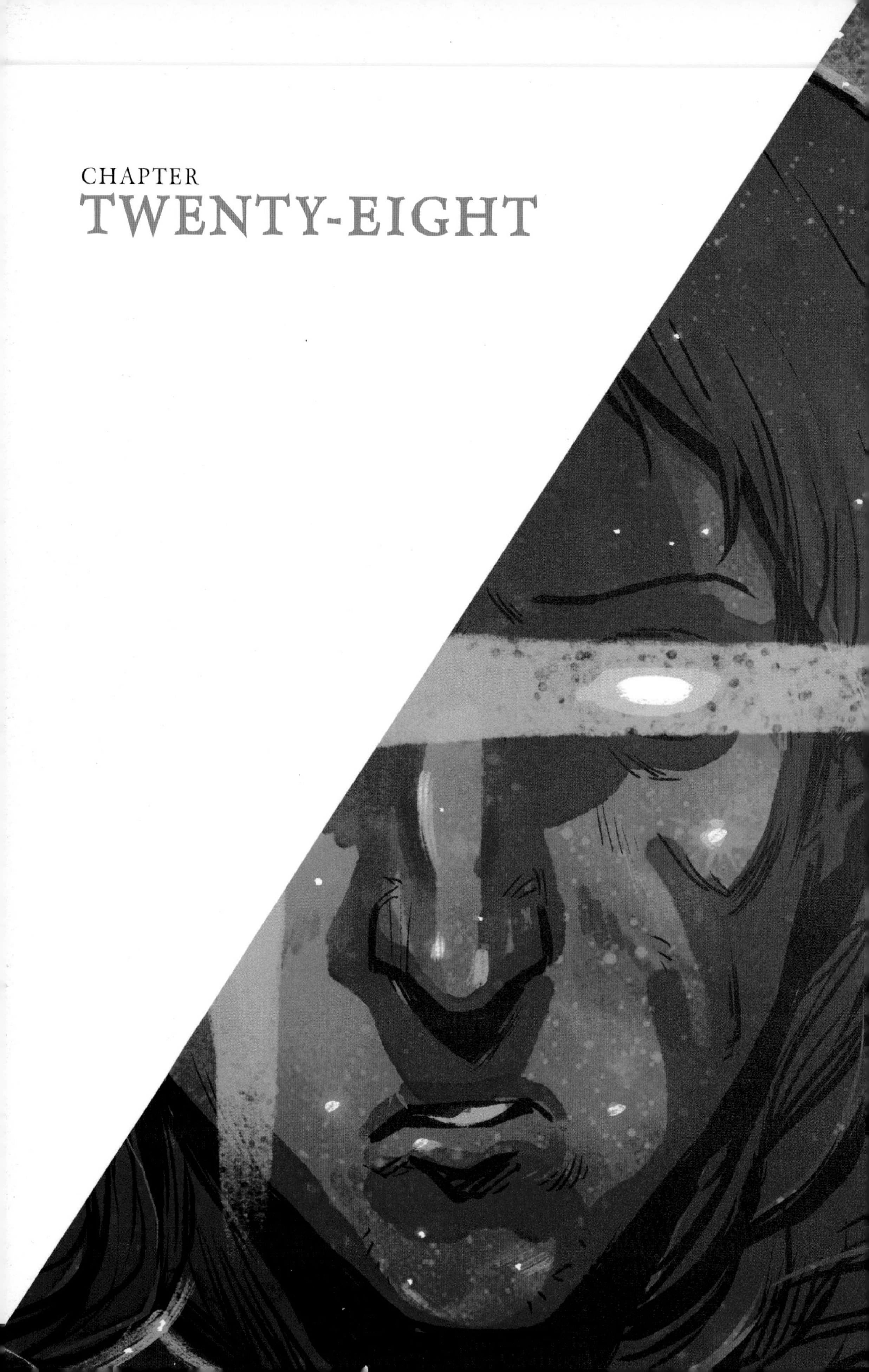

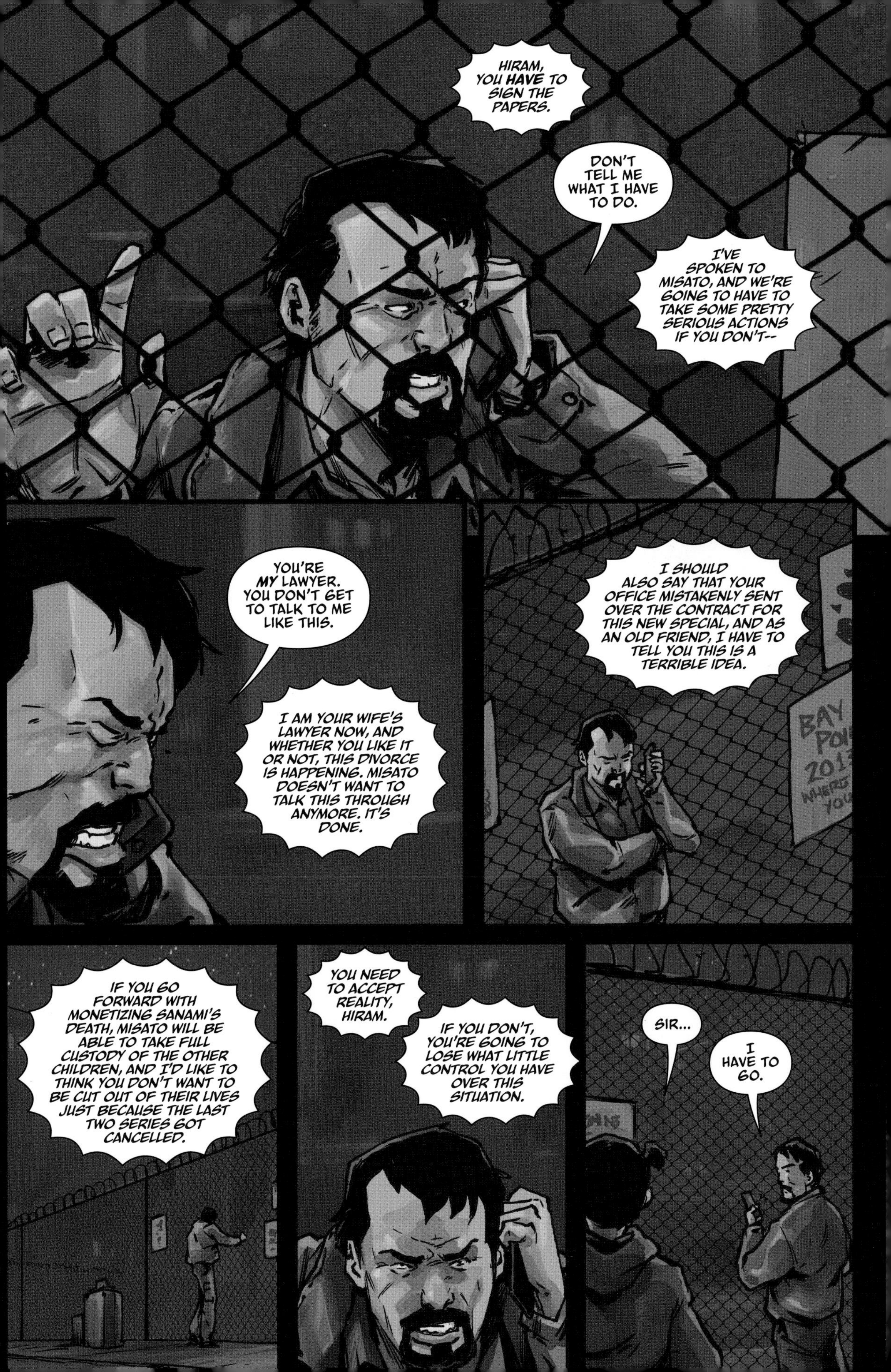
HIRAM, YOU HAVE TO SIGN THE PAPERS.
DON'T TELL ME WHAT I HAVE TO DO.
I'VE SPOKEN TO MISATO, AND WE'RE GOING TO HAVE TO TAKE SOME PRETTY SERIOUS ACTIONS IF YOU DON'T--
YOU'RE MY LAWYER. YOU DON'T GET TO TALK TO ME LIKE THIS.
I AM YOUR WIFE'S LAWYER NOW, AND WHETHER YOU LIKE IT OR NOT, THIS DIVORCE IS HAPPENING. MISATO DOESN'T WANT TO TALK THIS THROUGH ANYMORE. IT'S DONE.
I SHOULD ALSO SAY THAT YOUR OFFICE MISTAKENLY SENT OVER THE CONTRACT FOR THIS NEW SPECIAL, AND AS AN OLD FRIEND, I HAVE TO TELL YOU THIS IS A TERRIBLE IDEA.
IF YOU GO FORWARD WITH MONETIZING SANAMI'S DEATH, MISATO WILL BE ABLE TO TAKE FULL CUSTODY OF THE OTHER CHILDREN, AND I'D LIKE TO THINK YOU DON'T WANT TO BE CUT OUT OF THEIR LIVES JUST BECAUSE THE LAST TWO SERIES GOT CANCELLED.
YOU NEED TO ACCEPT REALITY, HIRAM.
IF YOU DON'T, YOU'RE GOING TO LOSE WHAT LITTLE CONTROL YOU HAVE OVER THIS SITUATION.
SIR...
I HAVE TO GO.

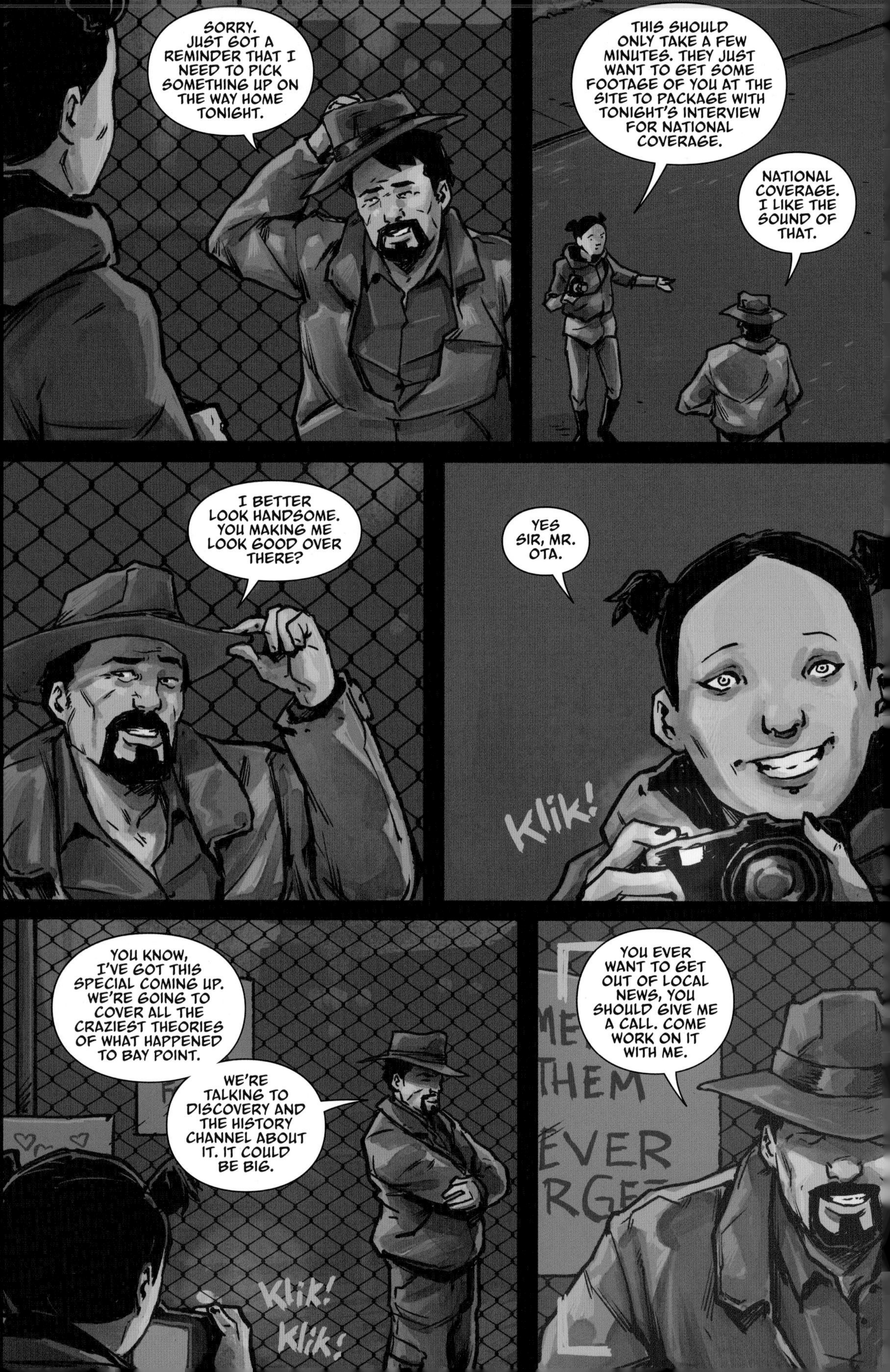
SORRY. JUST GOT A REMINDER THAT I NEED TO PICK SOMETHING UP ON THE WAY HOME TONIGHT.
THIS SHOULD ONLY TAKE A FEW MINUTES. THEY JUST WANT TO GET SOME FOOTAGE OF YOU AT THE SITE TO PACKAGE WITH TONIGHT'S INTERVIEW FOR NATIONAL COVERAGE.
NATIONAL COVERAGE. I LIKE THE SOUND OF THAT.
I BETTER LOOK HANDSOME. YOU MAKING ME LOOK GOOD OVER THERE?
YES SIR, MR. OTA.
Klik!
YOU KNOW, I'VE GOT THIS SPECIAL COMING UP. WE'RE GOING TO COVER ALL THE CRAZIEST THEORIES OF WHAT HAPPENED TO BAY POINT.
WE'RE TALKING TO DISCOVERY AND THE HISTORY CHANNEL ABOUT IT. IT COULD BE BIG.
Klik!
Klik!
YOU EVER WANT TO GET OUT OF LOCAL NEWS, YOU SHOULD GIVE ME A CALL. COME WORK ON IT WITH ME.

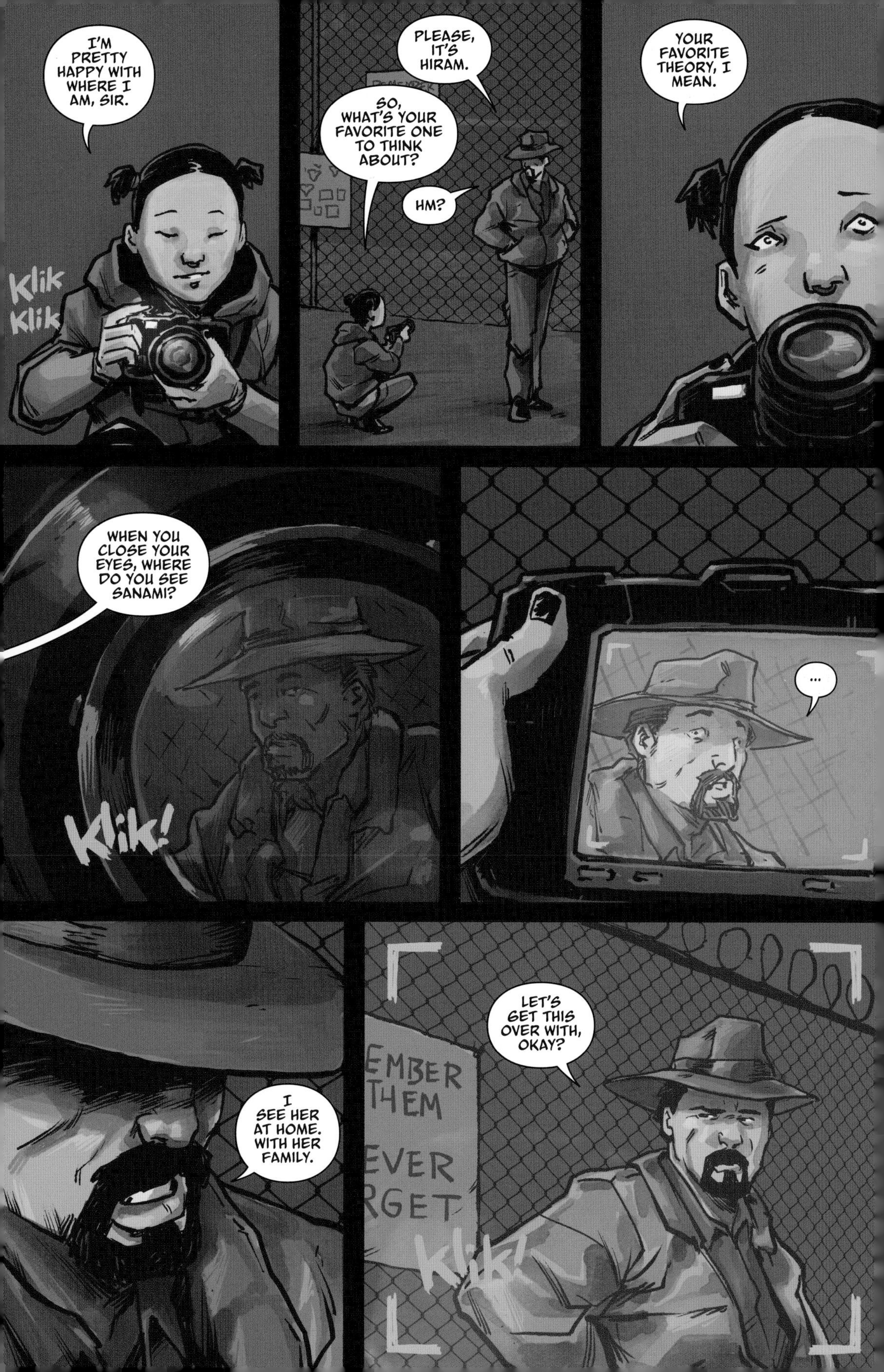
I'M PRETTY HAPPY WITH WHERE I AM, SIR.
Klik Klik
PLEASE, IT'S HIRAM.
SO, WHAT'S YOUR FAVORITE ONE TO THINK ABOUT?
HM?
YOUR FAVORITE THEORY, I MEAN.
WHEN YOU CLOSE YOUR EYES, WHERE DO YOU SEE SANAMI?
Klik!
...
I SEE HER AT HOME. WITH HER FAMILY.
LET'S GET THIS OVER WITH, OKAY?
EMBER
THEM
EVER
RGET
Klik!

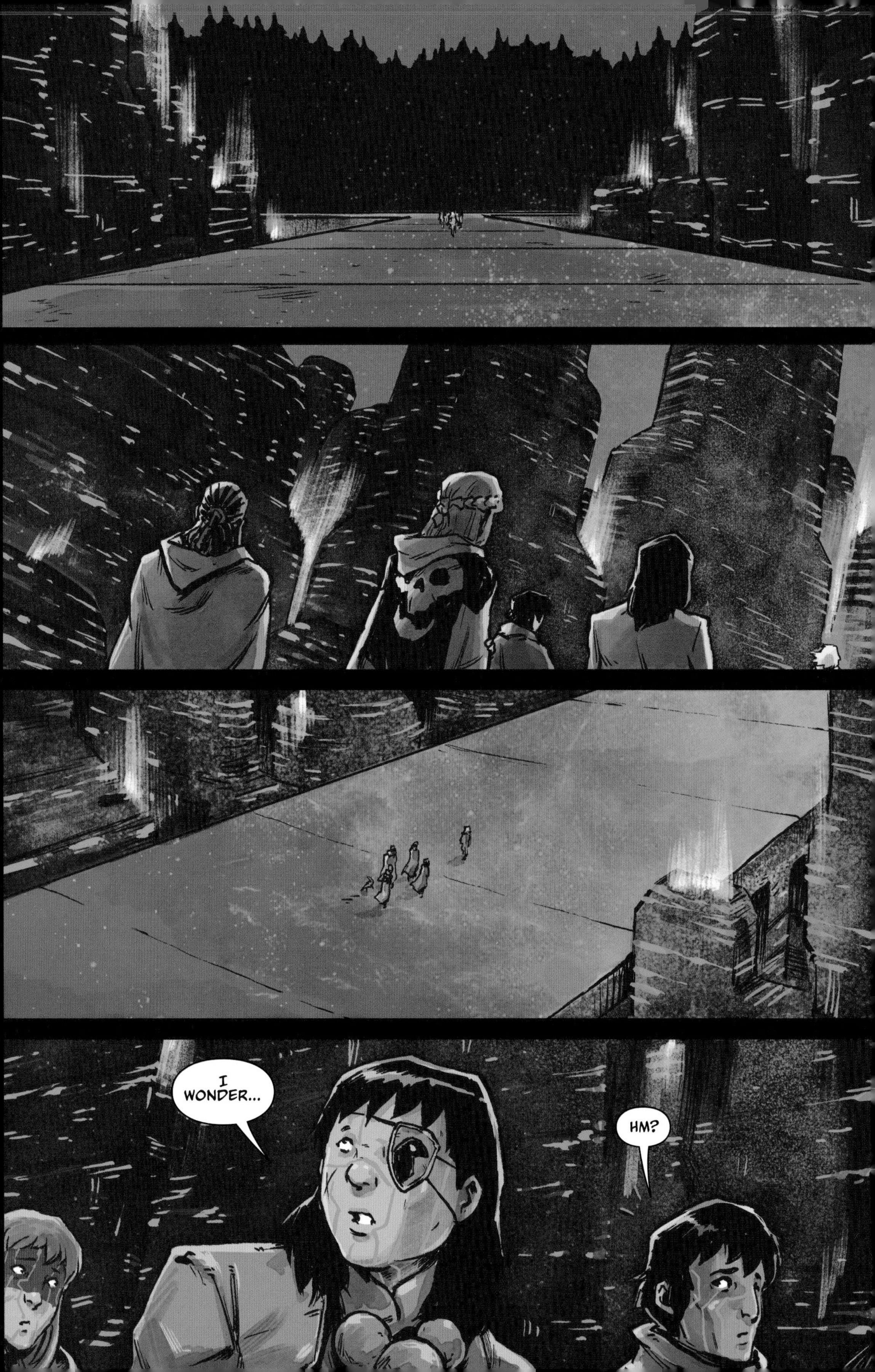
I WONDER...
HM?

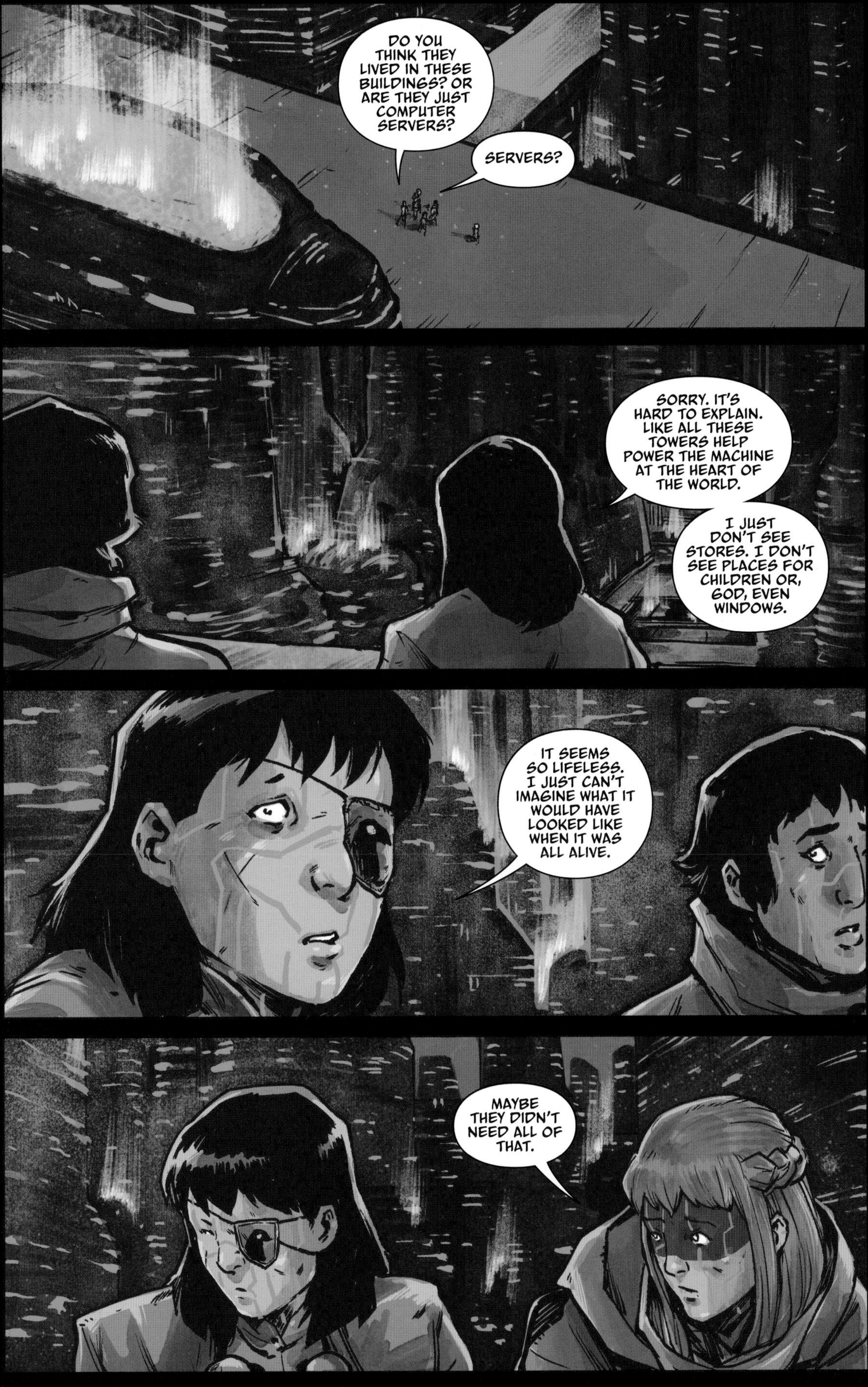
DO YOU THINK THEY LIVED IN THESE BUILDINGS? OR ARE THEY JUST COMPUTER SERVERS?
SERVERS?
SORRY. IT'S HARD TO EXPLAIN. LIKE ALL THESE TOWERS HELP POWER THE MACHINE AT THE HEART OF THE WORLD.
I JUST DON'T SEE STORES. I DON'T SEE PLACES FOR CHILDREN OR, GOD, EVEN WINDOWS.
IT SEEMS SO LIFELESS. I JUST CAN'T IMAGINE WHAT IT WOULD HAVE LOOKED LIKE WHEN IT WAS ALL ALIVE.
MAYBE THEY DIDN'T NEED ALL OF THAT.

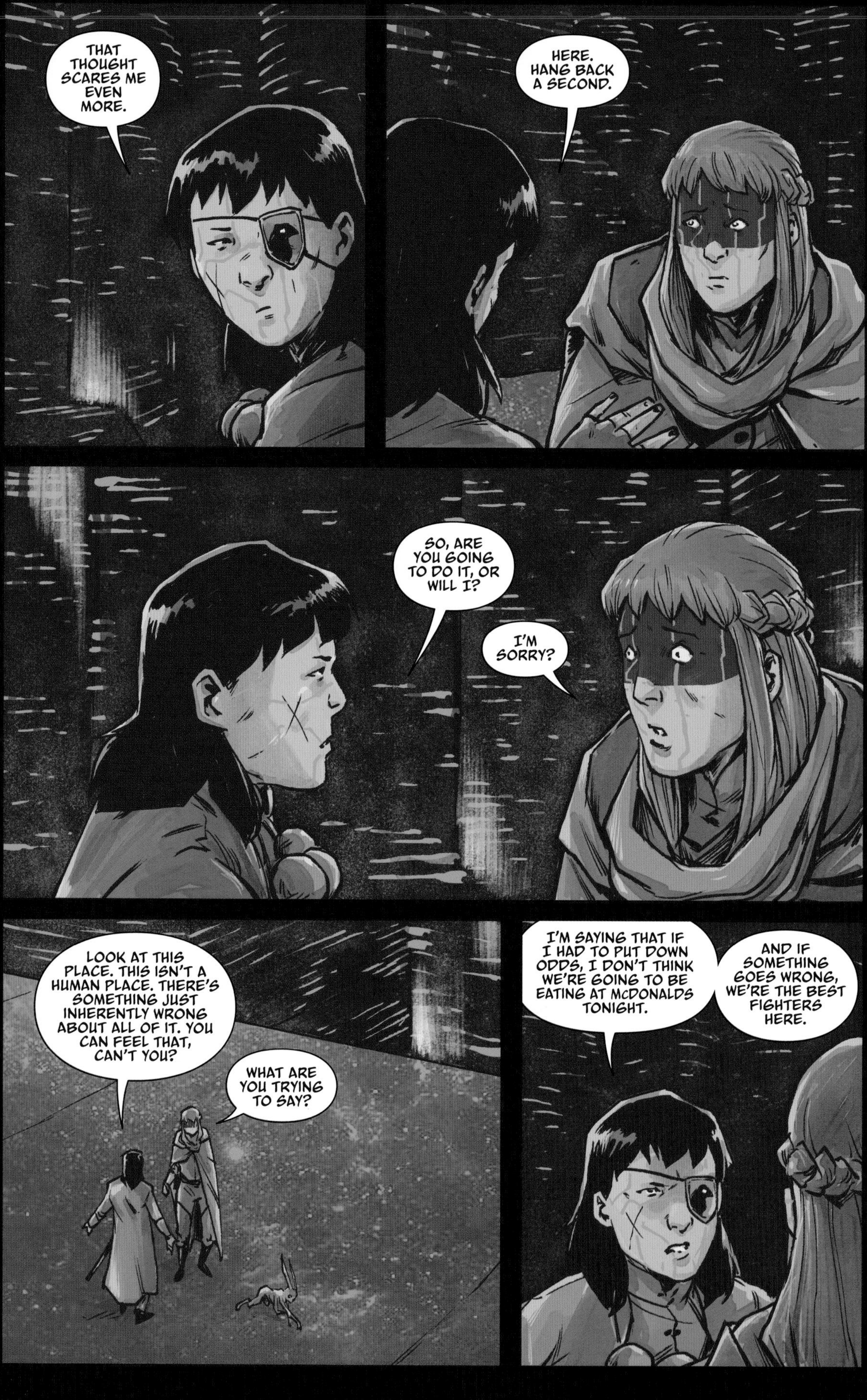
THAT THOUGHT SCARES ME EVEN MORE.
HERE. HANG BACK A SECOND.
SO, ARE YOU GOING TO DO IT, OR WILL I?
I'M SORRY?
LOOK AT THIS PLACE. THIS ISN'T A HUMAN PLACE. THERE'S SOMETHING JUST INHERENTLY WRONG ABOUT ALL OF IT. YOU CAN FEEL THAT, CAN'T YOU?
WHAT ARE YOU TRYING TO SAY?
I'M SAYING THAT IF I HAD TO PUT DOWN ODDS, I DON'T THINK WE'RE GOING TO BE EATING AT McDONALDS TONIGHT.
AND IF SOMETHING GOES WRONG, WE'RE THE BEST FIGHTERS HERE.

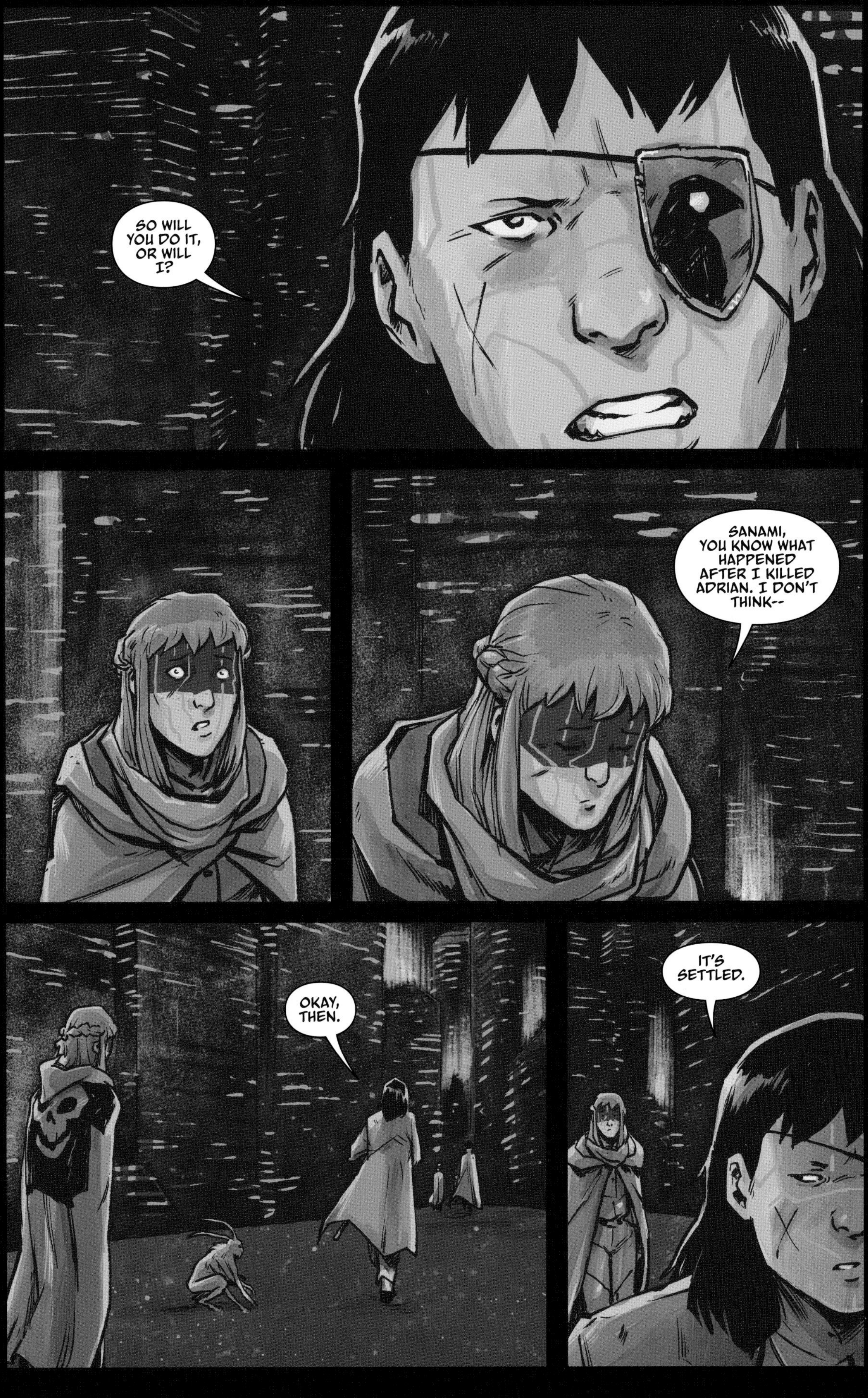
SO WILL YOU DO IT, OR WILL I?
SANAMI, YOU KNOW WHAT HAPPENED AFTER I KILLED ADRIAN. I DON'T THINK--
OKAY, THEN.
IT'S SETTLED.

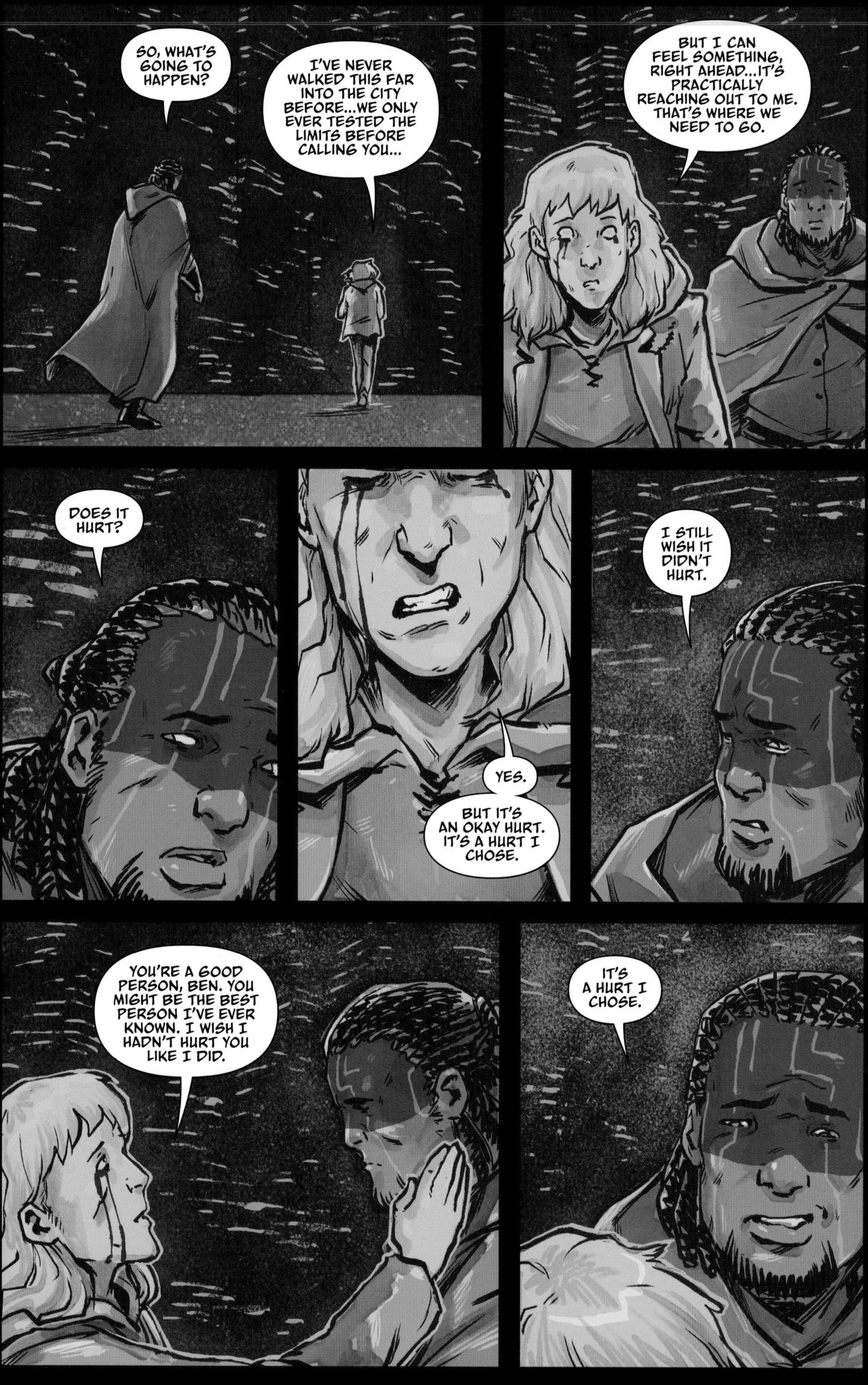
SO, WHAT'S GOING TO HAPPEN?
I'VE NEVER WALKED THIS FAR INTO THE CITY BEFORE...WE ONLY EVER TESTED THE LIMITS BEFORE CALLING YOU...
BUT I CAN FEEL SOMETHING, RIGHT AHEAD...IT'S PRACTICALLY REACHING OUT TO ME. THAT'S WHERE WE NEED TO GO.
DOES IT HURT?
YES.
BUT IT'S AN OKAY HURT. IT'S A HURT I CHOSE.
I STILL WISH IT DIDN'T HURT.
YOU'RE A GOOD PERSON, BEN. YOU MIGHT BE THE BEST PERSON I'VE EVER KNOWN. I WISH I HADN'T HURT YOU LIKE I DID.
IT'S A HURT I CHOSE.

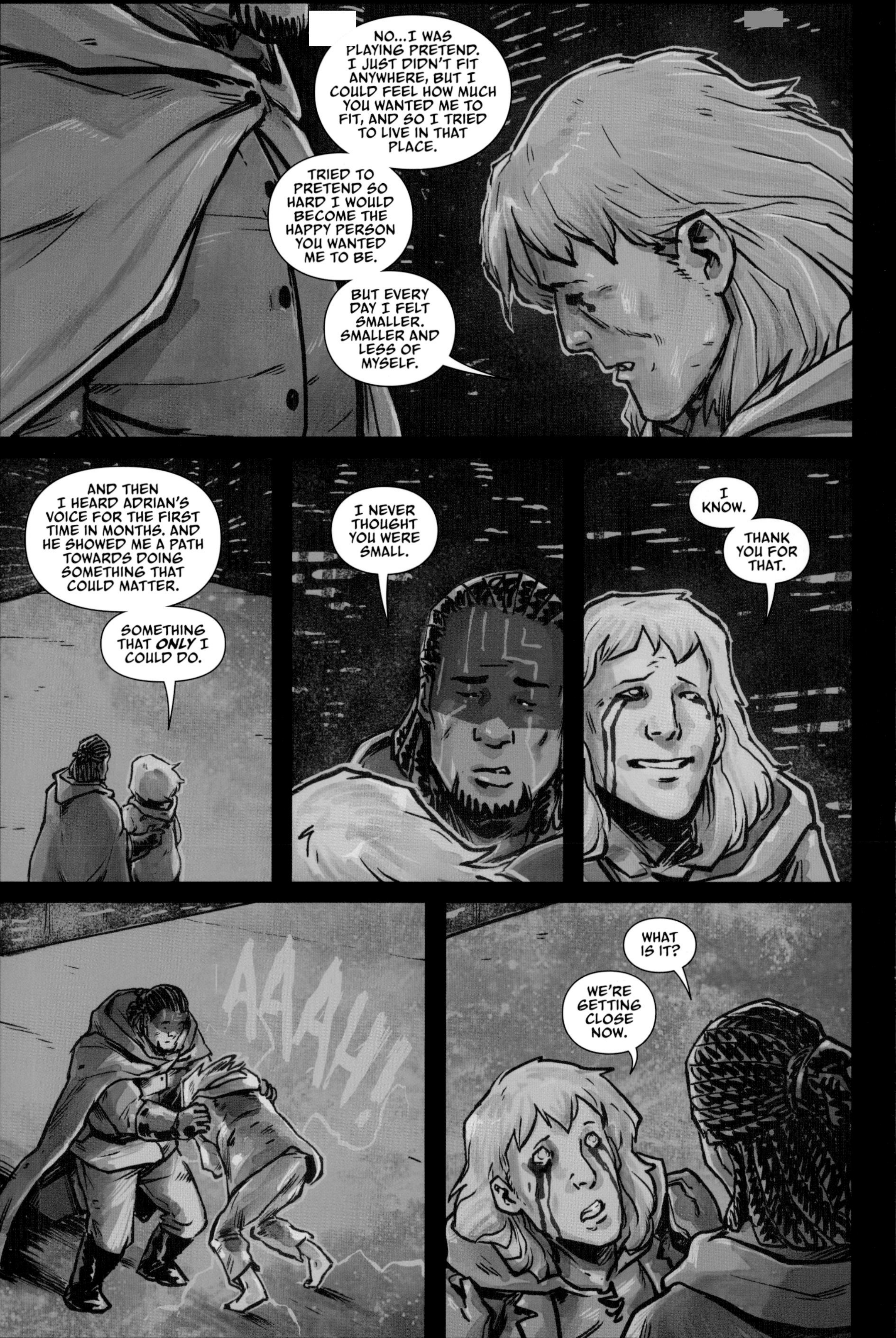

NO...I WAS PLAYING PRETEND. I JUST DIDN'T FIT ANYWHERE, BUT I COULD FEEL HOW MUCH YOU WANTED ME TO FIT, AND SO I TRIED TO LIVE IN THAT PLACE.
TRIED TO PRETEND SO HARD I WOULD BECOME THE HAPPY PERSON YOU WANTED ME TO BE.
BUT EVERY DAY I FELT SMALLER. SMALLER AND LESS OF MYSELF.
AND THEN I HEARD ADRIAN'S VOICE FOR THE FIRST TIME IN MONTHS. AND HE SHOWED ME A PATH TOWARDS DOING SOMETHING THAT COULD MATTER.
SOMETHING THAT *ONLY* I COULD DO.
I NEVER THOUGHT YOU WERE SMALL.
I KNOW.
THANK YOU FOR THAT.
AAAH!
WHAT IS IT?
WE'RE GETTING CLOSE NOW.

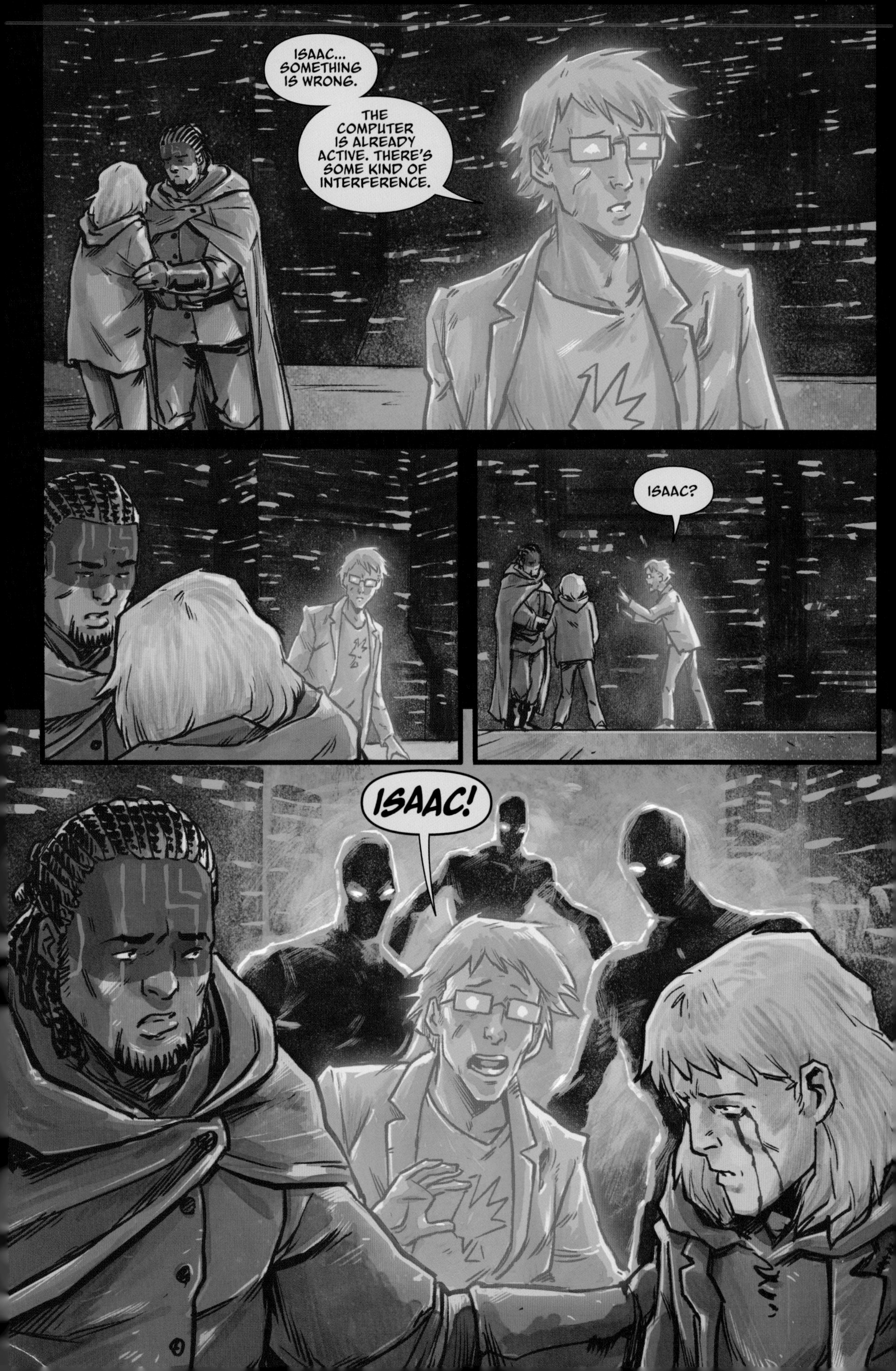
ISAAC... SOMETHING IS WRONG.
THE COMPUTER IS ALREADY ACTIVE. THERE'S SOME KIND OF INTERFERENCE.
ISAAC?
ISAAC!

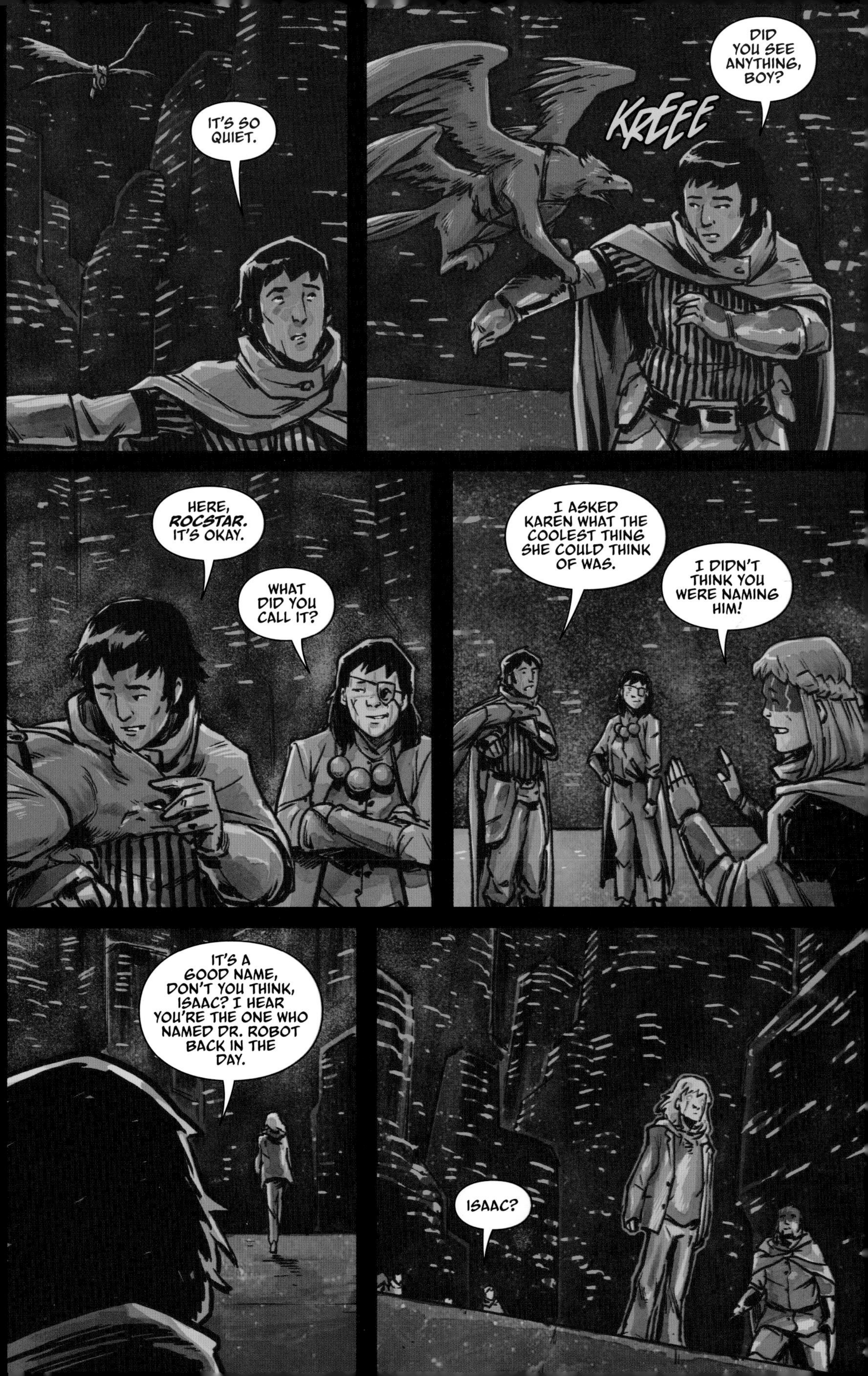
IT'S SO QUIET.
DID YOU SEE ANYTHING, BOY?
KREEE
HERE, *ROCSTAR.* IT'S OKAY.
WHAT DID YOU CALL IT?
I ASKED KAREN WHAT THE COOLEST THING SHE COULD THINK OF WAS.
I DIDN'T THINK YOU WERE NAMING HIM!
IT'S A GOOD NAME, DON'T YOU THINK, ISAAC? I HEAR YOU'RE THE ONE WHO NAMED DR. ROBOT BACK IN THE DAY.
ISAAC?

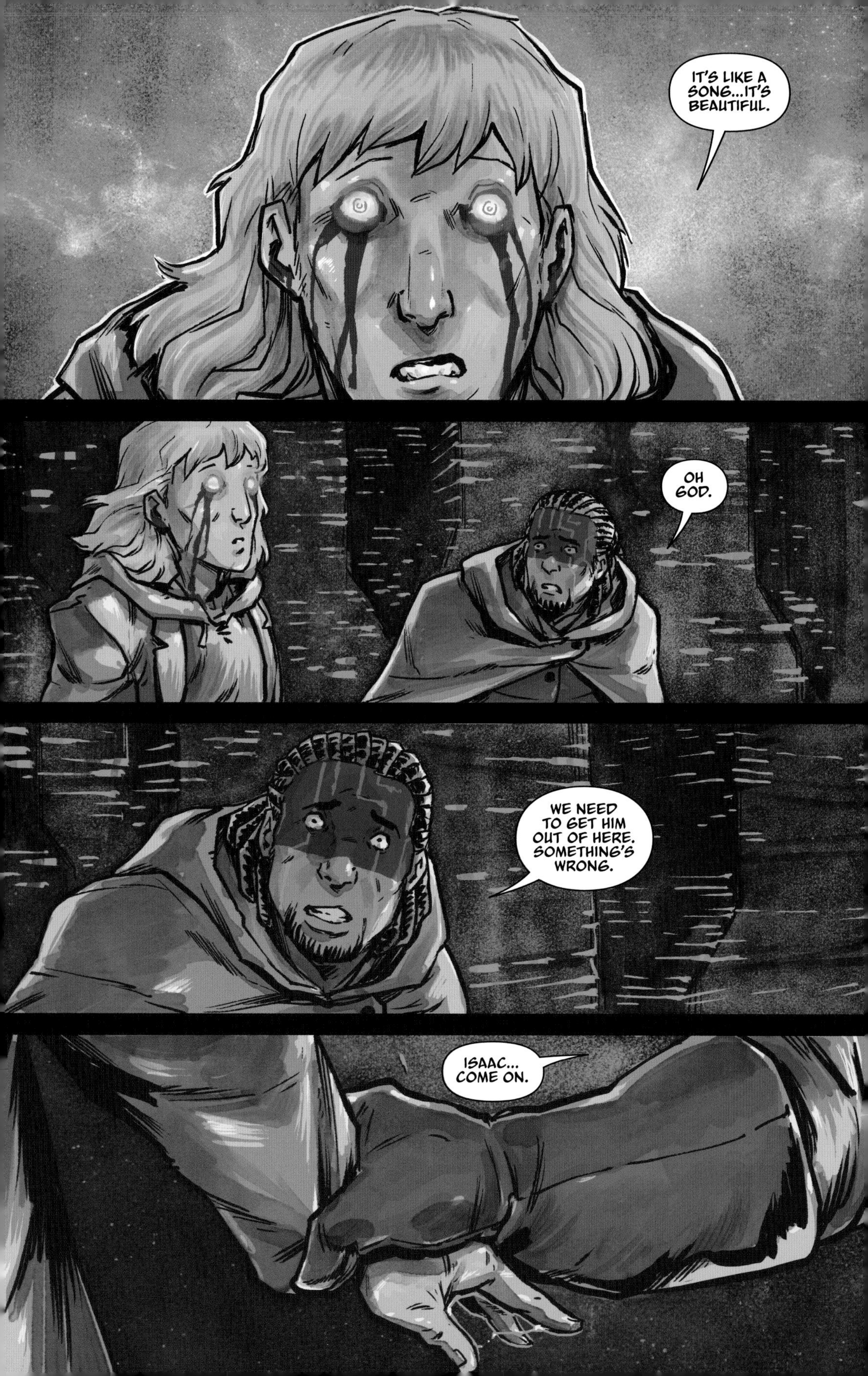
IT'S LIKE A SONG...IT'S BEAUTIFUL.
OH GOD.
WE NEED TO GET HIM OUT OF HERE. SOMETHING'S WRONG.
ISAAC... COME ON.

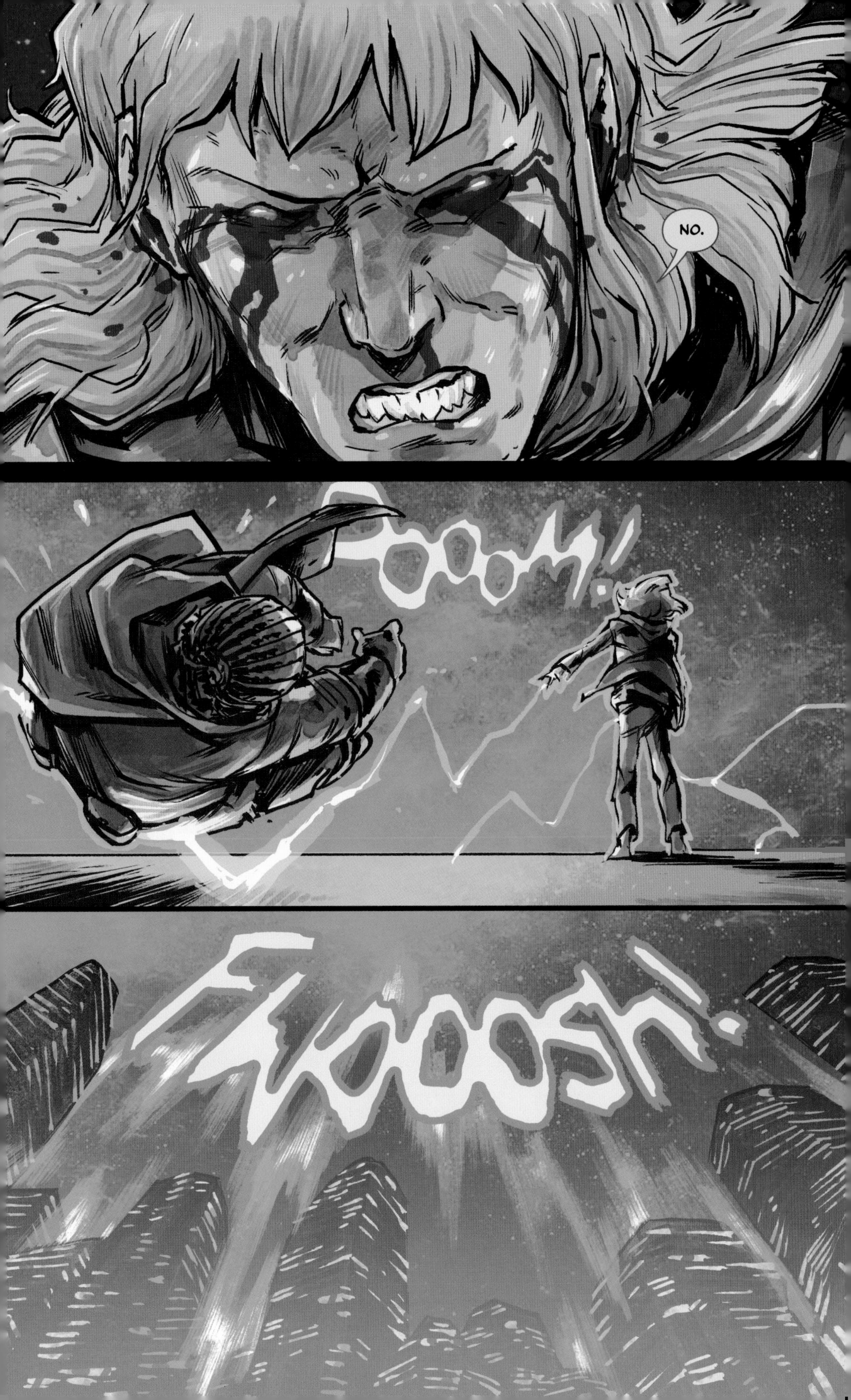
NO.
BOOOM!
FWOOSH!

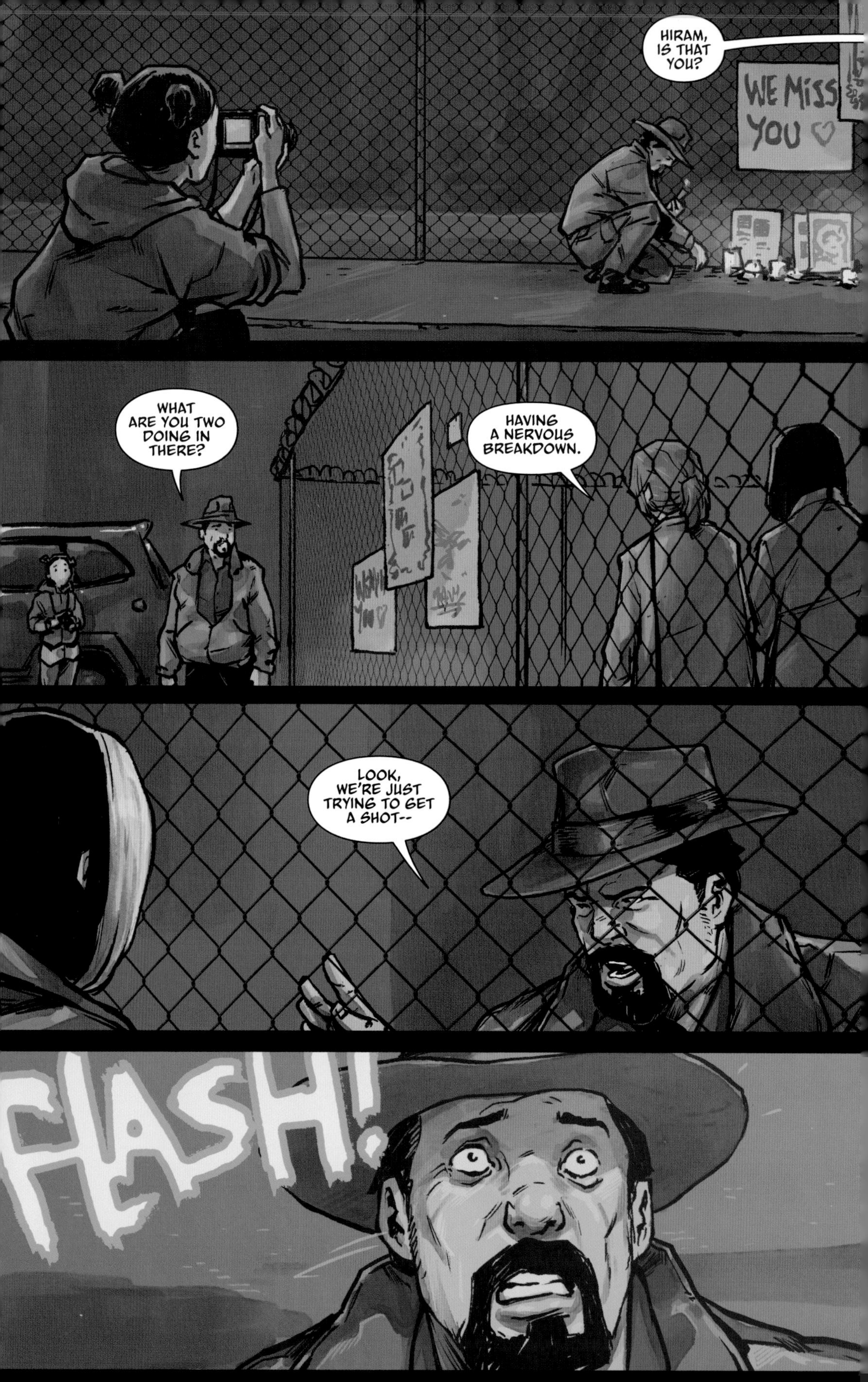
HIRAM, IS THAT YOU?
WE MISS YOU
WHAT ARE YOU TWO DOING IN THERE?
HAVING A NERVOUS BREAKDOWN.
LOOK, WE'RE JUST TRYING TO GET A SHOT--
FLASH!

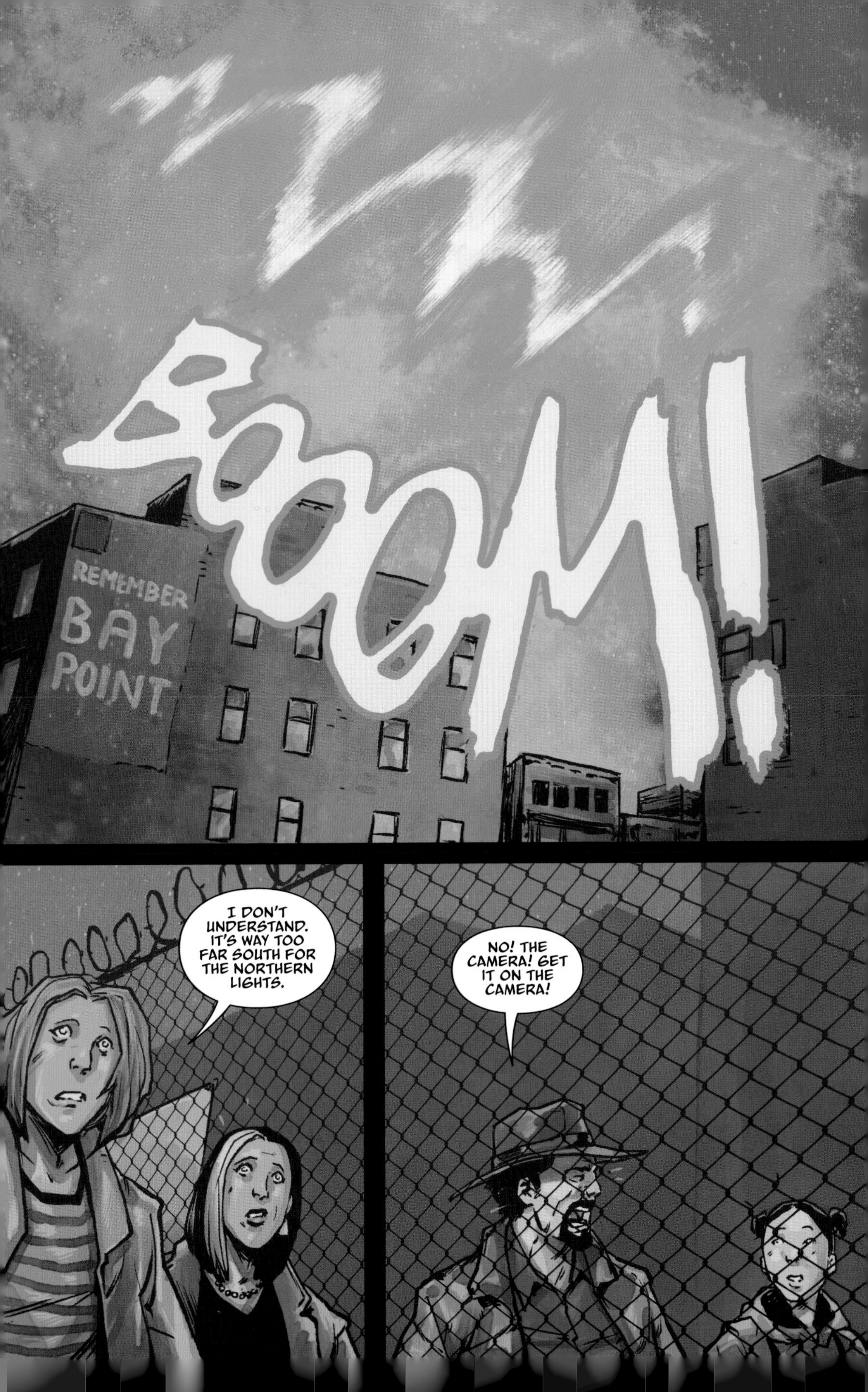
BOOOM!
REMEMBER BAY POINT
I DON'T UNDERSTAND. IT'S WAY TOO FAR SOUTH FOR THE NORTHERN LIGHTS.
NO! THE CAMERA! GET IT ON THE CAMERA!

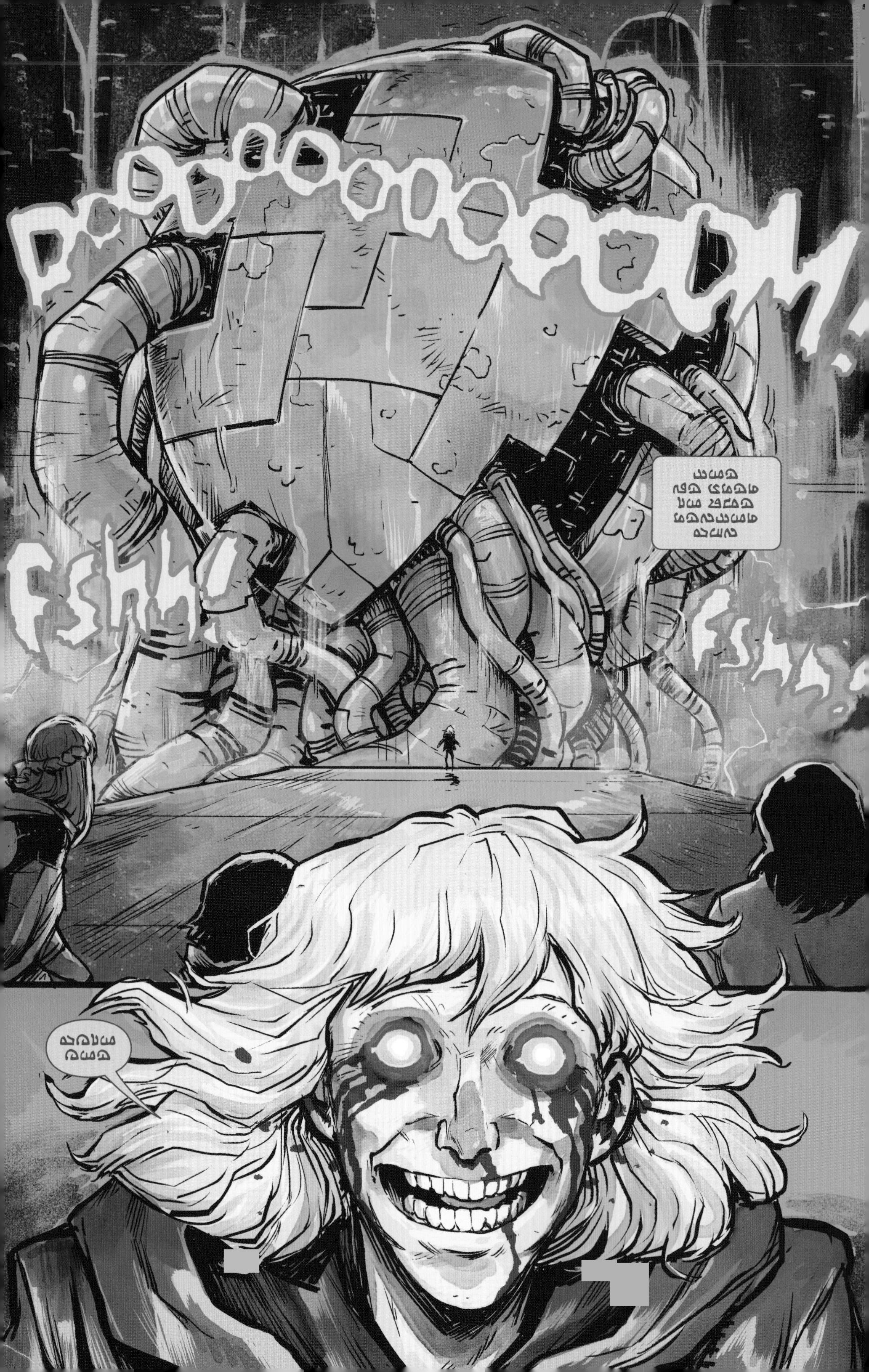

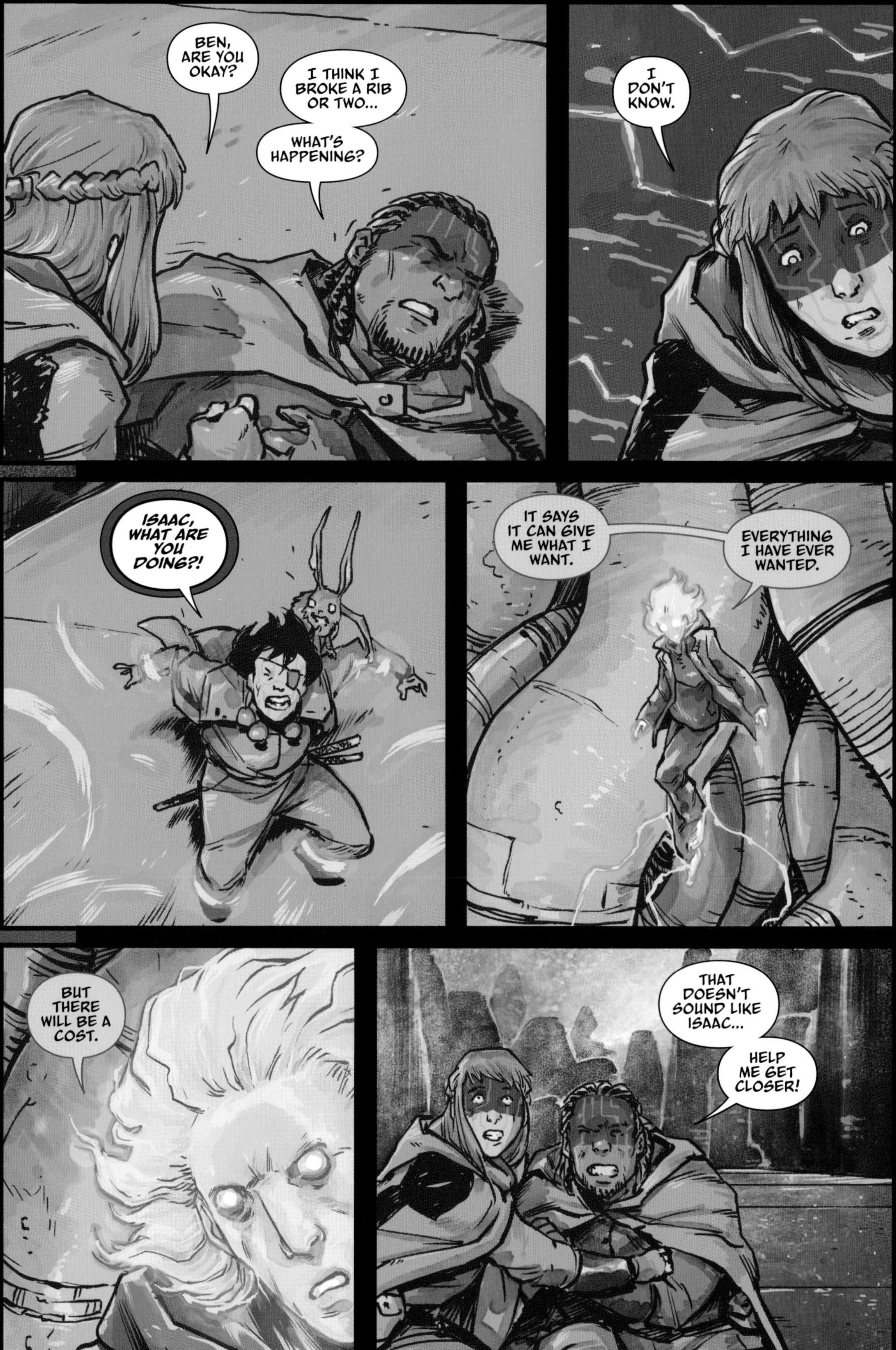
BEN, ARE YOU OKAY?
I THINK I BROKE A RIB OR TWO...
WHAT'S HAPPENING?
I DON'T KNOW.
ISAAC, WHAT ARE YOU DOING?!
IT SAYS IT CAN GIVE ME WHAT I WANT.
EVERYTHING I HAVE EVER WANTED.
BUT THERE WILL BE A COST.
THAT DOESN'T SOUND LIKE ISAAC...
HELP ME GET CLOSER!

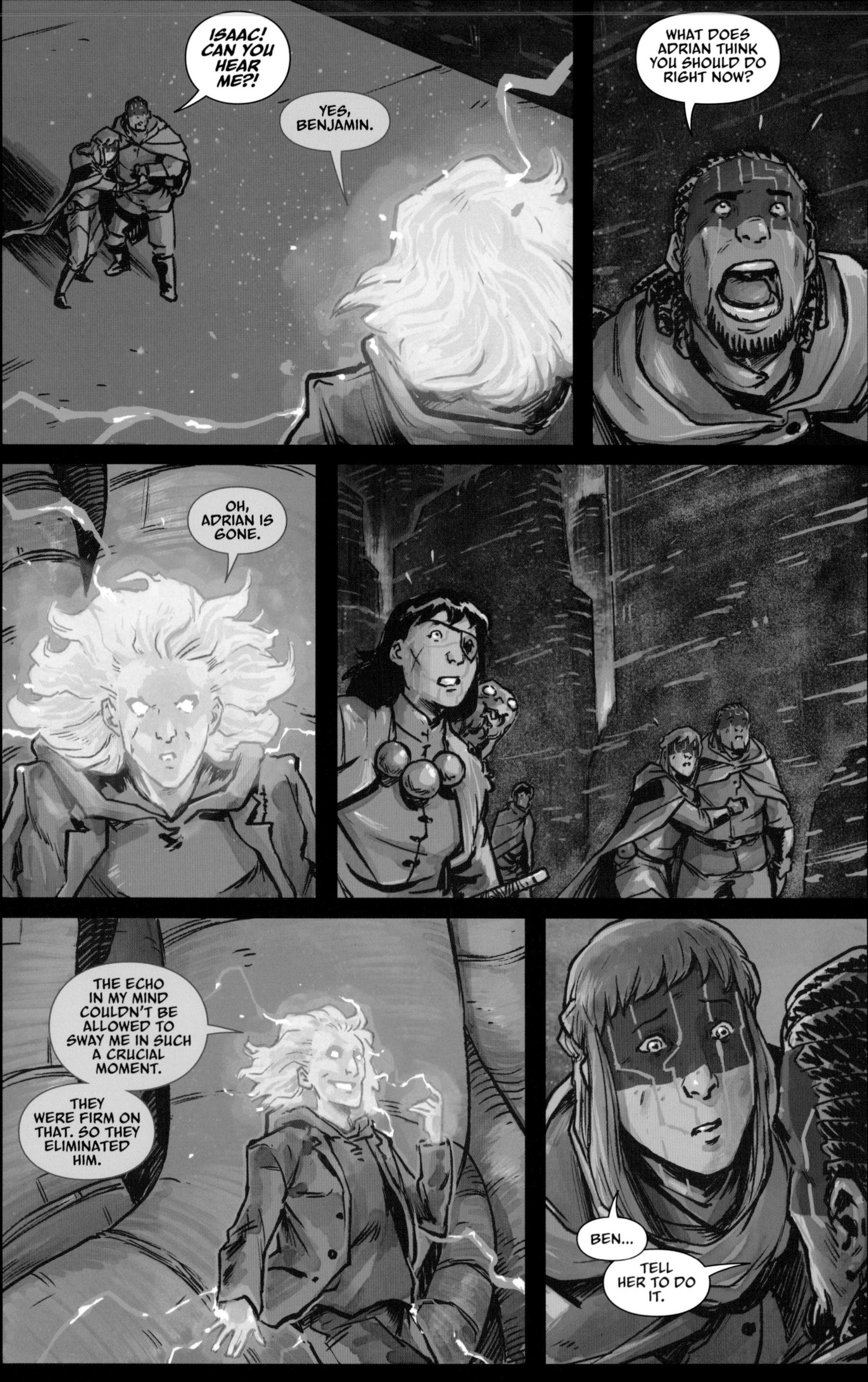
ISAAC! CAN YOU HEAR ME?!
YES, BENJAMIN.
WHAT DOES ADRIAN THINK YOU SHOULD DO RIGHT NOW?
OH, ADRIAN IS GONE.
THE ECHO IN MY MIND COULDN'T BE ALLOWED TO SWAY ME IN SUCH A CRUCIAL MOMENT.
THEY WERE FIRM ON THAT. SO THEY ELIMINATED HIM.
BEN...
TELL HER TO DO IT.

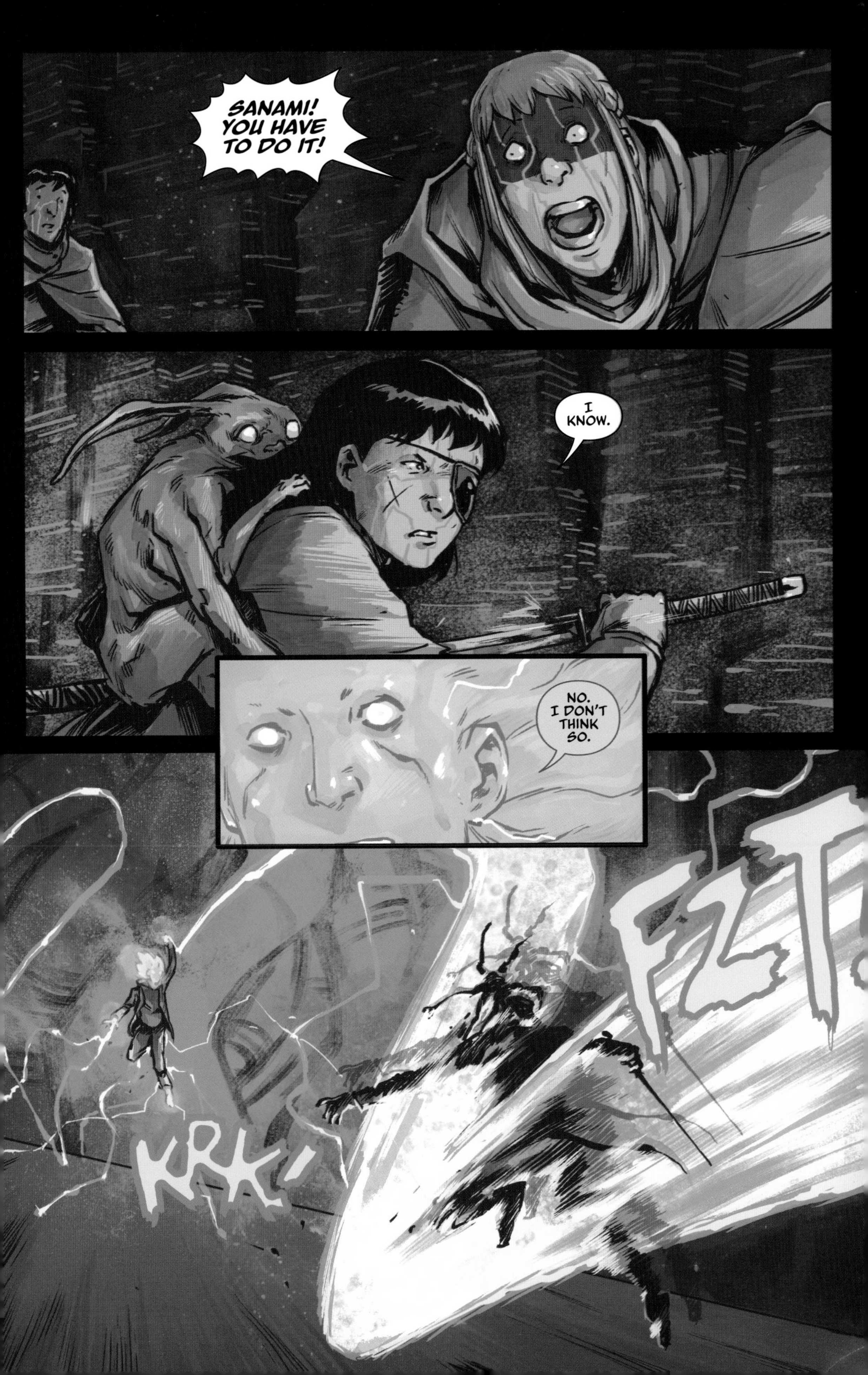
SANAMI! YOU HAVE TO DO IT!
I KNOW.
NO. I DON'T THINK SO.
FZT!
KRK!

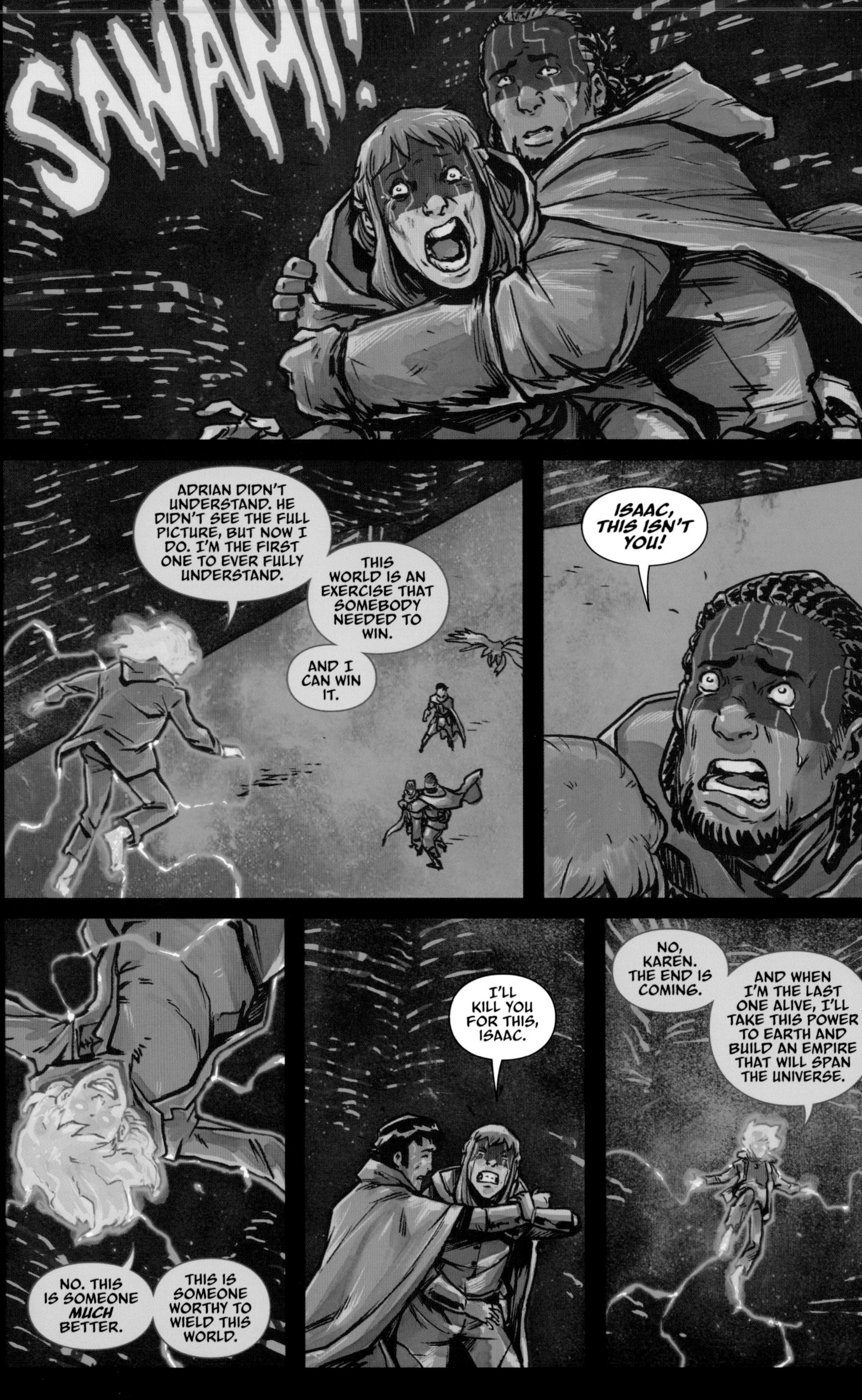
SWAM!
ADRIAN DIDN'T UNDERSTAND. HE DIDN'T SEE THE FULL PICTURE, BUT NOW I DO. I'M THE FIRST ONE TO EVER FULLY UNDERSTAND.
THIS WORLD IS AN EXERCISE THAT SOMEBODY NEEDED TO WIN.
AND I CAN WIN IT.
ISAAC, THIS ISN'T YOU!
NO. THIS IS SOMEONE *MUCH* BETTER.
THIS IS SOMEONE WORTHY TO WIELD THIS WORLD.
I'LL KILL YOU FOR THIS, ISAAC.
NO, KAREN. THE END IS COMING.
AND WHEN I'M THE LAST ONE ALIVE, I'LL TAKE THIS POWER TO EARTH AND BUILD AN EMPIRE THAT WILL SPAN THE UNIVERSE.

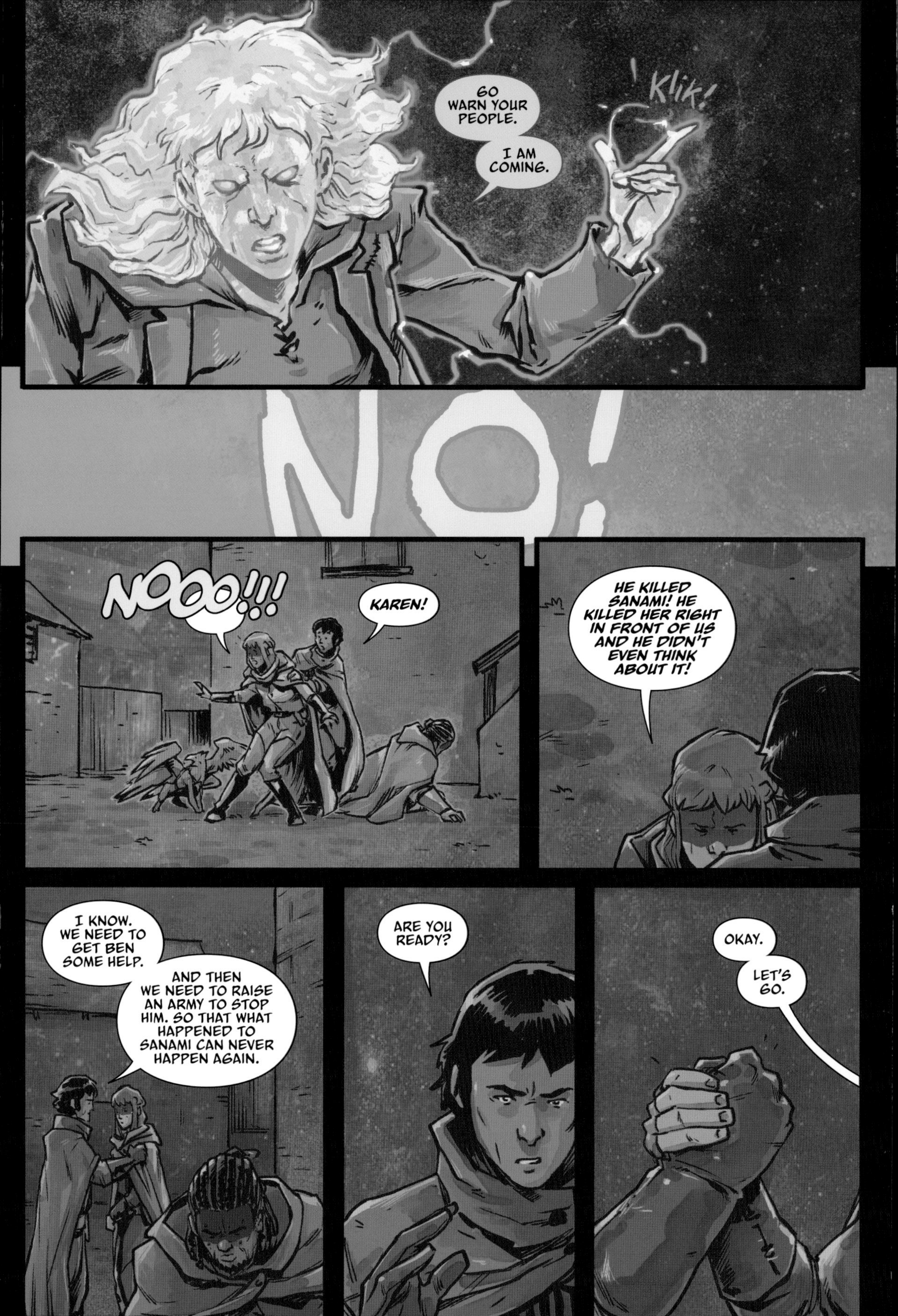

GO WARN YOUR PEOPLE.
I AM COMING.
KLIK!
NO!
NOOO!!!
KAREN!
HE KILLED SANAMI! HE KILLED HER RIGHT IN FRONT OF US AND HE DIDN'T EVEN THINK ABOUT IT!
I KNOW. WE NEED TO GET BEN SOME HELP.
AND THEN WE NEED TO RAISE AN ARMY TO STOP HIM. SO THAT WHAT HAPPENED TO SANAMI CAN NEVER HAPPEN AGAIN.
ARE YOU READY?
OKAY.
LET'S GO.

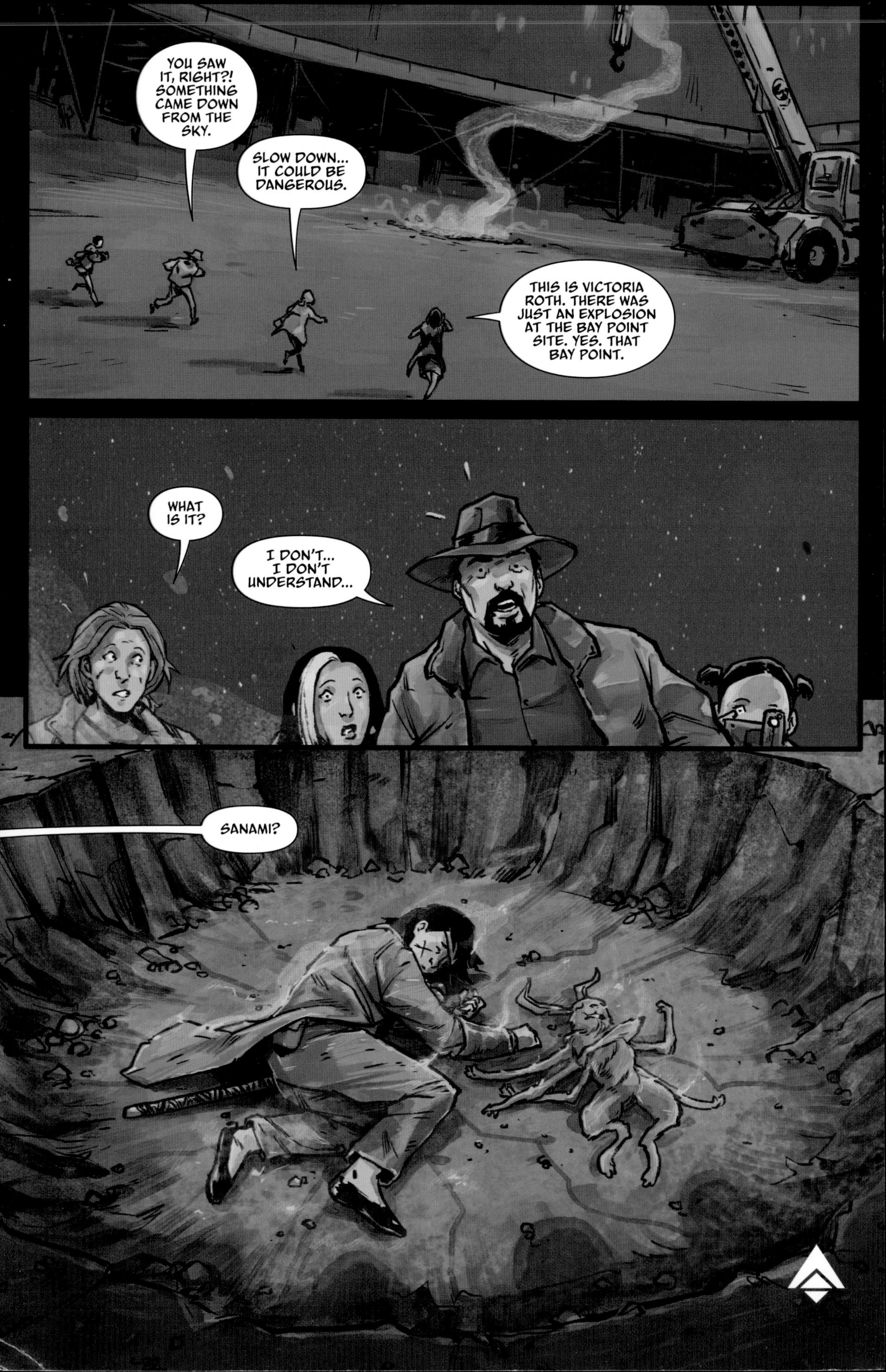
YOU SAW IT, RIGHT?! SOMETHING CAME DOWN FROM THE SKY.
SLOW DOWN... IT COULD BE DANGEROUS.
THIS IS VICTORIA ROTH. THERE WAS JUST AN EXPLOSION AT THE BAY POINT SITE. YES. THAT BAY POINT.
WHAT IS IT?
I DON'T... I DON'T UNDERSTAND...
SANAMI?

COVER
GALLERY

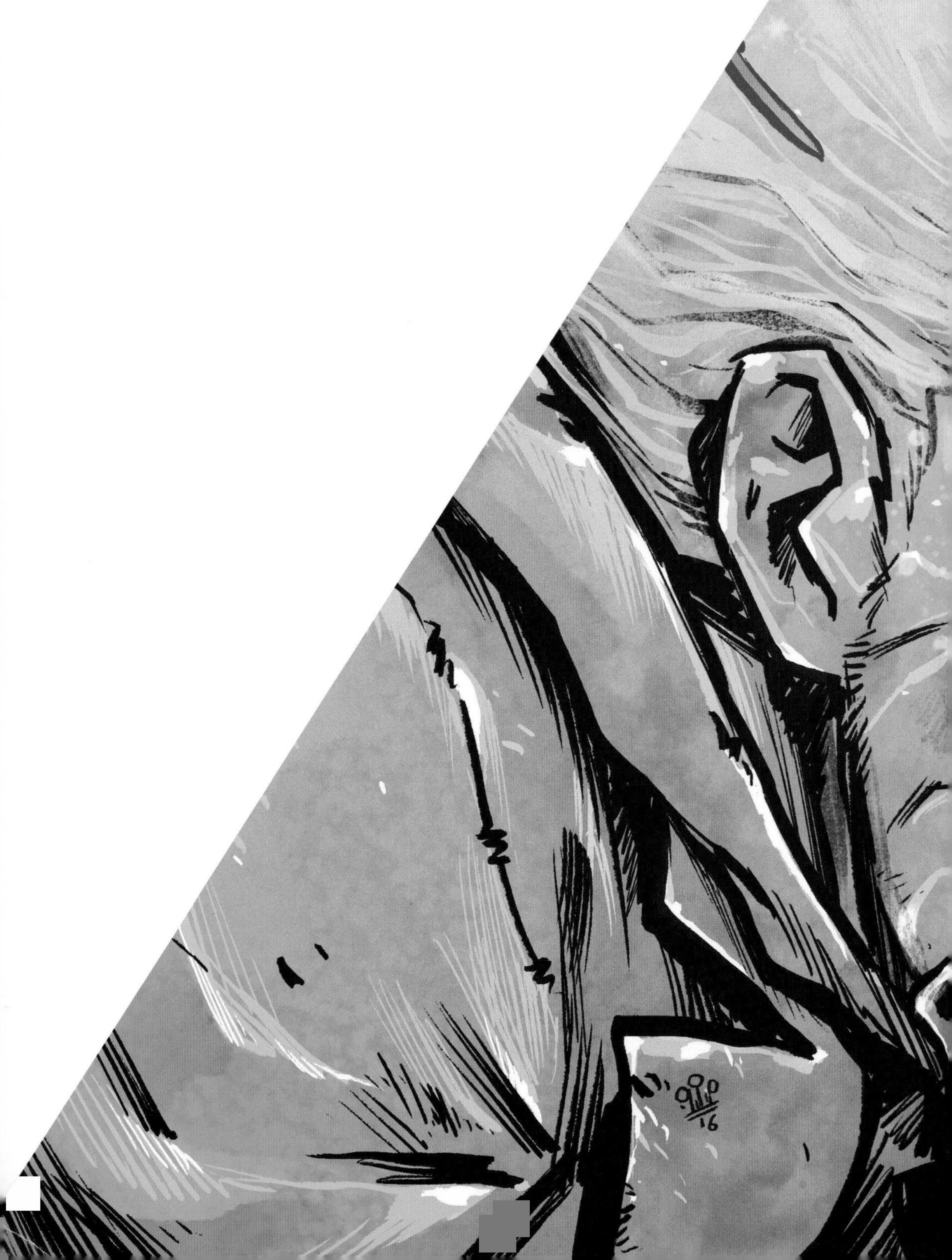

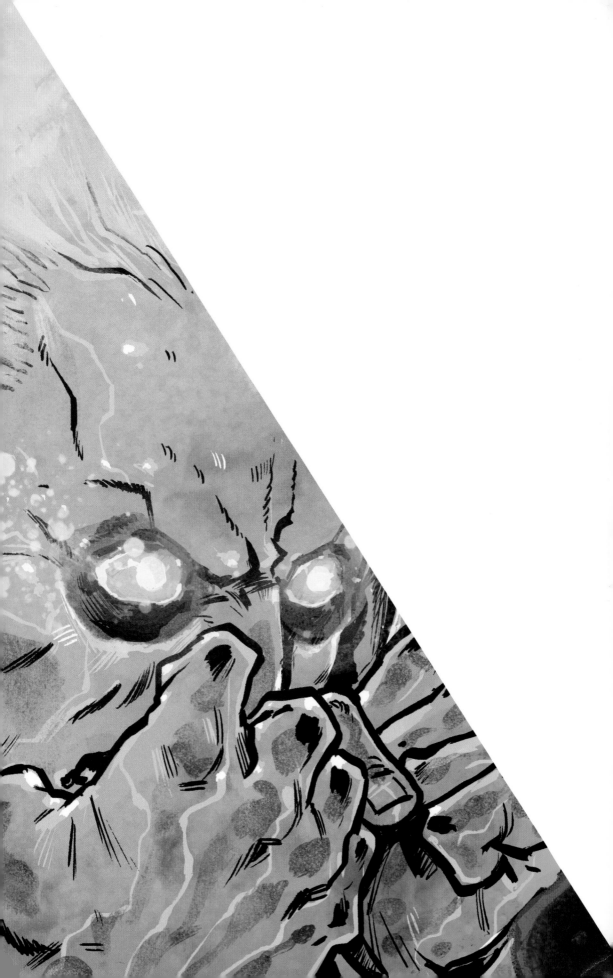

ISSUE TWENTY-FIVE COVER **MIC IAEL DIALYNAS**

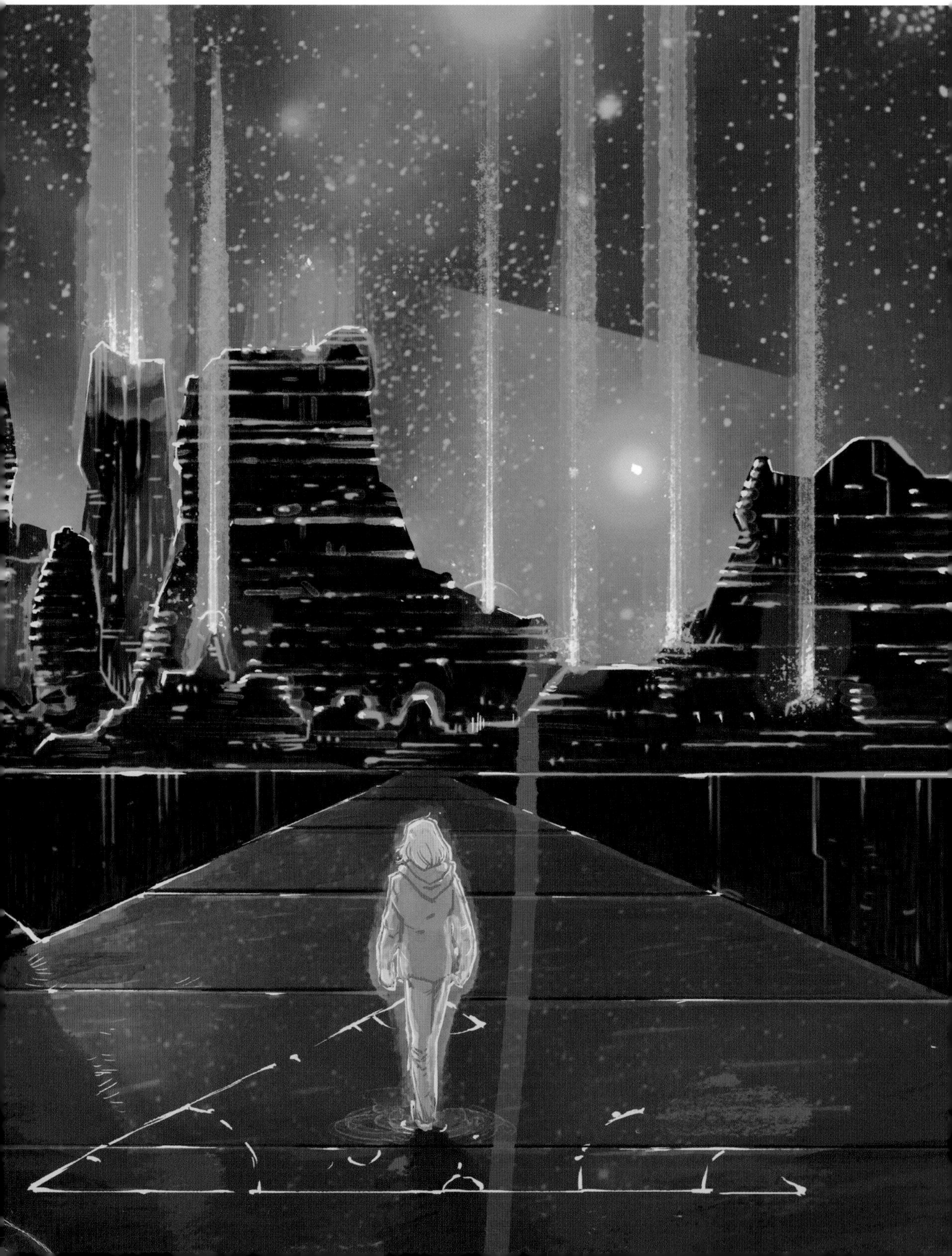

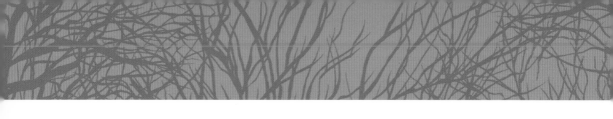

ISSUE TWENTY-SIX COVER **MICHAEL DIALYNAS**

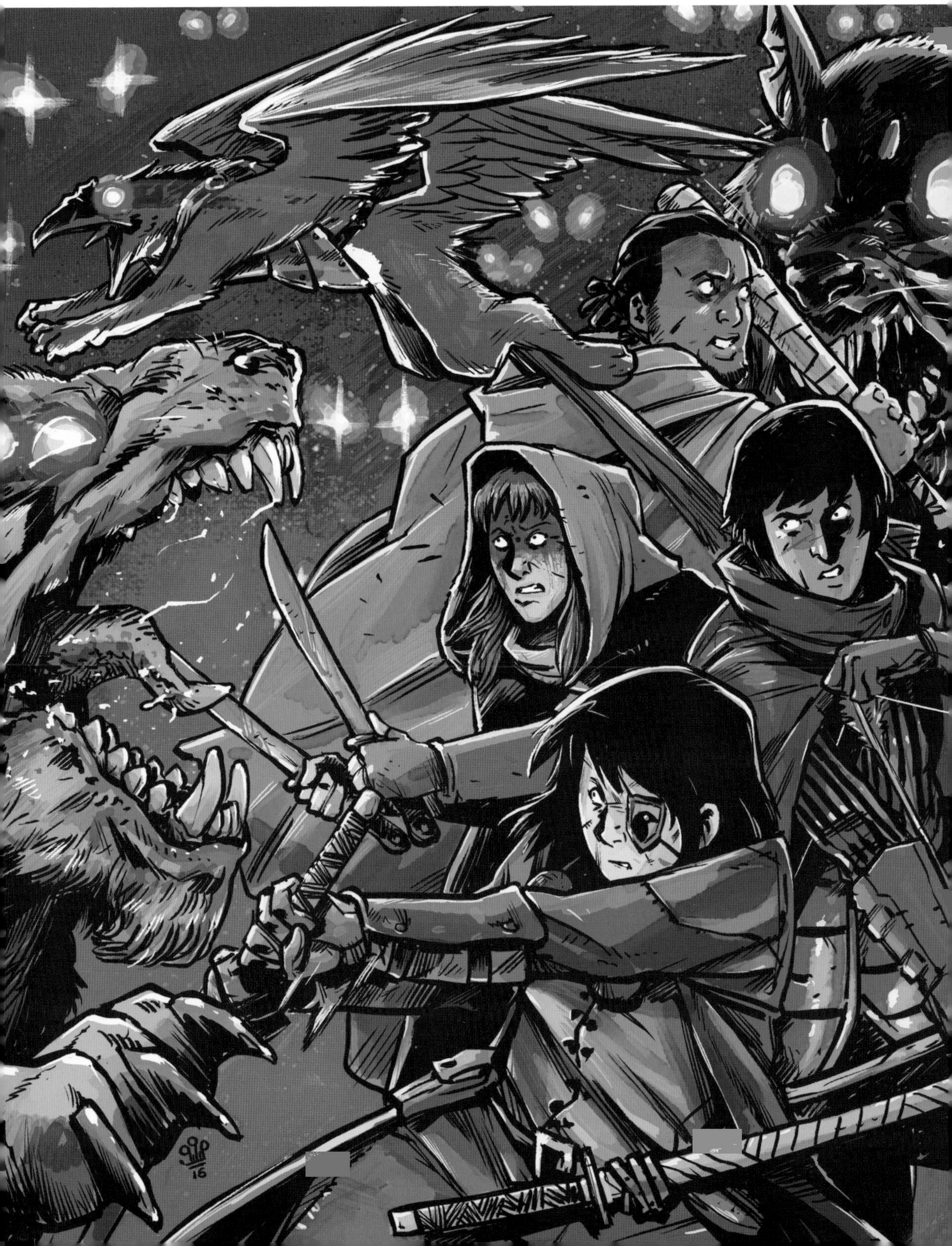

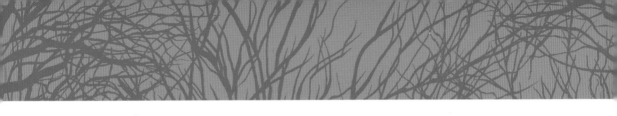

ISSUE TWENTY-SEVEN COVER **MICHAEL DIALYNAS**

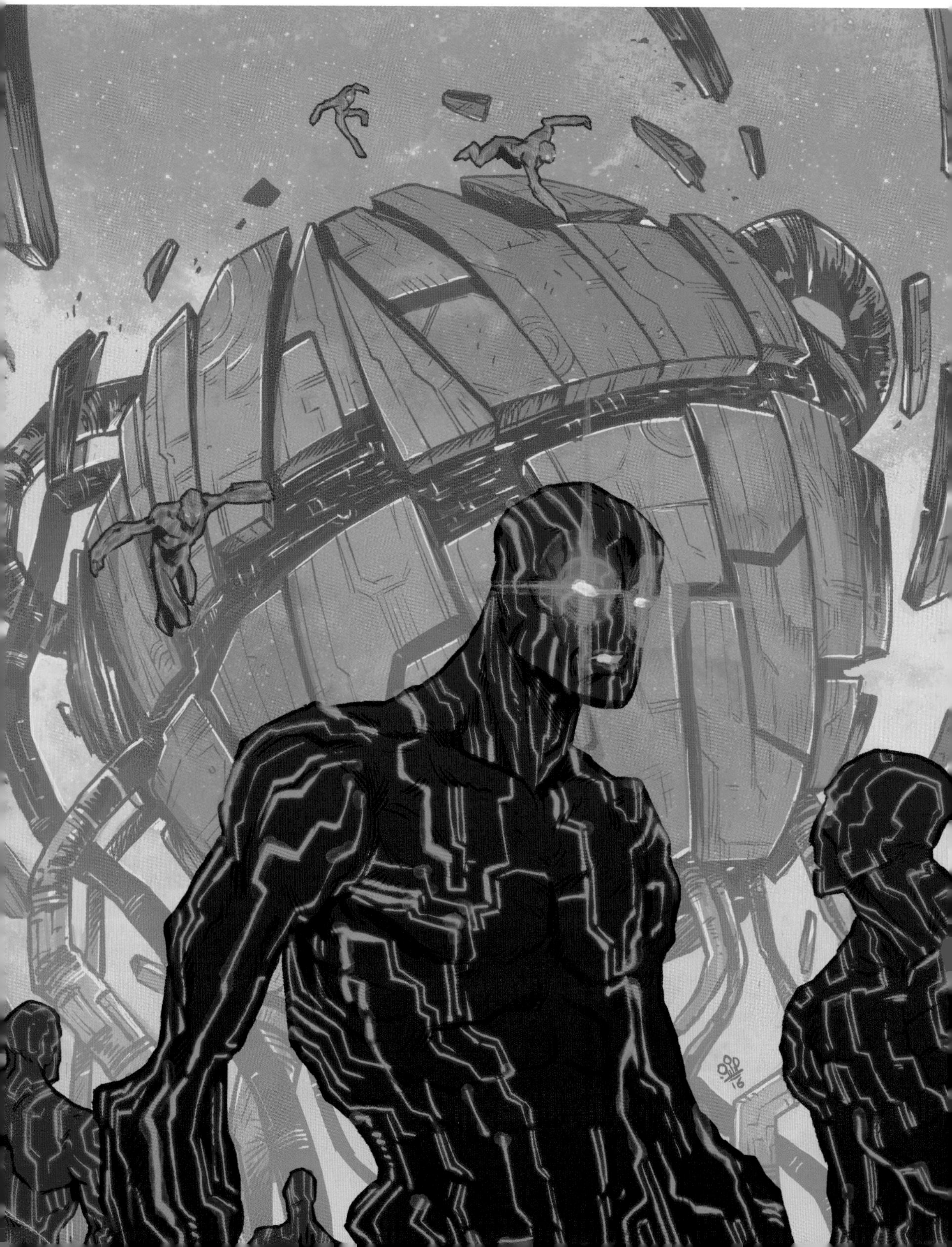

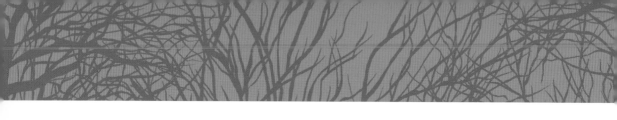

ISSUE TWENTY-EIGHT COVER **MICHAEL DIALYNAS**

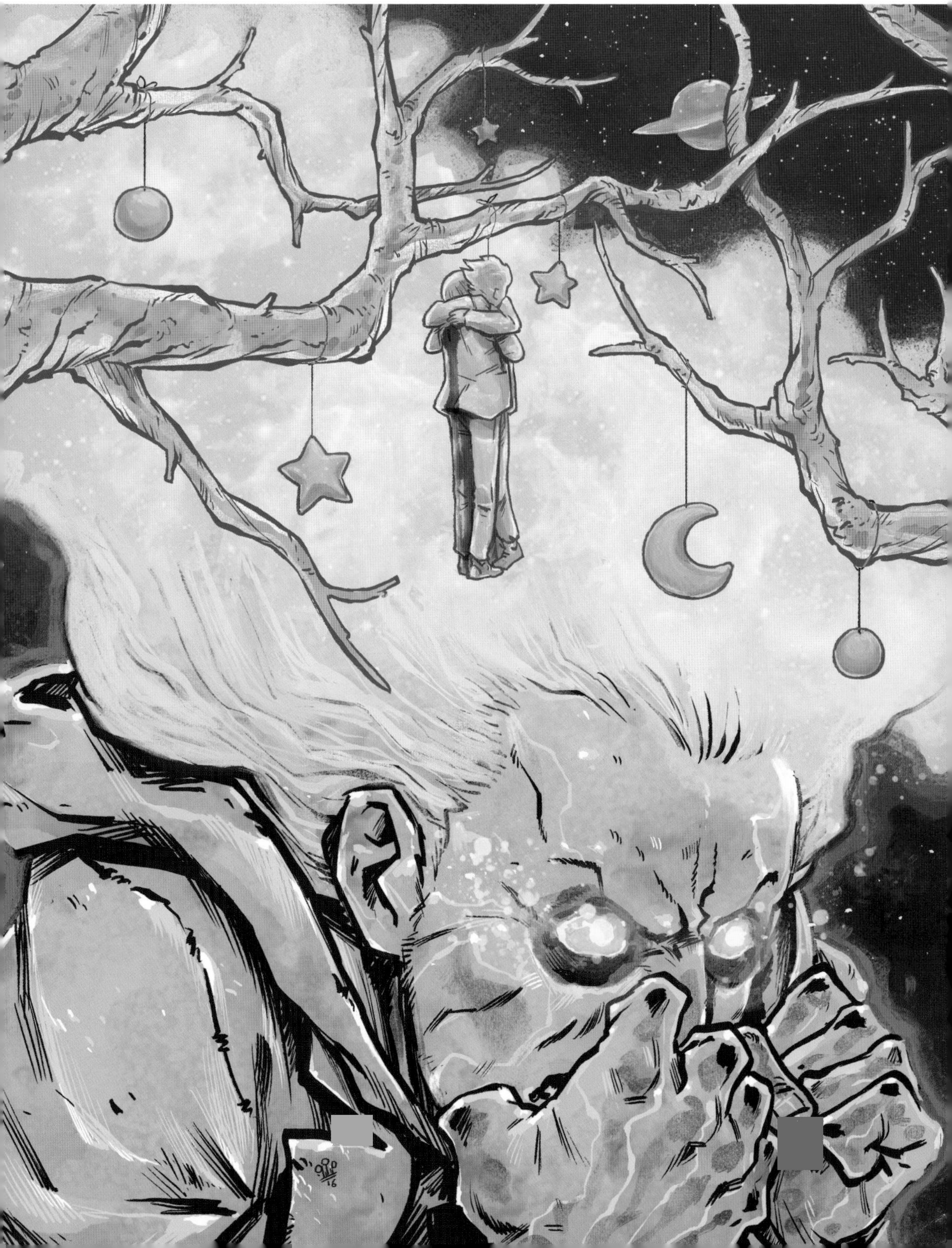

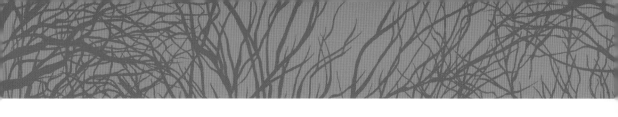

MICHAEL DIALYNAS

SKETCHBOOK

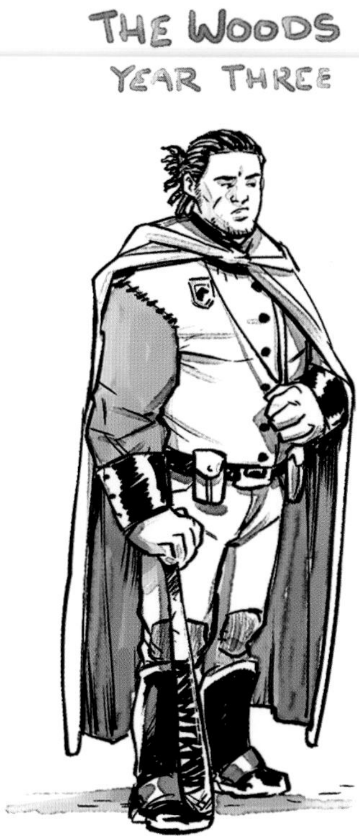
THE WOODS
YEAR THREE

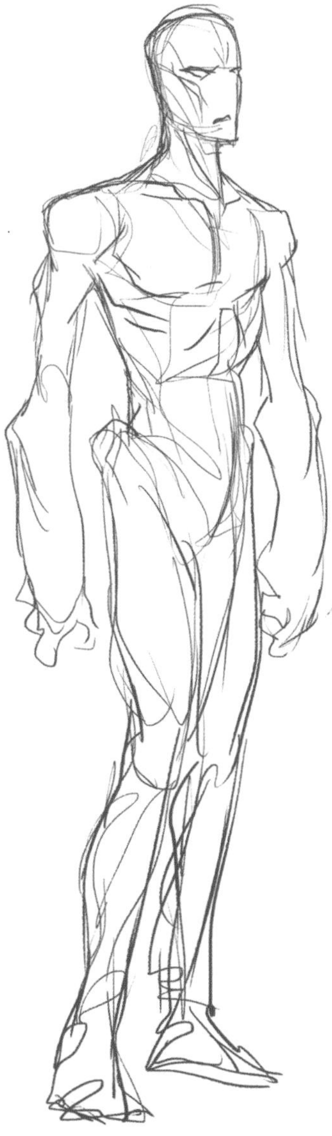

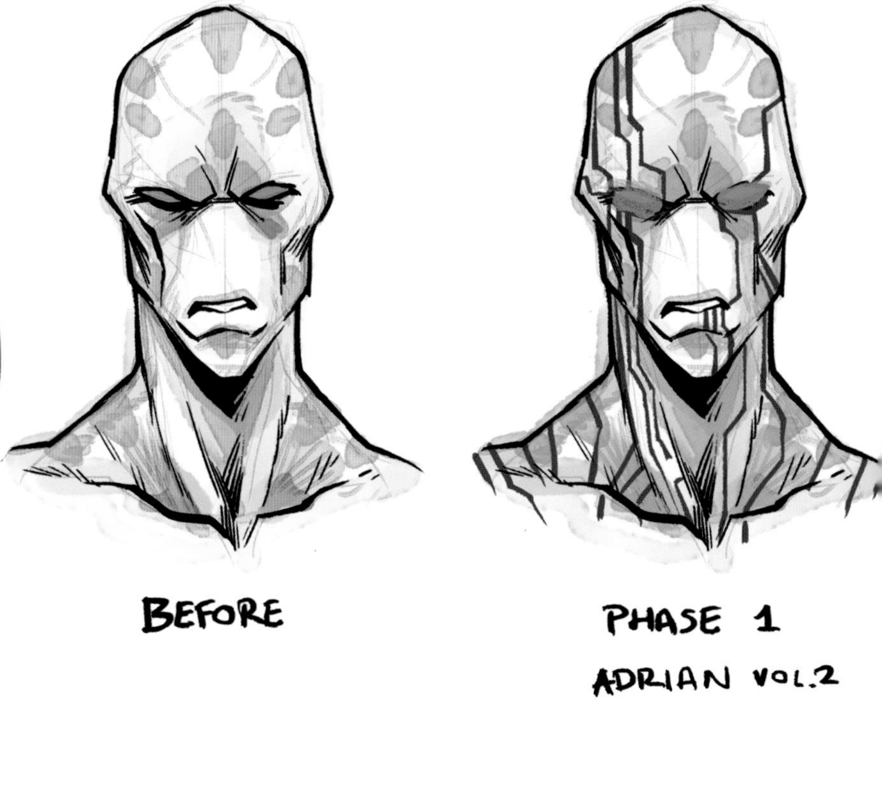
BEFORE
PHASE 1
ADRIAN VOL.2

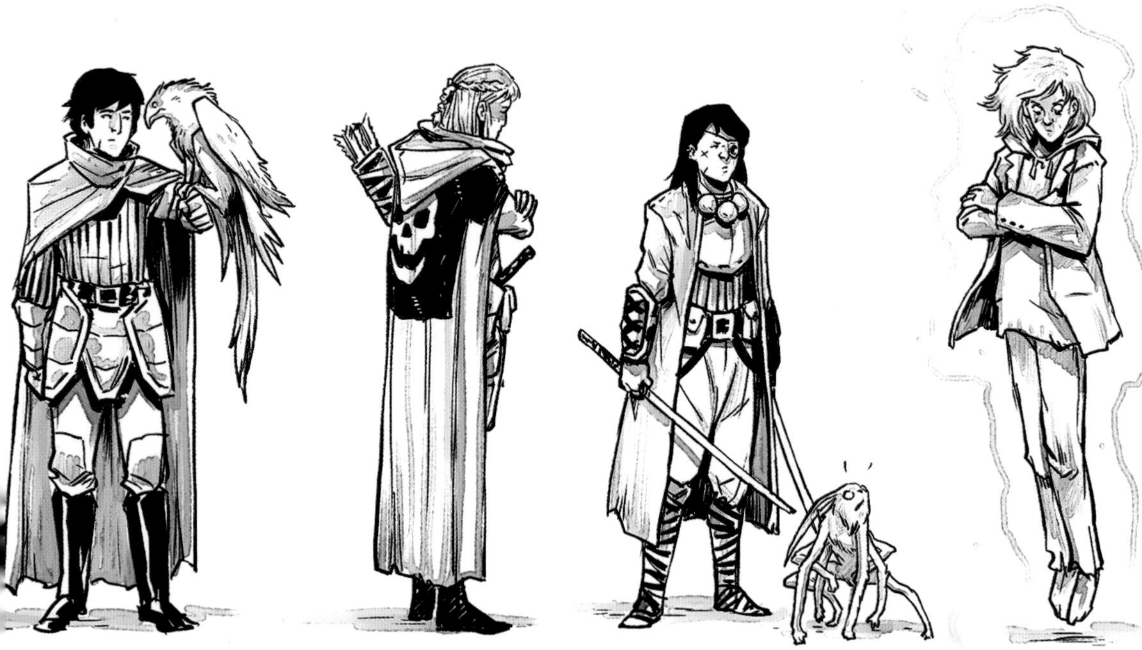

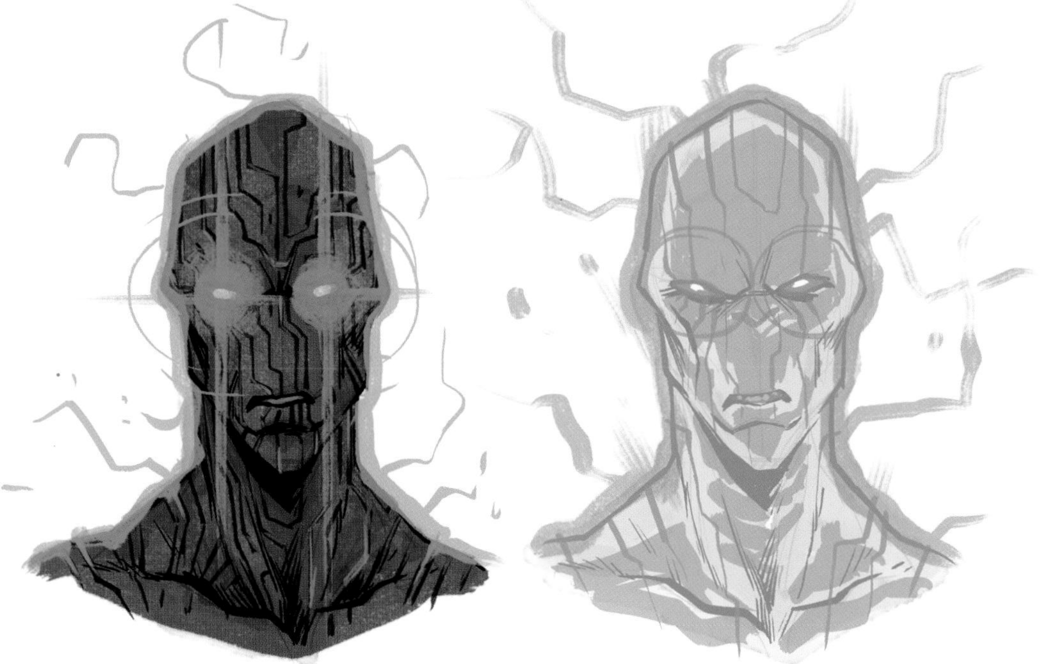

PHASE 2

PHASE 3

PURE ENERGY

DREAM ADRIAN

SHADOW ALIENS

ADRIAN VOL.3

ISAAC VO.5

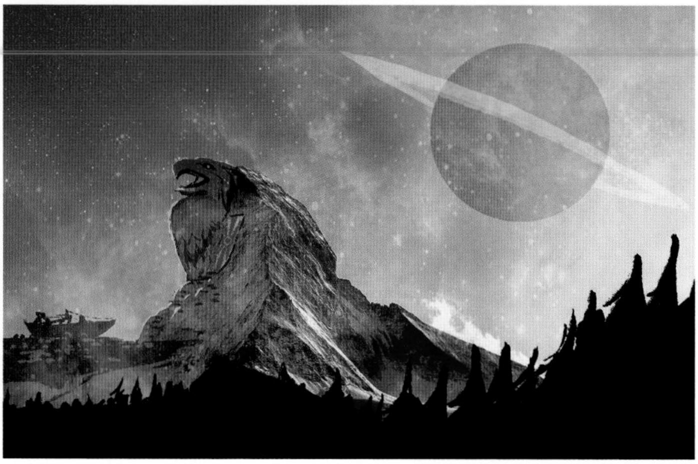

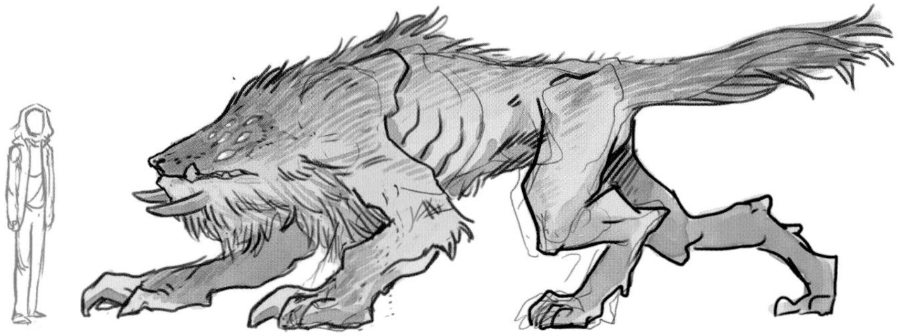

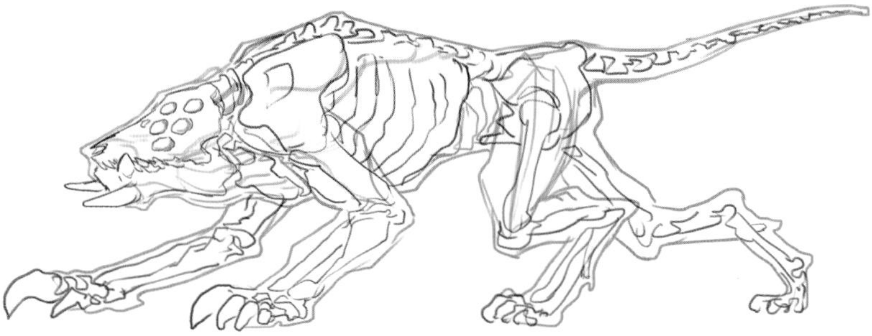

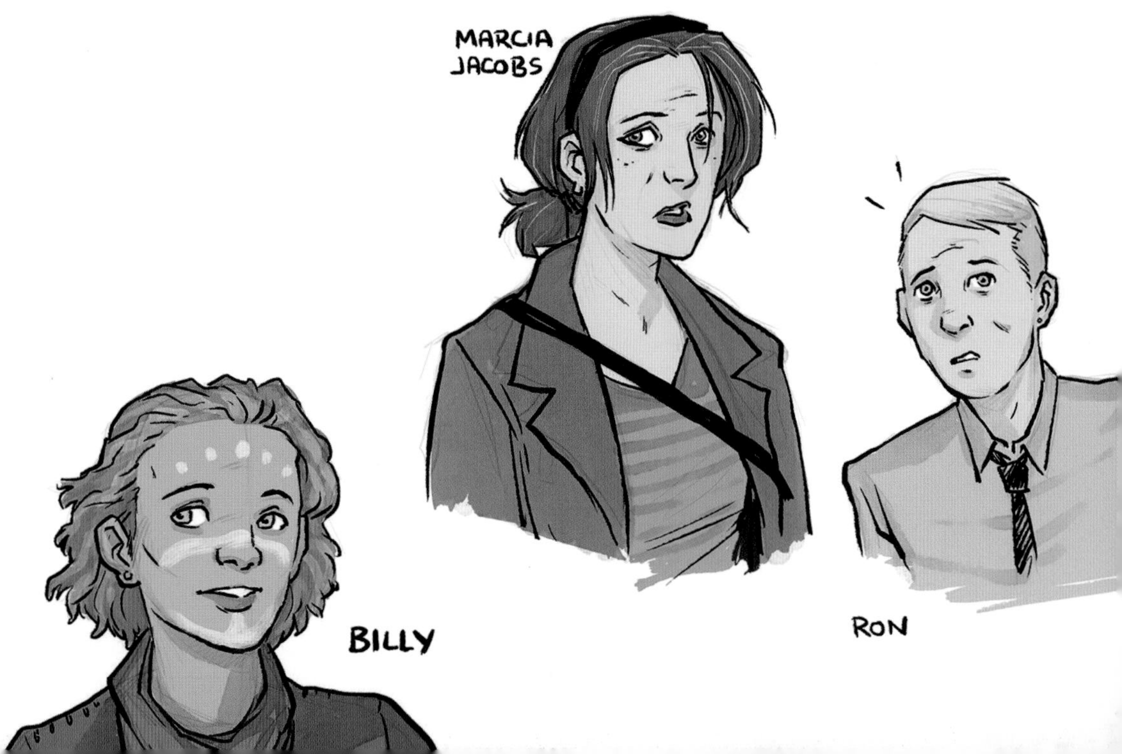
MARCIA JACOBS
BILLY
RON

BOOM! STUDIOS

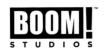

THE WOODS™

JAMES TYNION IV • MICHAEL DIALYNAS

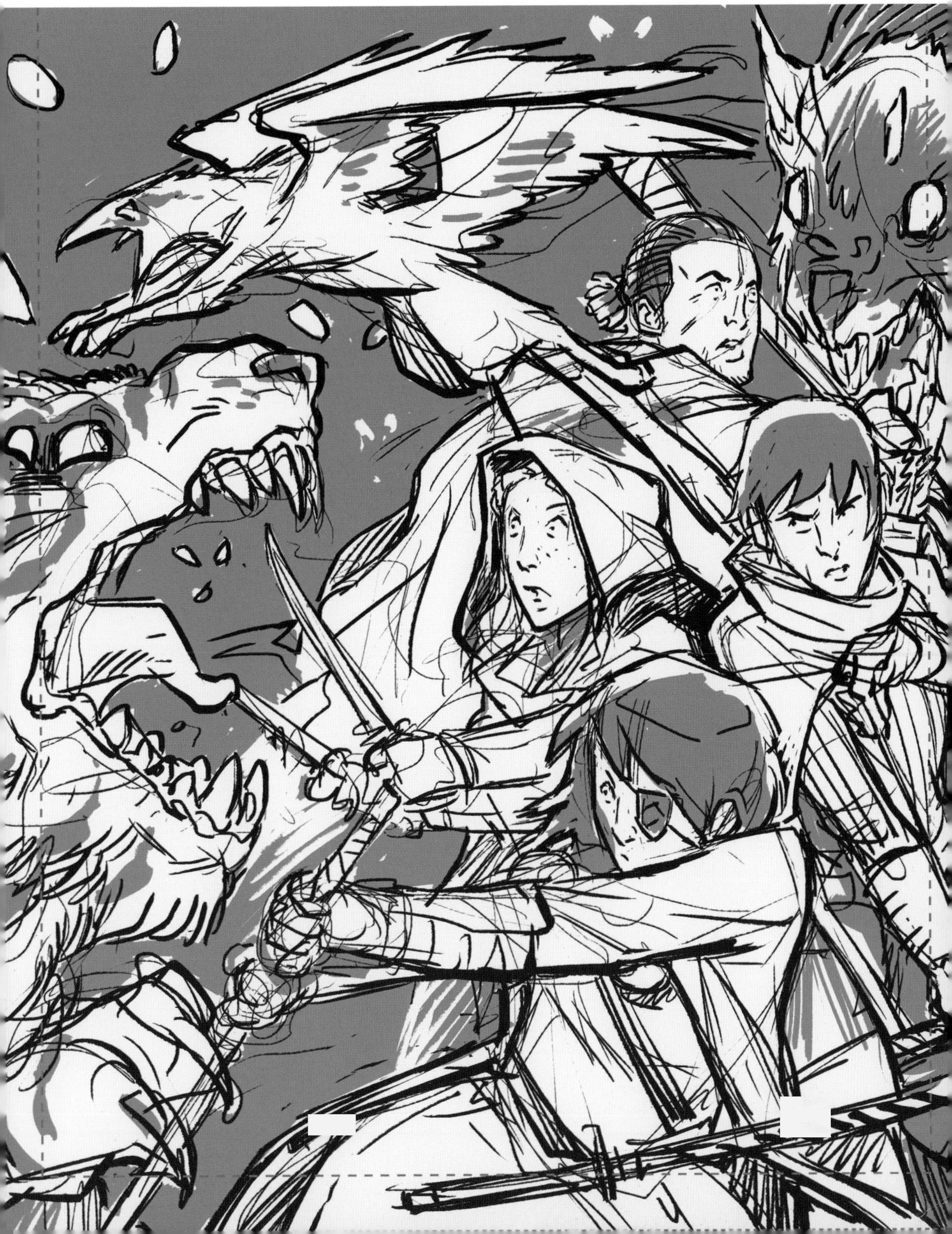